"This latest edition of Ted's go-to guide to LinkedIn is yet another example of his dedicated approach to delivering excellent, up-to-date information for the rest of us who rely on his expertise and guidance. Look at any of Ted's courses, articles—and especially the way he adds value through his answers in the LinkedIn community—and you will see the same focus on delivering dynamic, updated advice. Ted's consultancy skills and business proficiency are brought together in this book, bringing the same level of LinkedIn success to a wider audience."

—GEOFF CHEESEMAN, MBA, ACC, MANAGEMENT DEVELOPMENT CONSULTANT, THEMANAGERSMINDSET.COM

"Since working with Ted and optimizing my profile, I've added 208 connections in just 30 days and am in the top 20% of pros like me. My sales cycle is generally three months to three years since my services require so much education to the prospect . . . I took my best Facebook ad and put it on LinkedIn and already got seven clicks with an average CPC of $4.66."

—CRAIG PETRONELLA, CEO OF PETRONELLA COMPUTER, WWW.PETRONELLACOMPUTING.COM

"Ted is simply the master at communicating the best formulas for LinkedIn success! Ted helped me see that LinkedIn is so much more than the sum of its parts. He's guided me through creating a synergy on LinkedIn that yielded a greater understanding and fast, solid results."

—MICHAEL FLINT, CEO OF SWEET SUCCESS AND HISPANIC MARKETING SUCCESS

"Ted Prodromou is a LinkedIn Jedi Master. He's taught me more about LinkedIn than I could have ever learned trying to figure it out on my own. Truth is, I didn't even know where to begin with LinkedIn until I read Ted's book. He'll teach you the secret formula for getting the most out of LinkedIn within a very short period of time."

—CEDRIC CRUMBLEY, SALES TRAINER, CEDRICCRUMBLEY.COM

"I discovered Ted on LinkedIn and attended a webinar he was offering. It was the first in-depth training on LinkedIn I had ever had and it was an eye-opener. I've implemented as much of the training as I could and the results were immediate. The quality of the people responding to my group comments or postings, those viewing my profile and the number of connection requests have gone up significantly. My greatest success so far was following Ted's advice on building authority. My second publication on LinkedIn's Pulse had nearly 9,000 views, 460 "likes," and 59 comments within 2 days. The quality of the commenters was high and their comments provided me with a ton of content for further posts. Anyone who wants to take their LinkedIn presence to a new level should get this book."

—TOM DEWELL, FOUNDER, DEWELL CONSULTING

"The difference, they say, is in the details, and book has all the details that make the difference! Ted clearly knows how to be successful on LinkedIn and show others how to be successful, too. Ted made us aware of LinkedIn's scope, and all the subtle differences I would have missed."

—VIRGINIA AVERY, FOUNDER OF AVERY PRESENTATIONS, WWW.YOURSPEAKINGPOWER.COM

"Ted is the most knowledgeable authority on how to use LinkedIn profitably that I have ever met. He has provided insight on how to take maximum advantage of LinkedIn. I highly recommend Ted Prodromou as the #1 Authority in the world on LinkedIn strategies, and tactics. His book, which really is "The *Ultimate Guide to LinkedIn for Business*," is within easy reach on my computer desk and belongs on every successful business owner's library shelf."

—Joel Helfer, Founder of Quoted Authority, www.quotedauthority.com

"Everyone knows that it's smart to connect with over 300 million business people on LinkedIn. However, very few people know how to connect on LinkedIn profitably, without wasting tons of time and money. If you want to know the behind-the-scenes, real world strategies, you need to read and listen to Ted Prodromou. Ted has helped me tremendously and his book is jam-packed with nuggets of instantly applicable tips and tricks to save you time and money . . . and give you a road-map to actually making money on LinkedIn."

—Scott Keffer, #1 Amazon Best Selling Author, Coach and Speaker

"Ted, once again, I cannot say enough about your training. This has been an excellent program; I enrolled in the LinkedIn Jumpstart program because of all the value that you have been providing in your webinars over the past year and the credibility that you have earned with your level of knowledge and your passion for helping others to succeed. When I saw your offer for the Jumpstart program, I didn't hesitate for a moment and once again, you did not disappoint. It was definitely a worthwhile investment."

—Sandra Griffith, Training Client

"Ted Prodromou is an excellent trainer on the topic of LinkedIn. I knew quite a bit about LinkedIn, so I thought, but gained so much more useful knowledge from Ted's teachings. It was one of the best investments I have made in my social media education. LinkedIn is changing constantly and is getting better all the time. Ted is on top of all the new changes and is really passionate about LinkedIn and its use as a viable business-building tool. He teaches in a very down-to-earth manner, which I like, and he is very integral in his methodologies. I believe there is a very good window of opportunity in building a successful LinkedIn platform and Ted Prodromou can help you do that."

—Maggie Holbik, Business and Social Media Coach, www.MaggieHolbik.com

"Ted Prodromou absolutely blows my mind on the topic of LinkedIn. Our company teaches entrepreneurs all over the globe on LinkedIn prospecting, but whenever I have the opportunity to learn from Ted, I JUMP at it. This book is a must-read and I guarantee that if you take action on his teachings, then in a short amount of time, you will have more opportunity than you'll know what to do with!"

—Cory Michael Sanchez, Co-founder of MojoVideoMarketing.com

"This is a game-changing book on LinkedIn that is not to be read but to be DIGESTED! Ted is truly a pioneer and thought leader in the LinkedIn space! If you want to be relevant and highly competitive in this constantly changing market place you NEED to GET THIS BOOK TODAY!

—Ira Rosen, Co-Founder of MojoVideoMarketing.com

Entrepreneur
MAGAZINE'S

ULTIMATE
GUIDE TO

Linked in
FOR BUSINESS
Second Edition

- Quickly engage with ideal customers, partners, and employees
- Use insider tips and tactics to **create a steady flow of leads**
- Showcase your company and attract new opportunities

Ep
Entrepreneur
PRESS®

TED PRODROMOU

W

Entrepreneur Press, Publisher
Cover Design: Andrew Welyczko
Production and Composition: Eliot House Productions

Library of Congress Cataloging-in-Publication Data
Prodromou, Ted.
    Ultimate guide to LinkedIn for business/by Ted Prodromou.
      pages   cm.
    ISBN-13: 978-1-59918-560-6 (paperback)
    ISBN-10: 1-59918-560-1 (paperback)
      1. LinkedIn (Electronic resource) 2. Business networks. 3. Online social networks. 4. Internet
    marketing. I. Title.
    HD69.S8P75 2015
    650.140285′6754—dc23   2014039156

Printed in the United States of America

19 18 17 16   10 9 8 7 6 5 4 3 2 1

W

This book is dedicated to my parents, Sophia and Ted Prodromou. You continue to inspire me every day, and I'm thankful I had two loving parents who taught me how to be successful in life. I love you and miss you, Mom and Dad.

Contents

Foreword
by James Malinchak

As the Big Money Speaker, I've had the privilege to train thousands of authors, trainers, consultants, infopreneurs, consultants, coaches, speakers, and entrepreneurs on the importance of building their business and careers the right way.

I call my philosophy the "Five Millionaire Secrets," which are: mastering your mindset, money, marketing, making connections, and making a difference.

There is no question that in order to give back to those around you, first you must take control of your life and business. I'm passionate about enriching the lives of those around me using the Five Millionaire Secrets.

The question I always ask my students and clients is "What is the fastest way to the cash?" because they are often distracted in today's busy world. Social media is one of those distractions that keep us from staying on the fastest path to the cash.

Don't get me wrong. Social media is a very powerful tool when used properly. Never before could we create massive, instant web traffic and notoriety in seconds, for free. But you have to have a social media strategy so you stay focused on your desired result: making money.

In late 2012, I received an unexpected gift in the mail from Ted Prodromou. It was a copy of his first edition of *Ultimate Guide to LinkedIn for Business*.

At the time, I had a LinkedIn profile, but like most business professionals, I didn't understand the true power of LinkedIn. After exploring LinkedIn, I realized it's the perfect tool for three of my five Millionaire Secrets: money, marketing, and making connections. After reading Ted's book, I realized I was only a few clicks away from connecting with over 300 million business professionals. It doesn't get any easier than that.

Ted Prodromou has cleverly written a book that not only teaches you the ABCs of LinkedIn in an easy-to-understand way, he teaches you advanced LinkedIn strategies that make you more money.

If you are a LinkedIn beginner, Ted walks you step by step through setting up your profile so you are easily found by others. Next you learn how to build your professional network and how to engage people in such a way that they'll instantly know, like, and trust you.

The *Ultimate Guide to LinkedIn for Business* doesn't stop there. Ted teaches you real-world LinkedIn strategies that keep you on the fastest path to the cash. These simple strategies can be accomplished in just a few minutes a day, keeping your sales pipeline full while you close more deals than ever.

Today, it's easy to get distracted by the latest bright, shiny object and lose focus. No matter how many new social networks or online tools appear, the bottom line is relationships are the key to a successful business. Whether these relationships exist online or offline, your business will not succeed if you don't create strong relationships with your prospects and clients. LinkedIn is the perfect tool for creating new relationships and staying top of mind with your existing professional network.

Preface

Since I wrote *Ultimate Guide to LinkedIn for Business* in 2012, LinkedIn has transformed into an interactive, vibrant business community. In just two years, LinkedIn more than doubled in size from 130 million members to approximately 330 million members at the time of this writing. LinkedIn is adding two new members every second, growing faster than Facebook and Twitter combined. LinkedIn wants to become the largest publishing platform on the internet and has created easy-to-use tools to help you publish and share your content with millions of LinkedIn members.

What comes to mind when someone mentions LinkedIn? Most people think LinkedIn is a place to post your resume and someone will contact you for a job interview. Others think it's a business networking website where you can network with like-minded people and generate leads for your business.

Even today, most people don't understand the power of LinkedIn, but they signed up because they received an invitation from a friend or colleague.

I'm sure you created a profile on LinkedIn and wondered what to do next. Millions of business professionals have joined LinkedIn over the past few years, but most rarely take advantage of the vast opportunities on the site. They don't take the time to learn what LinkedIn can do for their career or business, so they're missing a huge opportunity.

When the economy turned in late 2008, millions of people lost their jobs. They may have heard on the news or from friends that LinkedIn was a good place to find a job, so they created an account. They partially filled out their profile and waited. And waited. And waited, but nobody contacted them for a job interview. They assumed LinkedIn was a waste of time and never returned.

In 2008, the bottom fell out for most businesses, too. Many large and small businesses filed for bankruptcy soon after the economy collapsed. Most of these businesses were running on very small margins and couldn't withstand the sudden downturn in the economy. While many businesses struggled, others thrived during the worst downturn in the economy since the Great Depression in the 1930s. My friend Perry Marshall expanded his business significantly in 2009-2010, releasing many new high-priced products. The worse the economy got, the faster his business grew.

Why did some companies thrive while others went out of business? Those that thrived during this downturn had already built a strong network of followers before the collapse. These businesses had loyal followers on social media sites such as LinkedIn, Facebook, and Twitter. These businesses built large email databases of these loyal followers and continued to communicate with them on a regular basis when times were tough. They created products and services that could help businesses survive the economic downturn. By building a loyal network of followers during the good times, these businesses had a huge safety net for outreach when times got tough. Surprisingly, these loyal followers were more than willing to open their wallets and invest in new products and training while others hoarded their money trying to ride out the storm.

What the companies that failed didn't know is that it takes more than filling out your company profile to succeed on LinkedIn (or in the business world, for that matter). Filling out your company profile on LinkedIn is like creating a flier to advertise your business. If you create an ad for your business but never send it to anyone, how do you expect anyone to know you are in business?

Most people don't understand how to use LinkedIn to its full advantage to promote their business or consulting practice. For example, I see a lot of great individual and company profiles, but I don't see those people participating in LinkedIn discussions. These are the people with a powerful, well-written resume and cover letter. They took the time to clearly define the services their business or practice provides skillfully, summarize their work history, and spell out their skills in an easy-to-read format. They know how to post their resume on the online job sites and get a response. Their weakness is they haven't taken the time to learn how to network. Business networking is a skill that takes time to hone, and you learn only by practicing. It takes years to become an expert business networker, but it's well worth the effort. Networking on LinkedIn is relatively easy if you take the time to learn how to use the tools.

I see others doing a fantastic job demonstrating their expertise in the LinkedIn Groups, but their profile suggests they are a "Jack of All Trades and Master of None." They have a diverse skill set and work history, so they end up creating a fragmented personal profile because they're trying to cover all the bases in their profile summary. To me, it's a sign of desperation when I see a mixed-bag profile. There is no focus or clarity, which makes it difficult to tell what products or services they are providing, and they don't exude confidence in any of their skills. Many of these people are good at networking because they're participating in the LinkedIn Groups. They know how to connect with others and help others without self-promoting, which will eventually turn into paid projects. If they would pick one expertise and focus their personal profile on that expertise, they would have unlimited opportunities coming their way.

It's pretty easy to succeed on LinkedIn if you know how to network in person. We've all been to networking events or cocktail parties where you meet the guy that can't stop telling you how wonderful he is or how great his product is. It's all about him, and you can't get a word in edgewise. You try to break away from the conversation, but he's like gum on the bottom of your shoe and won't let you escape.

I see those people on LinkedIn, too. Their profiles are full of self-promotion. They participate in LinkedIn Group discussions by promoting their own products or services instead of answering the questions. The focus is on them instead of focusing on building relationships with other LinkedIn Group members. It's a one-way monologue, and nobody's listening.

In addition to the information and instruction in this book, I recommend spending some time in the LinkedIn Help Center. Easy-to-follow articles and webinars show how to create a compelling, searchable profile and how to use the vast array of networking tools LinkedIn provides. The combination of a clear, complete profile and the ability to network will help you succeed on LinkedIn. But learning how to build a strong LinkedIn profile and how to network isn't enough. The key to success on LinkedIn is to take what you learn from this book and take action. Commit time in your schedule to build that complete personal profile and company profile. Schedule time every day to connect with others on LinkedIn and participate in discussions. Take action on a regular basis, and you will succeed on LinkedIn and in business.

By the time you read this book, LinkedIn will have added new tools and features. To keep up with the latest LinkedIn updates, I invite you to visit http://tedprodromou. com/LinkedIn frequently where I will be posting articles and videos demonstrating the latest LinkedIn features.

How much more powerful would LinkedIn be if everyone had a complete profile and used the networking tools effectively? LinkedIn would be exponentially more useful than it is today—which is hard to imagine.

MY PERSONAL LINKEDIN STORY

When I first moved to San Francisco in 1979, it was easy to find a job. Silicon Valley was growing like crazy, and the high-tech industry was desperately looking for skilled workers. Companies were growing so fast they posted job openings on billboards outside their sprawling tech campuses. I could drive around Silicon Valley, drop off my resume at the security desk, and have multiple job offers by the end of the day. For more than 20 years, I had the most secure career ever, knowing I could change jobs and get a significant raise whenever I wanted.

The high-tech boom of the 1980s and '90s was a very wild ride. I built a strong network of contacts in the high-tech industry over 20 years and felt on top of the world in my career as a network manager working for companies like IBM, Cellular One, and Digital Equipment Corporation. Life was great, and I was a recognized leader in my field. I was featured in trade magazines and even an annual report of a networking company.

The internet boom of the late 1990s was like pouring gasoline on a fire, accelerating the growth of the high-tech industry exponentially.

Then came Y2K and the turn of the century. The dotcom boom imploded, collapsing the entire tech industry. It was the end of an era. High-tech companies began laying off employees for the first time ever.

Soon many companies closed their doors. Others sold themselves off for pennies on the dollar as the entire industry collapsed. Within one year, more than 500,000 high-tech workers lost their jobs in Silicon Valley alone. Most of the remaining jobs were outsourced overseas. Salaries collapsed for those lucky enough to keep a job, but most of us were unable to find work for the first time in our careers.

When my consulting practice went under in late 2001, I began reaching out to my network of colleagues for work. I didn't care if it was a consulting gig or full-time job. I was looking to my network because I knew someone would have a lead for me.

A funny thing happened when I reached out. I couldn't get in contact with most of my network. Emails bounced back. Telephones were disconnected. I only had business cards with company email addresses and telephone numbers in my Rolodex (yes, that old-fashioned contraption). I didn't have a private email address for my network because email was still fairly new at that time and we didn't have private email addresses. Cell phones were also fairly new and not everyone carried one because it was still pretty expensive. Many of my colleagues moved out of the area because of the high cost of living and the lack of career opportunities.

I felt lost. I had no way to reach my network that took 20 years to build. I couldn't find them in the phone book (that's how we used to find people in the old days) and lost touch with most of them. My safety net was gone, and I was starting my career over from the beginning. This was devastating for someone in his early 40s in the high-tech arena where 20-somethings ruled the roost.

There were no online networking websites like LinkedIn in 2001, so I joined a local business-networking group. We met once a week for breakfast and traded leads. Most of the leads were worthless, but occasionally one would pan out. It also gave everyone in the network an excuse to get out of the house, since we were all struggling, work-at-home consultants.

My business treaded water for the next few years as the economy recovered from the dotcom crash and 9/11. The only way to get new projects was from referrals, in-person networking, and cold calling because I couldn't afford to advertise.

In 2004, I received an email invitation from a friend who wanted to connect with me on LinkedIn. I didn't know what LinkedIn was, but I registered to check it out. I am LinkedIn member number 2,239,835. You can determine your member number by going to Profile, View Profile on the LinkedIn main menu. Your member number is the number in your profile URL.

I signed in to LinkedIn and looked around a bit, but there wasn't much to see. I joined a couple of alumni groups, searched for some old co-workers, and then pretty much ignored LinkedIn for the next year.

I slowly filled out parts of my profile after people would invite me to connect with them but never spent much time on the site. When LinkedIn first launched, there really wasn't much you could do other than fill out your profile and connect with colleagues and former co-workers. I considered LinkedIn nothing more than an online resume website.

Eventually I reconnected with some of my original network. It was great to see most of them had landed on their feet, and some were doing extremely well. I was excited to see some of the people I hired right out of college were now directors and vice presidents at large tech companies. I guess my mentoring paid off for them, and we're still close today.

Over time, LinkedIn added more features, which made the site more useful. Answers and LinkedIn Groups were added, so there was more interaction between members. Adding the ability to interact with others was the turning point for LinkedIn, and membership began to increase. LinkedIn retired the Answers section in January 2013, but LinkedIn Groups continues to thrive.

I quickly discovered if I answered questions in the Answers sections, people started reaching out to me with contract opportunities. I also posted provocative questions, which attracted a lot of attention and created some interesting conversations.

LinkedIn became a useful tool for me to promote my own consulting practice. My network expanded significantly as I connected with more people and joined groups. After being a passive observer of LinkedIn for years, I realized the more I participated, the more consulting work came my way.

For a few years, I worked full time as an online marketing/SEO analyst for a large software company so I used LinkedIn in a very different way. I managed our company's LinkedIn Group, updated our company status with news items, scheduled events, and managed our company page. My job was to get exposure for our company on LinkedIn, which in turn gives us more exposure on Google. I used to generate leads by answering questions in LinkedIn Groups and the Answers section. Another way I generated leads was by posting provocative statements in our status, with links to landing pages where people could download valuable white papers. I also managed paid ad campaigns on LinkedIn, which are precisely targeted and very effective. Today I use all of these tactics to generate new business for my consulting practice and for my clients. I'll share more details about LinkedIn advertising later in the book.

WHAT YOU'LL FIND IN THIS BOOK

Throughout this book I'll share my perspective of LinkedIn from the keyword and search engine ranking perspective. I'll also share tips to help you get maximum exposure for your personal profile and your company.

Most LinkedIn books teach you the fundamentals of LinkedIn and don't go into much detail. You learn how to create a basic profile and how to use the LinkedIn tools from the 10,000-foot level, but you don't get into the nitty-gritty details that make you a LinkedIn Expert.

We're going to go deep in this LinkedIn book, very deep. We'll start with the basics of LinkedIn, and then I'll show you the advanced tips and tricks that will separate you from your competitors. I'll start out teaching you the fundamentals of LinkedIn to help first-timers or users with minimal experience using LinkedIn. Once you master the fundamentals, we'll move on to the advanced features of LinkedIn to help you get the most out of your LinkedIn experience. Throughout the entire book, you will learn lots of great tips to help you get maximum exposure and find what you are looking for to grow your business or advance your career.

First, I'll show you the ins and outs of LinkedIn by introducing you to the vast array of features and tools available to you. I'll explain each feature and tool in detail and show you some best practices for each. Some of the LinkedIn features you will learn about include:

- Your Homepage
- Profiles
- Jobs
- LinkedIn Groups
- LinkedIn Today
- Twitter
- Company Pages
- Tools
- Mobile
- Settings/Personalization
- Advertising
- LinkedIn Premium for Business, Sales, and Recruiters
- Job Seeker Premium

I'm going to show you how to leverage the power of LinkedIn so you and your company can appear in the LinkedIn and Google search results. I'll show you exactly how to create a searchable LinkedIn profile that will rise to the top of the search results in both LinkedIn and Google.

After you master the basics of LinkedIn, I'll show you how experts get the most out of LinkedIn. We'll review step-by-step case studies demonstrating how to use LinkedIn for various outcomes. If you are looking to grow your business, I'll show you how to use LinkedIn to find your perfect clients or customers. If you're looking to hire a new employee, I'll show you how to find your dream employee.

To help you see the effect LinkedIn can have on your business or career, I've included some real-world success stories from people just like you. These success stories include:

- Sales professionals/business development/lead generation
- Finding your ideal employees
- Recruiters

I'm sure you have a compelling business story to tell if you've survived the dotcom crash in 2000 to 2001 or the collapse of the economy in 2008. Maybe your business wasn't lucky enough to survive two major downturns in less than ten years. My business didn't, and from that experience I learned the importance of building and nurturing a strong business network.

Today, the business world is changing constantly. You need to be well connected so your business continues to thrive through the peaks and valleys of the economic swings.

You need to build a strong, stable professional network that can provide guidance and support during the trying times. During your boom times, you can provide guidance and support to those in your network who are struggling. In the next chapter, I'll show you the benefits of joining LinkedIn and show you how it can help you build your ideal professional network and grow your business.

Chapter 1

Why LinkedIn?

You know when you're thinking about buying a new car, and all of a sudden you see that car everywhere? You never noticed many on the road, but now that you're thinking about buying one, it seems like everyone is driving your new car.

I have the same problem when I see online ads and keywords. Sometimes I feel like Don Draper from the TV show *Mad Men*, analyzing every ad and keyword I see. Since I'm a search engine optimization and online marketing expert by trade, I see the internet from a different perspective than most. Whether I like it or not, I see the internet from the perspective of online ads, keywords, and search rankings. I'm always trying to figure out how a company gets top rankings or maximum exposure from their marketing campaigns. I look for the same patterns on LinkedIn. Which companies appear consistently in LinkedIn? Which people get the most exposure on LinkedIn? Which keywords get the most traction in LinkedIn?

THE INFO GOLD MINE

With more than 330 million members and growing, LinkedIn has become a gold mine of demographic information and business intelligence. Unfortunately, most LinkedIn members don't see LinkedIn as a powerful business tool. They see LinkedIn as a place to post their profile and expect others to hunt them down without providing any value to the site.

Today, LinkedIn has become a very powerful business-oriented search engine. With the advanced search features, you can find great employees to hire, find the perfect company to work for, find highly targeted leads to sell to, and network with the thought leaders of your industry.

You can mine deeply into the LinkedIn database and find a treasure trove of information that will change the way you do business. You'll know so much about a prospect, their company, their competitors, their industry, and their products before you ever meet the person. LinkedIn is changing the sales process and making it easier than ever to find targeted prospects for your business.

SOUPED-UP SEARCH ENGINE

Not many people consider LinkedIn a search engine, but I invite you to consider the possibility. What if your profile or company appeared when someone did a people search on LinkedIn? What if your LinkedIn profile or company profile appeared when a prospect searched Google for keywords related to your product or service? What would that do for your career or company? What would your bottom line look like if you could identify highly targeted prospects just by searching on LinkedIn or Google?

If you still don't believe LinkedIn is a powerful search engine, then why do LinkedIn search results appear in Google search results? If Google understands the power of LinkedIn, you should, too.

Throughout this book I'll be sharing my perspective of LinkedIn from the keyword and search engine ranking perspective. I'll also share tips to help you get maximum exposure for your personal profile and your company.

CONCLUSION

You now know that LinkedIn is the fastest growing and most successful business networking site in the world. You see the benefits of joining and participating in the networking groups and demonstrating your expertise by helping others. In the next chapter, I'll show you how to get started on LinkedIn, so you can begin growing your professional network and become a recognized thought leader in your industry.

To learn how to take advantage of the latest LinkedIn updates,
visit www.tedprodromou.com/chapter1

Chapter 2

Getting Started on LinkedIn

Why did you sign up for LinkedIn? Did your friend invite you when she signed up for LinkedIn and clicked on the automated invitation? You may have read about LinkedIn in *The Wall Street Journal* or your local newspaper. Maybe you read about LinkedIn in a magazine or on someone's blog. Or maybe your colleagues at work signed up and told you to sign up, too.

For whatever reason you joined LinkedIn, you are now a member of the largest professional business networking community in the world. At the time of this writing, LinkedIn just surpassed 330 million members. LinkedIn is often called a networking community, but it's becoming much more than just a networking website. It's become the largest job-related website with thousands of job postings. Recruiters and job seekers are finding LinkedIn the perfect place to connect.

Many people ask me if LinkedIn is better than Facebook for connecting with people. A couple of years ago, I preferred to use LinkedIn to build my professional network and use Facebook to connect with my personal network. Facebook is trying hard to become both a personal and professional network, and they're succeeding. Of course, I'm friends with some people on Facebook who are also connected with me on LinkedIn, which is fine with me. My differentiation is focused on what I put on both networks. I post personal comments and pictures on Facebook, while I post business-oriented information on LinkedIn. Personally I don't like to see people's business-oriented status updates or Tweets on Facebook. When I'm on Facebook, I want to turn off my business-oriented brain and have fun. When I'm on LinkedIn, my business-oriented brain is turned on, and I prefer to see only business-related information. That was my opinion a few years ago, but something interesting happened that changed my view of Facebook for business. My virtual assistant accidently scheduled some automated posts in Hootsuite to post on my Facebook page. I post excerpts from my *Ultimate Guide to LinkedIn for Business* and *Ultimate Guide to Twitter for Business* books on LinkedIn, Twitter, and other social media sites that link to landing pages where people can download free chapters of my books.

When I first saw the excerpts on Facebook I wasn't happy because I wanted to keep Facebook personal. Then I started receiving more downloads of my free chapters from Facebook than I was from Twitter and LinkedIn. After experimenting, I discovered Facebook is very effective at generating leads for business. Now I use Facebook for personal and business while keeping my LinkedIn activity purely business. The combination of Facebook, LinkedIn, and Twitter generates most of the traffic that comes to my website.

Do you have a preference? I'd love to hear what you think. Send me an email at ted@tedprodromou.com, and let me know whether you keep your business and personal networks separate.

LinkedIn is also becoming the largest B2B lead-generation website where businesses can connect with their ideal customers and potential business partners. LinkedIn is where you can reconnect with past co-workers and classmates. LinkedIn has become so much more than a job hunting website, which most people mistakenly think is its only function; it is invaluable for so much more. Here is just a small sampling:

- Keeping up with news and trends in your industry
- Demonstrating your particular expertise
- Finding great professional referrals
- Promoting your events
- Recommending people to others

LinkedIn has become the one-stop portal for you to connect with like-minded people. There is hardly anyone who doesn't benefit in some way from its network and tools. It's perfect for:

- An employee for a company
- Marketing and sales professionals
- Job seekers, HR personnel, and recruiters
- Entrepreneurs and small-business owners

Through LinkedIn Groups, you can demonstrate your expertise to attract new clients and connect with other industry experts. You can share your knowledge or keep up with the latest industry news on LinkedIn Today. LinkedIn is expanding its tools and services to attract the best business professionals, so the quality of the community continues to improve and exceed all other business networking communities.

Unfortunately, many people become LinkedIn members and don't take advantage of the unlimited opportunities in the community. They create their account, partially fill out their profile, connect with a few close friends, and never come back. They complain there is nothing for them on LinkedIn because they think it is only a job opportunity website and they are already employed.

The real reason they are frustrated with LinkedIn is because they don't have a reason for being a LinkedIn member. Like any community you join, you have to have a reason to join it if you want to take full advantage of all the opportunities it has to offer.

When people join Facebook, they expect to connect with past and current friends in a casual environment. Facebook is all about taking a break from our busy lives by viewing vacation pictures posted by our friends, engaging in chats, and playing games. Your expectations are very clear when you join Facebook, and the level of engagement is incredibly high.

When people join LinkedIn, they used to expect to find a new job, but today they can expect to connect with a lot of like-minded business professionals. As LinkedIn provides more networking tools and ways to engage others in conversation, the level of engagement increases proportionally. I spend most of my day logged into LinkedIn checking status updates from my connections and learning about industry news. When I leave work, I spend my personal time engaging with friends on Facebook. My expectations of both websites are very clear, so I have no problem engaging with people on both networks.

Do I think Facebook will ever replace LinkedIn or vice versa as an all-in-one networking site? My personal opinion is no, because most people like to keep their personal life separate from their work life. More and more businesses are building a presence on Facebook—which is making Facebook an effective way to engage business prospects—but I'm not ready to merge my personal life with my business life yet. I like the fact that LinkedIn is pure business and I can engage people on a business-level without distractions.

DETERMINE YOUR LINKEDIN OBJECTIVE

What is your LinkedIn objective? Most people don't have one when they join LinkedIn, which explains why many profiles are incomplete, and their profiles show little or no activity. They signed up because they were invited to connect with a co-worker or colleague, but they aren't looking for a job or looking to network with others so they rarely return. They assumed LinkedIn was only for job hunting, so they never took the time to explore the incredible networking opportunities and professional communities.

Even if you're gainfully employed and not looking for a job, it's more important than ever for you to be on LinkedIn and complete your profile. Your LinkedIn profile is a dynamic electronic billboard displaying your skills and expertise to millions of potential readers. By keeping your profile up to date, connecting with others, engaging in LinkedIn Groups, and demonstrating your expertise, you are showing the business world you are in touch with the latest trends and technologies. The more you participate on LinkedIn, the more your name will pop up in the LinkedIn sidebar and on Google, creating unexpected opportunities to help potential customers, partners, and employers find you.

You may not use LinkedIn on a regular basis, but other business professionals do. It's becoming a common business practice to view someone's LinkedIn profile before a meeting so they get to know you. Your LinkedIn profile is often someone's first impression of you, and as Will Rogers said, "You never get a second chance to make a good first impression."

With the uncertain job market and corporate instability, you never know when your company will be acquired or go out of business. It's also impossible to predict when you'll be restructured or downsized out of a job. There is no security in today's marketplace, and no one is safe when corporations downsize or get acquired. If your company is acquired or merges with another business, the chances of job loss increase.

My parents grew up in the generation where they got a job after they finished school, worked for the same company for 40 years, and retired. There was complete job security, and they never worried about being laid off or their company being acquired. If a company was acquired, they usually kept all employees whether they were needed or not. Layoffs were rare back then.

Unfortunately, those days are long gone, and today we have to be prepared to change jobs, or even careers, in an instant. If your LinkedIn profile is active and current, there's a good chance you will land on your feet in a short period of time if the worst happens. If you wait until you're unemployed to update your LinkedIn profile and build your connections, it will take longer for you to find your next job. So take a few minutes every day and complete your LinkedIn profile, get the minimum three recommendations, connect with some colleagues, and participate in some LinkedIn Groups. Take it one step at a time, and in no time you will be logging in to LinkedIn every day to participate in the vibrant community discussions.

Once you are on LinkedIn and you have finished your profile, you should determine how LinkedIn can best serve you. There are four basic functions of LinkedIn:

1. Establishing your professional profile
2. Staying in touch with colleagues and friends
3. Exploring opportunities
4. Finding experts and answers to your business-related questions

Your objective could be one of these functions, all of these functions, or any combination. You should have the objective of establishing your professional profile, even if you aren't actively looking for work. Remember, LinkedIn is your electronic business card that could be seen by more than 330 million professionals, so you want a complete, up-to-date profile. You never know when a once-in-a-lifetime opportunity will arise because the right person came across your profile in a LinkedIn search or read some of your comments in a LinkedIn Group discussion.

It's also good practice to keep in touch with colleagues and friends, even if it's just commenting on one of their status updates. By "pinging" your network on a regular basis, you keep your name in front of them, and they're more likely to consider you for an opportunity when it arises. Many great career opportunities present themselves when you least expect it. I have to say, since I completed my profile and optimized it to appear when people search for popular search terms, I have received numerous opportunities even though I am not looking for them. This proves to me that LinkedIn is a powerful tool, and I will never have to worry about finding a new job if something unforeseen suddenly happens to my current role.

LinkedIn has been working hard to make their site more interactive so we have a reason to log in every day. One of these new features is called Keep in Touch and is located under your Connections tab. LinkedIn now prompts you to Say Happy Birthday or congratulate people when they have a work anniversary or are starting a new position. With LinkedIn Premium accounts, LinkedIn now displays your recent email conversations with your connections. These new tools make it very easy to "ping" your connections to remain top of mind with them. One of my students recently "pinged" an old colleague whom he lost touch with, and it turned into a $3 million opportunity for him.

As I mentioned earlier, given the unstable business environment, you should always keep your eyes open for new opportunities. Companies are in a constant state of flux and won't hesitate to lay off thousands of workers if they see a downturn in business on the horizon. I'm not telling you to always be actively looking for new opportunities, but I am telling you to keep one eye open for better, more stable opportunities as they appear on your radar.

LinkedIn is a fantastic business resource if you're doing research or looking for expertise in an unfamiliar area. You will receive great advice from many experts in a matter of minutes by posting a question in the Groups section of LinkedIn. In the past you would have to hire a consultant to help you navigate unfamiliar areas of expertise. Today you have access to thousands of subject matter experts at your fingertips who will gladly answer your question for free in the LinkedIn Groups section. Many times you will end up hiring the consultant who provides quality recommendations or advice—I know this for a fact because I was hired many times after I answered questions—so it's a win-win for you and the subject matter expert.

WHAT ABOUT OTHER NETWORKING WEBSITES?

There are other professional business communities online, but none is as vibrant and dynamic as LinkedIn. Friendster was the original online social network, but it wasn't focused on business networking. It was the most popular personal social networking site for years until MySpace and Facebook came along.

Ryze was launched a few years ago with a lot of fanfare, and they claim to have more than 500,000 members in 200 countries. Since then they've lost momentum. Like the early days of LinkedIn, it seems people don't know what to do once they log in. The idea behind Ryze is that you "rise up" through quality networking. I see some current postings on the site, but they have disabled the ability to create new accounts so it looks like Ryze's days are numbered.

Xing is the most popular business networking website in Germany and has a strong following in Europe. Xing is free to join, and they offer premium accounts for about $10 per month. The premium accounts let you see who searched your profile, filter your searches for better targeting, and allow you to send messages to people you are not connected to. Xing has a lot of the same features and tools as LinkedIn, including groups, jobs, events, apps, and company pages. It's very user-friendly and a great business networking community for Europeans.

Some people prefer to network on these other sites for various reasons, but I think they're missing out by not focusing on LinkedIn. Maybe they have a nice niche network on one of these other sites that's working for them, but there is so much opportunity on LinkedIn that they're crazy not to build a network on LinkedIn, too. LinkedIn is exponentially larger than Xing (LinkedIn has more than 330 million users, while Xing has more than 7 million users primarily in the DACH region [Deutschland, Austria, and Switzerland]), so why not belong to both networks and expand your reach significantly? Why be the salmon swimming upstream against the current, when you can easily ride the wave to success by using LinkedIn?

CONCLUSION

There are other business networking websites, but none is near the quality of LinkedIn for growing your professional network. You've established your reason for joining LinkedIn and your networking strategy is beginning to take shape. In the next chapter, we'll create your LinkedIn account, start creating your optimized profile, and begin expanding your professional network.

For additional updates and how-to videos, visit
www.tedprodromou.com/chapter2

Chapter 3

Creating Your LinkedIn Account

When you create your LinkedIn account, you will be prompted to answer some questions as you populate your profile. Filling out your profile completely will help you connect with others faster than if you leave out important details.

You will be asked if you are Employed, a Job Seeker, or a Student. You will be led through a custom wizard, as you see in Figure 3–1 on page 12, which is tailored to your selection so you can easily build a profile optimized for your objective.

After you enter your country, ZIP code, job title, and company and click "Create my profile," your profile will be created.

Next you will be asked if you want to import your contacts into LinkedIn. If you choose this option, LinkedIn will automatically import all of your contacts from Outlook, Gmail, or any other email program you use. LinkedIn will tell you which of your contacts are already on LinkedIn, so you can send them invitations to connect automatically. If your contacts are not on LinkedIn, you can send them an email from LinkedIn inviting them to connect with you on LinkedIn. This is an easy way to quickly connect with your existing network on LinkedIn.

Personally, I do not like using automated connection tools. I feel it's impersonal and almost like spamming your current network. LinkedIn sends a canned invitation message to your existing contacts, and you can't customize the message for each person. I prefer to reach out to my existing network manually and choose whom I want to connect with on LinkedIn. I prefer to build my LinkedIn network with a small number of quality contacts instead of everyone who is in my address book. I may have met a person at a networking event and corresponded with him a few years ago, but he may not be appropriate for my LinkedIn network today.

I do have clients who successfully used the automated connection tool to quickly build their network. Their perspective is they're already connected to these people from previous business ventures so they feel it's fine to send the standard LinkedIn connection message. This approach allowed them to quickly grow their network, but only a small percentage of the emails sent resulted in LinkedIn connections. Eventually they manually connected with the rest of their email address book.

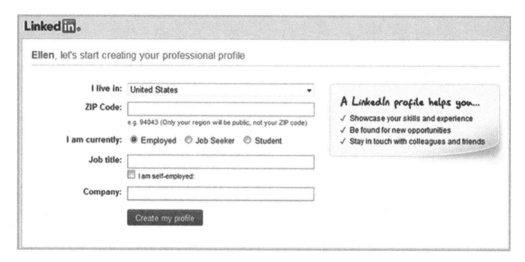

FIGURE 3–1. Using the LinkedIn Profile Wizard

I'll leave it up to you if you want to use the automation tools to build your network quickly, but most professionals prefer the "quality over quantity" method of building their network.

Next you will be prompted to share on Facebook and Twitter that you just joined LinkedIn. When people click on the link you will be connected to them on LinkedIn. Again, I don't like this method of connecting with people because you are sending a blind invitation to all of your friends on Facebook and your followers on Twitter. I connect with people on Facebook on a personal level, not as a business networking venue. I like to keep my Facebook life separate from my business life, which I share on LinkedIn. As I mentioned in Chapter 2, Facebook is becoming a great venue for business, but I still use Facebook primarily for personal posts. With Twitter, I have no control of who follows me, and I may not want them to be part of my professional network on LinkedIn. Again I'll leave it up to you if you want to automatically share an open invitation on Facebook and Twitter, but I don't recommend it.

The next step in the registration wizard will ask you if you want to sign up for the premium paid version or use the free basic version of LinkedIn. I'll go into greater detail about the premium version throughout this book, but I highly recommend staying with the free version for now, unless you have an immediate need for the advanced LinkedIn features.

The wizard will now prompt you to enter your current job information including your hire date and details about the position. The wizard will continue to prompt you to complete your past job titles, responsibilities, and the dates you worked at that position. You can enter up to five past positions in LinkedIn.

As you enter your job information, the wizard will ask you: "What did you do as *your job title will appear here*?" Enter the details of your job responsibilities, and remember to add your skills when possible. Some people write a brief description of their responsibilities in the first person, while others create a bulleted list of responsibilities. An example of a first-person job description would be, "I was responsible for search engine optimization and online advertising for our regions around the world. I was also responsible for email marketing campaign development, brand development, and website traffic growth."

Some people write their summaries in the third person. An example of a third-person summary would be: "Ted was responsible for search engine optimization and online advertising for the company's regions around the world. Ted was also responsible for email marketing campaign development, brand development, and website traffic growth."

I prefer to use the first-person voice when I write my profile summary because it sounds like it's coming from me personally. To me, third-person narrative sounds like it was written by someone else so it's less personal and not as friendly as a first-person profile summary. I know there is an ongoing debate about which style works better, so I suggest trying first person for a few months and switch to third person to see which gets the best result for you.

Another way to phrase your summary would be like this:

A dynamic online marketing manager with over ten years of experience, including search engine optimization (SEO), pay-per-click (PPC) advertising, and search engine marketing (SEM).

- Thrives in chaotic environments, cool-headed in stressful situations; able to manage multiple projects concurrently and get things done
- Excellent communicator; often serves as the liaison between other departments, customers, and offshore teams

- Flexible and resourceful, applying exceptional organizational, time-management, and planning skills to deliver projects on time and on budget
- Drives adoption of new technologies and innovative solutions

Here's another example of a bulleted-list job description:
Responsibilities included:

- Search engine optimization (SEO)
- Online banner advertising for regions around the world
- Creating and managing pay-per-click (PPC) ad campaigns internationally
- Email marketing campaign development and management
- Brand development
- Website traffic growth

Notice how the list contains keyword phrases and three-letter acronyms where appropriate. I added SEO after search engine optimization, so the LinkedIn search algorithm can find these keywords and related acronyms in my profile. Now I'm easily found when someone searches for SEO or search engine optimization.

There is no right or wrong way to create your profile summary. The main objective is to use your keyword phrases so you're easily found and people can get a quick overview of your skill sets as they scan your professional profile.

Once you've entered your current and past jobs, the LinkedIn wizard will prompt you to enter your education. Here you enter the school you attended, the degree(s) you earned, if any, and the dates you attended the school. If you are a current student you can enter your expected graduation date. If you didn't graduate from that school, you can just note the dates you attended the school and the courses you studied. The wizard will continue to prompt you to enter more schools until you've entered all of those you attended.

A lot of people ask me if they should include their high school in the education profile if they have college or advanced degrees. If you enter your high school, LinkedIn will show you people who also attended your high school so you can easily add them to your network. If you think it would be valuable to have people from your high school in your professional network, then you should add your high school in your education profile.

After you complete the education portion of your profile, the wizard will move to your skills. It's important to use your keyword phrases in the skills section of your profile so your profile is search friendly. You can add up to 50 skills to your profile, which will dramatically increase the chances of someone finding you when they search for that skill set. As you start typing, the system will suggest skills that are already being used on LinkedIn. Select as many variations of your keywords as possible to optimize your profile.

At this point you have a basic LinkedIn profile, and you will start seeing new items appear in your sidebar. LinkedIn is reading your profile and building a list of recommendations based on the keywords you post in your jobs, education, summary, and skills. The People You May Know section will begin recommending new, targeted connections you may want to add to your network. As you add connections, Your LinkedIn network will update automatically. It will tell you how many connections and how many new people are in your network. You will also see recommended jobs and groups you may want to join based on your profile and network data. You will also see a list of companies you may want to start following so you can keep up with your industry trends or watch them to see if you may want to work there some day.

Keep adding appropriate connections to your network; this sidebar data continues to update automatically. LinkedIn is constantly learning and suggesting appropriate recommendations as your extended network grows. You receive targeted information automatically, which saves you a ton of time when you're looking for people to connect with or looking for companies to learn more about.

Your personal profile should complement your company profile using the same terminology and keywords. People like to see congruency when they view your company profile and then visit your employee profiles. This helps present a more professional image for you and your company, which gives potential clients a positive and lasting impression.

CONCLUSION

Your basic LinkedIn profile is now live, and you will start receiving invitations to connect with others. You will also have the opportunity to reach out to others, but I recommend waiting a bit before connecting with others until you are more familiar with LinkedIn.

In the next chapter, I'll show you how to optimize your LinkedIn profile so you will appear near the top of LinkedIn and Google search results for your skills and target keyword phrases.

For additional updates and how-to videos, visit
www.tedprodromou.com/chapter3

Supercharging Your LinkedIn Profile

Your LinkedIn profile represents your professional image on the internet and can be found through searches on LinkedIn or search engines like Google, Bing, and Yahoo!. When people search the internet for your name, your LinkedIn profile will most likely be one of the top search results, so you want to make a great first impression.

Think of LinkedIn as your online resume and your profile as the introductory paragraph of your resume. As people scan your profile, they should be able to understand exactly what you do as they read your headline.

Your LinkedIn profile provides people with a comprehensive summary of you, your education, work experience, and your achievements. Your LinkedIn profile also links people to other social media properties and websites where you can showcase your expertise.

Your LinkedIn profile consists of:

- Your headline
- Your photo
- Status updates
- Vanity URL
- Summary
- Applications

- Experience
- Education
- Recommendations
- Additional information
- Personal information
- Contact information

PROFILE HEADLINE

Your profile headline is the single most important part of your profile. Your profile headline will appear next to your name in the search results. As your name appears in the search results, your headline must be compelling enough to make people want to click on your profile to learn more about you. You should never put just your name and company name in your headline.

> **LINKEDIN PROFILE TIP**
>
> In this age of text messaging and autocorrect, our society has become very careless about spelling and grammar. Your LinkedIn profile is a reflection of your professional image, so be 100 percent sure your profile is correctly formatted and free from spelling and grammatical errors.

Some people like to add symbols to their profile headline to attract attention. Some of the symbols I've seen include ™ ♦ # * ◊ and many other unprofessional symbols. I searched Google to see how people added the symbols to their profile, and they just copy and paste them from other people's profiles. You can also add the symbols from a Word document by using Insert, Symbols or Insert, Shapes.

Personally, I don't think it's professional to add symbols to your profile, and it diminishes your credibility. If you are really good at what you do you shouldn't have to trick people into reading your profile. When I see symbols in someone's profile, I think of those cheap restaurants with the flashing signs out front advertising their specials and cheap prices. You know the restaurant is a dive and the food is horrible, but they catch your attention with the flashing lights and cheap prices. You regret eating there because you always leave with a stomachache, but you were seduced by the bright, flashing lights.

I usually feel the same way after wasting my time reading a LinkedIn profile that contains flashy symbols. If the symbols do catch my attention, I take a moment to read the profile, and it's usually very unprofessional. The person typically overuses keywords, overstates his experience, and uses tricks to rank well in the LinkedIn and Google searches. Eventually, LinkedIn and Google catch up with profiles like this and lower their rankings, although they do get their 15 minutes of fame and maybe even a few clients.

You will also select your location and industry in this section of your profile setup. You can also create multilingual profiles in the Basic Information section of your profile as shown in Figure 4–1 on page 19.

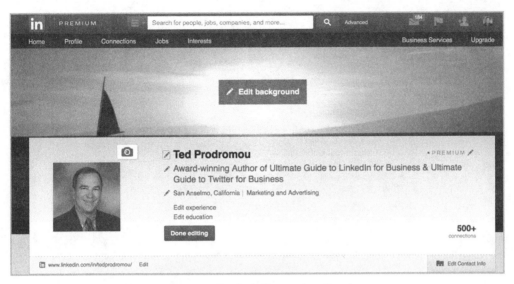

FIGURE 4–1. Basic Information Section

Here's my profile headline in Figure 4–2 with my name and profile headline, using my target keyword phrases, location, and industry.

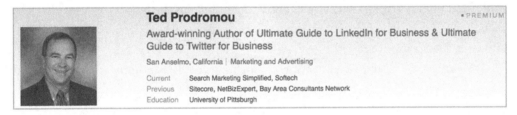

FIGURE 4–2. Location and Industry Headline

Figure 4–3 shows us the profile headline for Viveka von Rosen, a well-known LinkedIn expert. You know exactly what she does for a living within seconds of reading her profile headline.

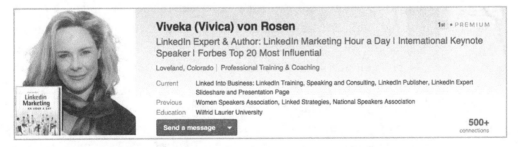

FIGURE 4–3. Profile Headline for Viveka von Rosen

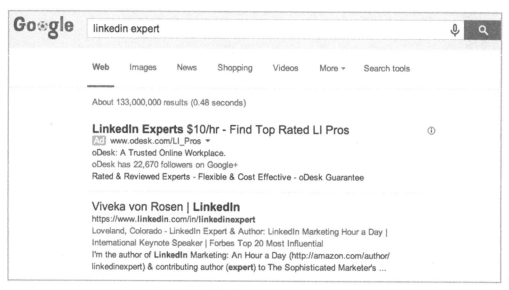

FIGURE 4–4. LinkedIn Expert Google Search

And here's why it's important to use your target keyword phrases in your LinkedIn profile headline. Viveka is the top organic search result in Google for "LinkedIn expert" out of 133 million search results. Also notice her public profile link, www.linkedin.com/in/linkedinexpert, which makes it very easy for prospective customers to find her, as shown in Figure 4-4.

Take the time now to create your compelling profile headline using your target keyword phrases.

PROFILE PICTURE

It's very important to use a professional picture in your LinkedIn profile. You are trying to project a professional image on LinkedIn, and a professional profile picture will make a lasting impression when people view your LinkedIn profile. First impressions are very important, and people will judge you within a few seconds when they see your LinkedIn profile. Save your casual pictures for Facebook and Twitter. The best LinkedIn profile pictures are engaging and inviting. I recommend a headshot focusing on your smiling face. You are establishing your professional brand on LinkedIn, and your profile photo is your personal logo. Your profile will be associated with your company so you want to present a consistent, professional image. This is why I recommend using a professional headshot of yourself instead of avatars, caricatures, or other images that aren't congruent with the image you are establishing for you and your business.

Never use your company logo as your personal profile picture. First, it's not engaging and doesn't give people a chance to get to know you. Second, it's a violation of the LinkedIn End User License Agreement (EULA; http://www.linkedin.com/legal/user-agreement).

Your profile photo must meet the following format:

- You can upload JPG, GIF, or PNG files
- Maximum file size is 4MB
- Your photo should be square
- Pixel size: 200 x 200 minimum and 500 x 500 maximum. If either width or height exceeds 4000 pixels, your photo will not upload.

As you upload your profile picture, you can choose who will be allowed to view your profile picture. I recommend choosing "Everyone," so people may see your picture when they are viewing your profile even if you are not connected with them.

In addition to users I message, my profile photo is visible to:

- My Connections
- My Network
- Everyone

I like to see a person's picture when I'm deciding whether that person is a good fit for my network. I've never rejected linking with a person because I didn't like a profile picture, but I have turned down invitations to connect with people if they don't have a picture in their profile or have chosen not to make it available. To me there is nothing worse than a LinkedIn profile with a missing picture.

I feel strongly that you should have a complete profile on LinkedIn, including a professional picture. When I see a partial LinkedIn profile or a profile without a professional picture, I feel this is a negative reflection on that person. If those individuals don't take the time to complete their LinkedIn profiles, chances are they don't take the time to complete other work tasks as thoroughly as they should. I judge this based on the fact that some people I know don't have a complete LinkedIn profile and they are not very detail-oriented. They finish 80 to 90 percent of a project but don't complete it. These are not people I want working for me, and I would not want to recommend these people to others because it could reflect negatively on me. This is just my personal opinion, and while it may not hold true in all cases, I feel very strongly about finishing what we begin.

STATUS UPDATE

Below your LinkedIn toolbar is your Status Update section. Your updates for "Share" will appear right under your Basic Information as well as under All Updates on the LinkedIn homepage. You can choose how you will share your updates, as you see in

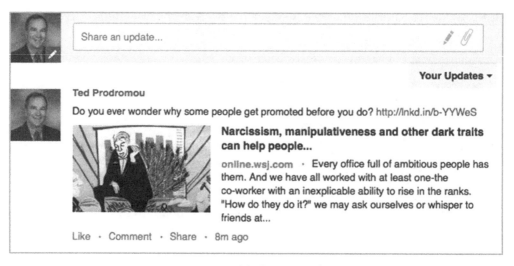

FIGURE 4–5. My Status Update

Figure 4–5. By default your update will be shared to Public only and you can select whether to share it on Twitter too or just to your Connections.

You can share an update using this box, which is located on the LinkedIn home page. By checking the box you see in Figure 4–6, your share will also be tweeted.

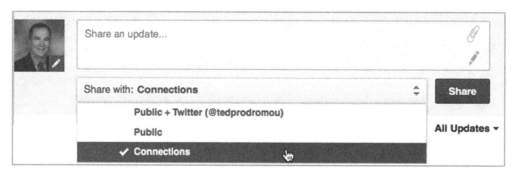

FIGURE 4–6. Tweet Status

EXPERIENCE

Now we'll move into your Experience or Employment section. To add your current and previous positions, click **+** Add a position, as seen in Figure 4–7 on page 23. Your current position and your past three positions will be displayed in your profile. Up to three additional positions will be displayed if the viewer clicks on View All.

Simply fill out the form and click Save Changes. Figure 4–8 on page 24 shows you the Add Position form. Make sure you add a brief but clear description for each position. Use your target keywords in your description, so you will be found when people search

Experience

Award-winning Author of Ultimate Guide to LinkedIn for Business, LinkedIn Expert, LinkedIn Trainer

Search Marketing Simplified

February 2013 – Present (1 year 6 months) | http://tedprodromou.com

An award-winning LinkedIn and Twitter author, LinkedIn consultant and trainer, international speaker and an online advertising expert, Ted Prodromou helps small to medium-sized companies use the internet to grow earnings, global presence and business. http://www.tedprodromou.com

With the latest techniques, including social media, podcasting, online advertising, video, blogging, Google AdWords and more, Ted takes websites from so-so to successful.

The author of the growing "Ultimate Series" for businesses, Ted has written Ultimate Guide to Linked in for Business: How to Get Connected with 150 Million Customers in 10 Minutes and Ultimate Guide to Twitter for Business, which help companies of all sizes reach more customers with dynamic, low-cost social media strategies. He is also a regular contributor to Entrepreneur.com, writing columns with strategic business advice based on his consulting practice and experience.

▸ 1 project

▾ 2 recommendations

 Emma Laming
Direct Marketing Consultant

Ted is the author of "The Ultimate Guide to LinkedIn" from Entrepreneur press. If you're a newbie, it'll kick start your... View↓

 Betty Louise
Founder, "Wisdom of Your Body" Progra...

Ted's knowledge of social media, SEO, and internet marketing is second to none. He has been looking at internet strategies... View↓

FIGURE 4–7. My Current Experience Summary

for your skill sets. If you are going to use the Request Recommendations option, I recommend sending personal invitations to one person at a time.

Notice you can create another professional headline in your Experience section. This lets people instantly get to know you and learn how you can help them when they view your profile.

If you are going to Request Recommendations, I recommend sending personal invitations to one person at a time. Often I receive mass requests from people using the standard LinkedIn message:

I'm sending this to ask you for a brief recommendation of my work that I can include in my LinkedIn profile. If you have any questions, let me know.

Thanks in advance for helping me out.

I am going to cover giving and receiving recommendations in greater detail in Chapter 10. For now, I'll provide you with some important pointers as you get started. First, it is critical you know that I rarely recommend someone who sends me a mass

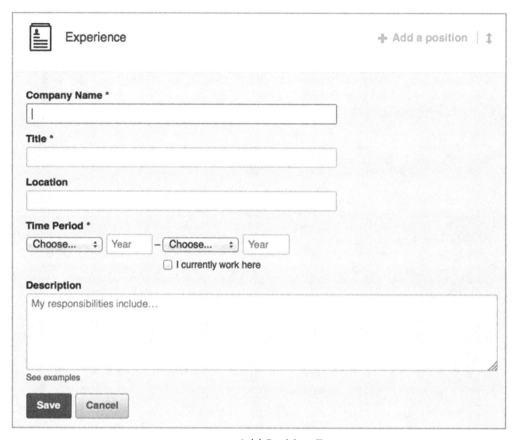

FIGURE 4–8. Add Position Form

request and doesn't take the time to write a personal invitation. This is a huge pet peeve of mine, and I will reiterate it numerous times throughout this book. *Don't use the tools in LinkedIn to send mass invitations!* LinkedIn is about building strong personal connections, and using automated tools is not the way to build a strong connection with me or with others. If you want a good recommendation from someone, take the time to write a personal invitation, and you will receive a much better recommendation than you would from a mass invitation.

You can Ask for a Recommendation in this section by clicking on the link. Fill out the form shown in Figure 4-9 on page 25, and a recommendation request will be sent to the contacts you choose.

Make sure you include personal details about how you met, projects you've worked on together, and other details about your working relationship. Specify exactly what you want in the endorsement, such as a specific project you worked on together or to highlight a certain skill set of yours. Some people even prefer that you send them a brief endorsement you've written about yourself they can edit or modify to save them time.

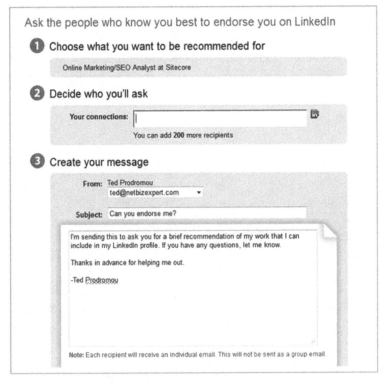

FIGURE 4-9. Recommendation Form

Your Recommendations are displayed next, as shown in Figure 4–10.

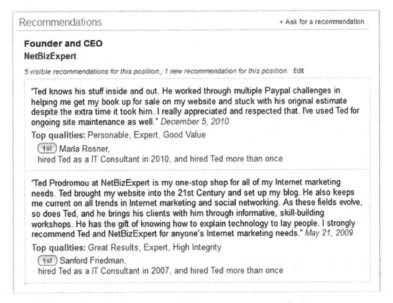

FIGURE 4-10. Some of My Recommendations

EDUCATION

Once you've added your current and previous positions, you'll move to your education. Simply click Add a School to enter your schools, years attended, and your major. Figure 4–11 shows the Add Education form.

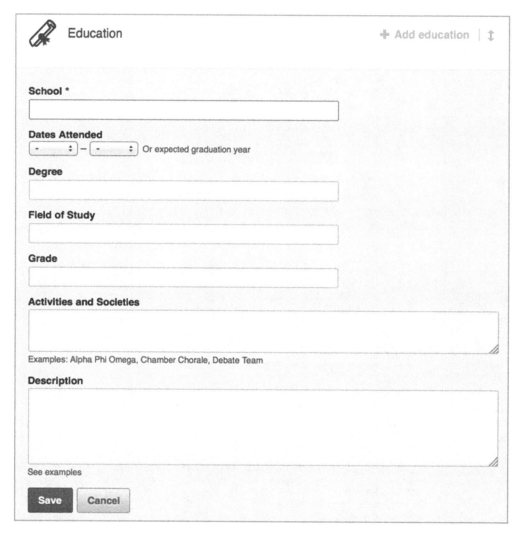

FIGURE 4–11. Add Education Form

You can also add multimedia content and links to articles on websites, as shown in Figure 4–12 on page 27.

CONTACT INFORMATION

This is the section where you can add links to your website and blog, which will generate lots of web traffic and help your search rankings. Links from popular sites

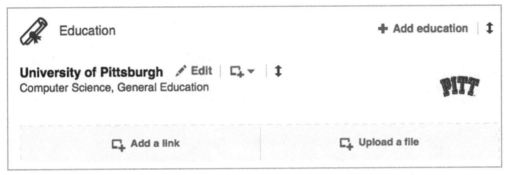

FIGURE 4–12. Education List with Multimedia Content Links

like LinkedIn are very valuable, so you want to use this trick when you enter your website or blog URL.

One of the most common mistakes people make when adding their website or blog URLs to their LinkedIn profile is to choose one of the default options like Personal Website or Blog.

If you choose Company Website or one of the other options in the dropdown list as shown in Figure 4–13, your listing will look something like Figure 4–14 on page 28. I chose Company Website so you can see how it displays Company Website instead of my actual company name or target keyword phrase. This helps add valuable links and keyword phrases in your LinkedIn profile that will help your Google search rankings.

LINKEDIN SEO TIP

Choose Other and enter your company name or keyword phrases in the middle box shown below.

FIGURE 4–13. Contact Information

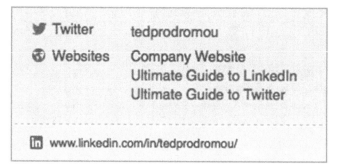

FIGURE 4–14. The Default Option—Company Website

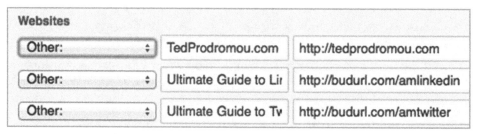

FIGURE 4–15. Displaying Your Keywords Instead of the Words "Company Name"

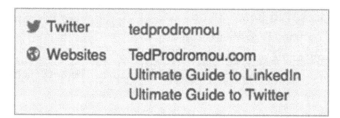

FIGURE 4–16. Search-Optimized Links to Your Website

Now your listing will look like Figure 4–16, and your company name or keyword phrases are clickable links to your blog or website.

ADDING YOUR SOCIAL MEDIA ACCOUNTS

LinkedIn lets you add social media feeds to your LinkedIn profile. This lets your profile visitors see what you're up to on the social media front.

Adding Your Twitter Account

Open your LinkedIn profile, click on Add Twitter Account, and enter your Twitter user name. I prefer to display my Twitter account on my LinkedIn profile by checking the

FIGURE 4–17. Adding Twitter to Your LinkedIn Profile

box. This allows me to tweet my LinkedIn Status Updates in one step. Figure 4–17 shows you how to manage your Twitter settings.

Now my Twitter account is connected to my LinkedIn profile, so I can share my LinkedIn Status Updates on Twitter, as you see in Figure 4–18.

FIGURE 4–18. Profile with Twitter

You can easily see your full status activity by clicking on See Your Updates, where they will see a full listing of your LinkedIn activity, as shown in Figure 4–19 on page 30.

PUBLICATIONS

One of the new additions to your profile is Publications where you can display your published books. You must have a valid ISBN number for your published book to use this section. As you see in Figure 4-20 on page 30, your publication listing includes your book title, publisher, publication date, and a description of your book. You can also add a link to your website, Amazon, Barnes & Noble, or any other website where people can purchase your book.

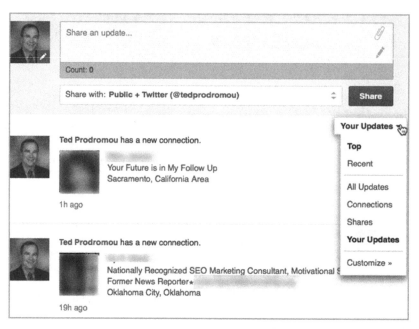

FIGURE 4–19. See Your Updates

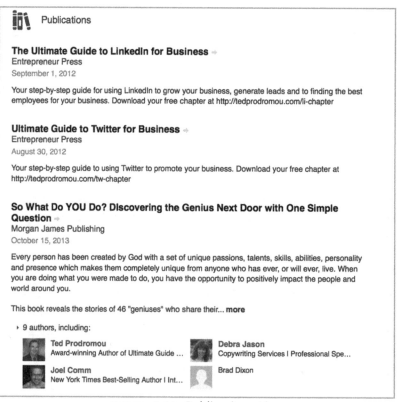

FIGURE 4–20. Publications List

A great feature of Publications is the ability to link to the LinkedIn profiles of other authors if you co-wrote the book. One of my books was co-authored with *New York Times* best-selling author Joel Comm so our LinkedIn profiles are displayed in my profile, Joel's profile, and all of the other book authors' profiles. This is a great way to associate yourself with famous authors, adding to your credibility.

CONCLUSION

Your LinkedIn profile is now optimized for the search engines and ready to promote. Edit your public profile and choose Create a Profile Badge to promote your LinkedIn profile or use your Public Profile link. Add links to your LinkedIn profile from your website, blog, and email signature to generate traffic and improve your search rankings. LinkedIn is frequently adding new sections to your profile, which lets you share more information about yourself. This lets people get to know, like, and trust you faster, which accelerates the sales process dramatically. As you notice additional sections in your LinkedIn profile, fill out the new sections to keep your profile as complete as possible.

In the next chapter, I'll introduce you to the LinkedIn Privacy settings, where you can control when and where LinkedIn and its partner websites may use your profile information. I'll show you why it's important for you to configure your privacy settings properly to prevent your profile from appearing in inappropriate places like an ad near your competitor's company profile.

For additional updates and how-to videos, visit
www.tedprodromou.com/chapter4

LinkedIn
Privacy Settings

Now that your LinkedIn profile is complete, we can configure your privacy settings. LinkedIn lets you control how your data is displayed and who is allowed to see your activity on LinkedIn. Internet privacy is a very controversial topic these days because people are becoming concerned about how much personal and private information is being collected by websites and how they are using it. Your LinkedIn profile does not contain any personal information like your home address or telephone numbers, unless you voluntarily add them to your profile. I do not recommend adding any such personal information on your account. It is appropriate to include your work telephone number and office address so prospects and customers can easily reach you, and I'll leave it up to you if you want to include your cell phone number. Remember, more than 330 million people potentially have access to this information, which could be a blessing or a curse depending on who gets access to your cell phone number. People will also be able to get your company telephone number from your LinkedIn company page, so you want to add a link to your company page in your profile. Make it easy for prospects and customers to connect with you.

You have two profiles on LinkedIn. Your primary profile is the profile people see when they are logged in to LinkedIn. They will see the details of your current and past jobs, the details of your education, your recommendations, your websites, Twitter account information, and which LinkedIn Groups you have joined. In the right column of your profile, people will see all of your LinkedIn activity, including your tweets and shared updates.

People can also see all of your connections and get a sense of who you are and whom you're associated with. This helps people connect with like-minded people, so they can grow their network. Many believe this is a great way to grow your professional network because you're being totally transparent with other LinkedIn members.

If you don't want to let people see your connections, you can change your privacy settings so you are the only one who can view your connections. Some people do believe that not sharing their connections with others gives them a competitive advantage. A common practice of LinkedIn members is to find out whom their competitors are connected to and reach out to these connections to see if they are interesting in bringing their business to your company. If the person doesn't share their contacts with other LinkedIn members, you wouldn't have the opportunity to connect with their customers and steal them away from your competitor.

When you recommend others on LinkedIn, your recommendation will appear in their LinkedIn profile, if they choose to display their Recommendations. This lets people see whom you do business with and helps them find great resources when they need assistance. People always prefer working with service providers who have been recommended instead of working with unknowns.

The last section of your profile sidebar displays Viewers of This Profile Also Viewed . . . . After people view your profile, they often view your connections' profiles. This section shows you the other profiles viewed after yours. This lets you see people LinkedIn has associated with your profile because you work for the same company, work in the same industry, have similar job skills, or have other similarities. This often shows you people you should be connected with on LinkedIn because of these similarities.

PUBLIC PROFILE

One profile is called your Public Profile, which can be viewed by people who are not logged into LinkedIn. This profile appears in Google searches if you choose to make it visible to the search engines. You can edit Public Profile settings and control which parts of your profile are displayed publicly. You can open up your profile completely so all information is accessible to the search engines and people not logged in to LinkedIn. You can also make your Public Profile completely private if you don't want to be found in the search engines. The third option is to customize the display of different elements of your profile. For example, you can display your basic information, headline, and summary and block the rest of your profile from the search engines. Most people use the custom configuration and display some of their profile and block sensitive information if it's included in their profile.

CONCLUSION

If you are a consultant or small-business owner and want to get your name out there, I see no reason to block any of your content from the search engines. You are on LinkedIn so people can find you, and blocking your listing from search engines is self-defeating. It would be similar to owning a small business and having an unlisted telephone number. Opening up your profile completely will get your target keywords into the search engines, giving you maximum exposure.

In the next chapter, we'll take a tour of your LinkedIn homepage. I'll show you how to customize your homepage layout so you can easily see a snapshot of your important LinkedIn data.

For additional updates and how-to videos, visit
www.tedprodromou.com/chapter5

A Tour of Your LinkedIn Homepage

et's take a tour of your LinkedIn homepage. Every LinkedIn member
has his or her own customizable homepage, which is like your start
page on Yahoo!, Google, or MSN. You select what you want to
appear on your homepage so you can easily see what's important to you
in a single glance. Figure 6–1 on page 38 is a view of a typical LinkedIn
homepage.

1. *LinkedIn Search*. This is where you search for people, companies, and
   groups on LinkedIn. I'll show you how to do advanced searches on
   LinkedIn in Chapter 8, "LinkedIn Search."
2. *Notifications*. This is your notifications section. When you have new
   LinkedIn email or notifications, like someone commented on your
   status update or accepted your connection request, the icon will
   show the number of new notifications. Currently I have 184 unread
   emails and 1 new notification.
3. *This is your LinkedIn toolbar or menu*. The menu options include:
   - *Home*: Obviously, this takes you back to your LinkedIn homepage.
   - *Profile*: This is where you can view and edit your LinkedIn profile.
   - *Connections*: This is where you can add and manage your LinkedIn
     connections. You can also Keep in Touch, Add Connections, and
     Find Alumni from this menu item.

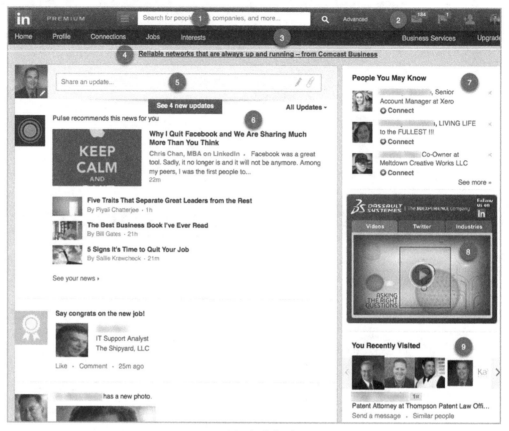

FIGURE 6–1. A Typical LinkedIn Homepage

- *Jobs*: You can post job openings for your company. This is where you can look for a job, post and manage jobs, and access premium services like Job Seeker Premium and Recruiting Solutions. I'll explain the premium solutions in Chapter 19, "Recruiting New Employees," and Chapter 23, "Finding a Job on LinkedIn."
- *Interests*: This is where you access Companies, LinkedIn Groups, Pulse, and Education.

4. *Self-Service Text Ads*. Near the top of Figure 6-1 you will see where your LinkedIn self-service text ads will be displayed.

5. *Share an Update Box*. This is where you post your status updates.

6. *All Updates*. This is where status updates and company news will appear. You can control the updates you see in this area by clicking on the down arrow next to All Updates.

7. *People You May Know*. This is where the LinkedIn search algorithm will recommend people you may want to connect with based on who you are connected with, companies you have in your profile or follow, or former co-workers.

8. *Content Ads.* This is where LinkedIn Premium Content ads are displayed.

9. *You Recently Visited.* This widget shows you profiles you recently viewed, company pages you visited, and status updates you commented on. Figure 6–2 shows additional widgets displayed on your LinkedIn homepage.

10. *Who's Viewed Your Profile.* This widget lets you know how many people viewed your profile in the past week. Clicking on the link will give you some details about who clicked, and LinkedIn Premium members will get full contact information about who viewed your profile.

11. *Who's Viewed Your Updates.* A new widget that shows Premium LinkedIn members detail analytics of who viewed your updates, commented and shared them, and how viral the updates went. You see how many first-, second-, and third-degree connections saw your updates.

12. *Your LinkedIn Network.* This is where you see how many first-level connections you have and how many people are in your LinkedIn network including first-, second-, and third-degree connections.

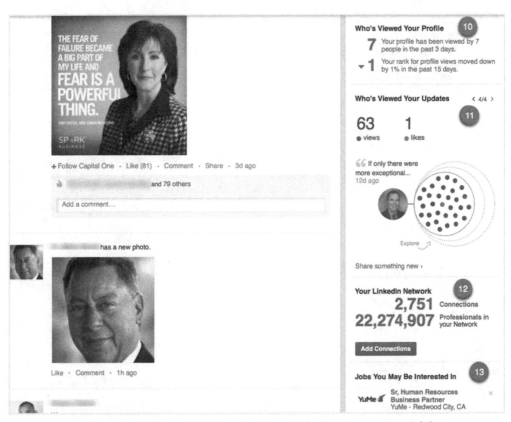

FIGURE 6–2. Additional Widgets in Your LinkedIn Homepage Sidebar

13. *Jobs You May be Interested In*. Based on the job titles and keywords in your profile, LinkedIn will recommend jobs you may be interested in.

As LinkedIn adds more analytical data to your profile, additional widgets will appear in your sidebar. Figure 6–3 shows the rest of the sidebar widgets.

14. *Groups You May Like*. LinkedIn will recommend groups for you to join based on your LinkedIn profile, your industry, your network, and your LinkedIn activity.

15. *Companies You May Want to Follow*. This LinkedIn widget displays companies you may want to follow based on your professional network, your industry, and people you follow on LinkedIn Pulse.

CONCLUSION

You are now familiar with your LinkedIn homepage and how you can configure it to display the content that is most appropriate for you. You can change many of the

FIGURE 6–3. Additional Sidebar Widgets Displayed on Your LinkedIn Homepage

content modules so your homepage gives you an efficient snapshot of the data you want to see.

In the next chapter, I'm going to show you how to set up your LinkedIn company page and customize it to give your company maximum exposure.

For additional updates and how-to videos, visit
www.tedprodromou.com/chapter6

LinkedIn
for Companies

LinkedIn company pages are like a LinkedIn personal profile for your company. Your company page is a mini-website for your company, but it's located on LinkedIn so it's easy for LinkedIn members to find. You'll want to use the same search optimization techniques that you used when you set up your personal profile when you're setting up your company page.

LinkedIn revamped company pages in 2014 to improve the user experience by making the pages more engaging and to increase brand awareness. Showcase pages replaced the product pages so it's easier for companies to feature their products and services. It's now easier to recruit new employees using the updated company pages by featuring job openings and letting job seekers learn more about your company and your culture.

Your company page will always appear when a member types your company's name in LinkedIn's search box on their homepage or on the Companies link on the top toolbar. Your LinkedIn company page will also appear in Google search results. Because LinkedIn is a very popular and trusted website, LinkedIn company pages rank well in Google. This is very significant because your LinkedIn company page will rank highly in Google search results and people can view your LinkedIn company page without logging into LinkedIn, giving your company significant exposure. For this reason, you want to make sure your LinkedIn company page is complete and updated frequently with your latest company news and product offerings.

Other ways your company page will appear include:

> **LINKEDIN COMPANY PAGE TIP**
>
> Your LinkedIn company page URL will be www.linkedin.com/company/ YourCompanyName.

- When you view the LinkedIn profile of one of your employees
- Receive a notification when your products or services are recommended by one of your employees' connections
- See an open position from your company via a job search under Jobs You May Be Interested In
- See your company under Companies You May Be Interested in Following, which appears in the right sidebar on your homepage
- Follow your company and receive status updates

For LinkedIn members, company pages are a great way to research companies. There is a treasure trove of detailed information about almost any company—even if the company does not have a company page. When you do a search from the LinkedIn top toolbar and switch the search type to companies, you will see search results from the company page (if there is one) and all companies who work closely or partner with that company.

For example, when you do a company search for Microsoft, you will see the Microsoft company page followed by a list of Microsoft Certified Partners. Click on the Microsoft company page and you'll find a list of people in your network who are affiliated with Microsoft. You'll also be provided with a list of Microsoft employees who are in LinkedIn and are your first-, second-, or third-degree connections.

You can follow companies on their company page so you can stay up to date with their new products or services, review their products or services, and see who they are hiring. You can also follow competitors and know what they're up to!

Company pages let your customers and prospects get to know the people in your company. You can feature the employees behind your brand and show how customers use your products. Your company page is a great way to solidify your reputation and build trust with your clients and prospects.

COMPONENTS OF A COMPANY PROFILE

Figure 7–1 on page 45 shows you a typical company profile and the options you have to customize it for your needs.

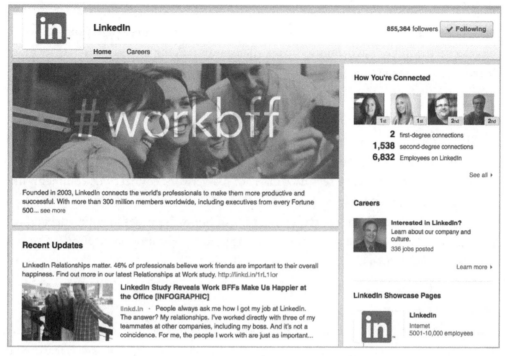

FIGURE 7–1. A Typical Company Profile

Overview of Your Company Homepage

The Home tab shows the viewer a snapshot of your company, including your Recent Updates, a brief description of your company, and all employees in the network, including first-, second-, and third-degree connections. You can also display your company's blog posts on the Home tab. It's a great way to give people a quick overview of your company and an opportunity for you to make a direct connection with them if they follow your company.

How You're Connected

This sidebar widget shows you to whom you are directly connected in this company and the number of second-degree connections you have. You'll also see how many employees of that company are within your current network and second-degree connections.

Careers

This is where any job openings you've posted on LinkedIn will appear. If you purchase a Silver or Gold Career Page, you can also add a brief description of your company culture, and people can get a good idea of how fantastic it is to work there. The Silver and Gold Career

Pages also let you feature top employees and create targeted messaging to help fill your open positions quickly with the best talent. If you have a Gold Career Page, your jobs will be targeted to the individual member viewing the page. For example, you can target members based on industry, job function, seniority, and geography, so your message to a programmer in Silicon Valley is different from your message to a sales professional in Sydney.

Showcase Pages

You can feature your products and services on this sidebar widget. When a prospect or customer visits this page, he sees how many of his network connections comment, like, or share posts on the Showcase page.

You can create a directory-style listing of your Showcase pages in your sidebar. Each product or service can have its own showcase page including descriptions, features, images, display banners, videos, and special offers.

Sponsored Posts

LinkedIn Advertising lets you promote posts from your Company page as Sponsored Updates. When you sponsor an update, the post from your Company page is featured in the timeline of a target audience using the same targeting you use in normal LinkedIn ads. This lets you get your message in front of your target audience, and they'll see your Sponsored Update in their personal timeline. I'll teach you more about LinkedIn advertising in Chapter 21.

Analytics

This tab is visible only to an administrator of your Company page. The Analytics tab shows you who your visitors are, what they do, and which other companies they follow. You gain valuable insight into what content they are most interested in, their job function, industry, company, and which products they are researching.

Updates

This data tells you exactly how many impressions your Company page updates reach, how many people click on the content, how many interactions (likes, shares, and comments), how many new followers resulted from the post, and the engagement percentage.

Followers

This is where you see the demographics of who's following your company. You'll see how many people organically followed you compared with the number of people who followed you from promotions. You can sort your followers by seniority, industry, company size, function, and employee/non-employee. This gives you valuable insight into the professionals who follow your company so you can structure Sponsored Updates and promotions targeted to your audience. You'll also see Follower Trends and How You Compare with companies similar to yours.

Visitors

This data is similar to Google Analytics. You'll see the number of page views and unique visitors to your Company page so you'll know which content and products they're most interested in. You can also sort your Visitor data by Seniority, Industry, Company Size, Function, and Employee/Non-employee.

COMPANY STATUS UPDATES

Company status updates are posts made by the company to share company news, product releases, promotions, or relevant industry news. Company status updates are a powerful communication tool, allowing you to send messages and links directly to your followers.

Company posts can be seen on the company's Overview tab by any LinkedIn member and in a member's network update stream. If you follow the company, you will see the company status updates directly on your homepage so it's easy to know what's happening with that company, your competitors, or in your industry. All LinkedIn members have the ability to view company status updates, click on embedded links, or view posted videos. They can also comment on, like, or share a company status update, allowing your updates to spread virally to grow your following and engage your members.

CREATING YOUR COMPANY PAGE

When you are ready to create your company page, go to Interests, Companies on the top toolbar. On the right side of the page near the top, click on Create. Enter your company name and company email address, and check the box next to the verification message: "I verify that I am the official representative of this company and have the right to act on behalf of my company in the creation of this page." You must use an email address from your company, not a Gmail or other free email address.

Next you will enter a wizard shown in Figure 7–2 on page 48 that will guide you through the setup of your new company page.

You can select any language for your company page. When you select any language other than English, the wizard changes; this eliminates all configuration options on the

Companies Home   Following (49)

Add a Company

Company Pages offer public information about each company on LinkedIn. To add a Company Page, please enter the company name and your email address at this company. Only current employees are eligible to create a Company Page.

Company name:

Your email address at company:

☐ I verify that I am the official representative of this company and have the right to act on behalf of my company in the creation of this page.

[Continue]   or Cancel

FIGURE 7–2. Company Page Setup Wizard

Overview tab, except Company Description. You can still add items to the Careers and Products & Services tabs if you select a language other than English.

If you choose English for your company page, you need to choose who will be authorized to be the company page administrators (admins). The default choice is "All employees with a valid email registered to the company domain," which I don't recommend. It's best to manually designate your admins, so you have consistency of and control over what is posted on your company page. Allowing every employee to have admin access to your company page can result in inappropriate content being posted and inconsistent management of your company page.

Designate at least two administrators for your company page. You may want to add more if you work for a large company and will have a lot of activity on your page. For example, if you will be posting a lot of job openings on your company page, you can designate a member of your human resources department as administrator and allow her to post and remove job openings. It would be smart to have an administrator from human resources, sales, public relations, and marketing, so they can each efficiently manage their respective areas of your company page. The marketing person could manage the Products & Services section; public relations could post your Share updates with current company news and product announcements; and sales could monitor the discussions, in case any pre-sales questions are posted on your company page.

It's imperative that someone is assigned to constantly monitor your company page, in case inappropriate content is posted. Any offending content should be removed immediately.

Negative remarks don't necessarily have to be removed, if you address them in an appropriate way. Every company has at least a small number of dissatisfied customers who may post negative comments about their products. Instead of just removing the negative comment, you can respond in a positive way by addressing the issue publicly. Sometimes the issue is a simple misunderstanding of how to use the product, which you can explain. On other occasions, there could be a legitimate problem with your product or service. If this is the case, then proper communication with the customer not only leads to resolution, it may even build your company's reputation. Admitting mistakes, offering speedy solutions, and showing strong commitment to respectful communication demonstrate that you care about your customers and provide excellent customer service.

CONCLUSION

Your LinkedIn company page is a mini-website where you can share company news, updates, and current job openings. Your LinkedIn company page is easily found in LinkedIn searches giving your company great exposure to millions of LinkedIn members and in Google search results.

In the next chapter, we'll explore LinkedIn Search, which is your most powerful tool on LinkedIn. Mastering LinkedIn Search will give you access to the invaluable data available in the rapidly growing LinkedIn database.

For additional updates and how-to videos, visit
www.tedprodromou.com/chapter7

LinkedIn Search

L inkedIn is essentially a business-oriented search engine and works
the same way as other search engines like Google and Yahoo!.
LinkedIn has its own proprietary search algorithm, which isn't as
sophisticated as the Google search algorithm (no search engine is as
sophisticated as Google's), but it's evolving rapidly. When you master
LinkedIn Search, you will have access to an unlimited number of
prospects at your fingertips.

LinkedIn Search has two functions. First, it can be used to find
other people, companies, and groups on LinkedIn so you can build your
professional network, follow companies, and join industry-related groups.
The second function of LinkedIn Search is for people to find you. Most
people don't think of LinkedIn Search from that perspective, but I think
you need to stop and consider the possibilities. What would it do for your
business or career if you appeared when people searched for specific skills
or industry terms? With more than 150 million of the best top business
professionals looking for industry experts by searching LinkedIn, you
career would skyrocket if you appeared on the first page of the search
results. If you want to optimize your LinkedIn profile so you appear
in search results, I invite you to visit Chapter 4, "Supercharging Your
LinkedIn Profile."

Let's start with using LinkedIn Search to find people, companies, and groups. As you can see in Figure 8–1 the LinkedIn search box is located right in the middle of the LinkedIn menu or toolbar.

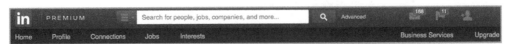

FIGURE 8–1. The LinkedIn Menu or Toolbar

The left side of the search box gives you eight search options in a dropdown box. This is called LinkedIn Smart Search. You have the ability to narrow your search results to All, People, Jobs, Companies, Groups, Universities, Posts, and Inbox. If you leave the search box on the default search All and just click the magnifying glass, LinkedIn will display a list of all of your first- and second-degree connections plus people in your LinkedIn Groups. You can also see a full list of your connections if you go to the Connections tab on the LinkedIn menu. On this page you will see recent communications with your contacts if you imported your contacts from Outlook, Gmail, or another email service provider. If you want to find people outside your network, you need to enter specific keywords like a job title, company name, industry, school, or skill in the search box.

LinkedIn People Search is a very powerful tool that can help you find new customers, recruit new employees, and build your professional network. You can also use LinkedIn People Search to:

- Find an industry expert to speak at an event your company is hosting
- Find an industry expert to hire as a consultant for a project
- Find people you want to meet with when you are traveling to another city
- Find speaking engagements
- Find consulting engagements
- Connect with other industry experts to join you in a project or business venture.
- Find people who want to join you for charity events
- Find people who want to start a local networking group

When you have the ability to search a database of more than 330 million business professionals, the benefits of LinkedIn People Search are endless.

KEYWORDS ARE KING

Keywords, keywords, keywords! You are going to get tired of hearing me talk about keywords, but they are the foundation of LinkedIn Search so it's important that you understand how to use them effectively. In the next chapter, "Getting Found on LinkedIn," I'm going to teach you everything you ever wanted to know about keywords (and probably a little more!), but for now let's focus on the fundamentals of using the LinkedIn Search function.

LinkedIn Search works a little differently from a Google search. If I search Google for "web marketing expert," without the quote marks, I will see results that contain the word *web* or *marketing* or *expert*. This is called a broad match search because Google will return all results that contain any of the keywords I used in my search.

I can also do a phrase search to narrow my results. If I search Google for "web marketing expert" with the quote marks, I will see only results that contain the entire phrase "web marketing expert." This gives me a more focused search result, saving me time.

When I search for "web marketing expert" on LinkedIn, the search results will show every person who has the phrase "web marketing expert" in their profile, and you will also see Companies, Showcase Pages, and LinkedIn Groups appear in a dropdown menu. This dropdown menu acts just like the Google Instant dropdown you see when you do a Google search. By default the initial search will show you first- and second-degree connections and Groups if you don't choose one of the dropdown search results.

Competitive Analysis

Let's get into more detail about doing a competitive analysis search, and I'll show you how to use the Search sort option to expand your search results and find exactly who or what you are looking for. A great example of a competitive search is one to see what keywords your competitors are targeting. Let's say you're in the cloud computing business and want to see who's ranking well in LinkedIn search results. Figure 8–2 on page 54 shows your competitors you entered in your initial search.

The search results begin to appear and suggest the top search results as you type your keyword phrase. In this example we see the top search results for Companies, Showcase Pages, and People. The top company for the phrase "cloud computing" is Cloud Computing Centre. Let's reverse-engineer the search result and see how Cloud Computing Centre achieved its top ranking and which other keywords they're targeting. Your goal is to outrank them for the search term "cloud computing." Note that you will receive different search results if you search for cloud computing, which looks for LinkedIn profiles that contain the word *cloud* or *computing*. We're looking for companies using the entire phrase "cloud computing."

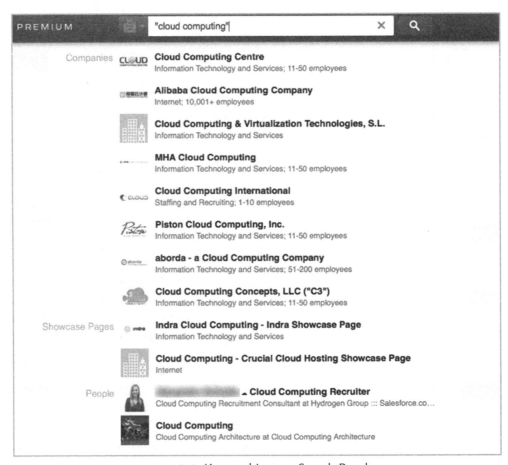

FIGURE 8–2. Keyword Instant Search Results

Reverse-Engineering

As I examine the Cloud Computing Centre company page, I searched for "cloud computing" in my browser by selecting CTRL F on my PC browser or Command C on my Mac browser, as you see in Figure 8–3 on page 55.

Keywords

From my experience, using your target keywords in your Company page title helps your search rankings significantly. It's also important to use the target keyword phrase a few times in the first two paragraphs of your summary. This strategy is almost identical to SEO best practices for ranking in search engines like Google, Bing, and Yahoo!. Be careful not to overuse your keyword phrases too often in your summary. The summary should read naturally and provide a comprehensive overview of your company offerings in the 2,000-character space you are provided.

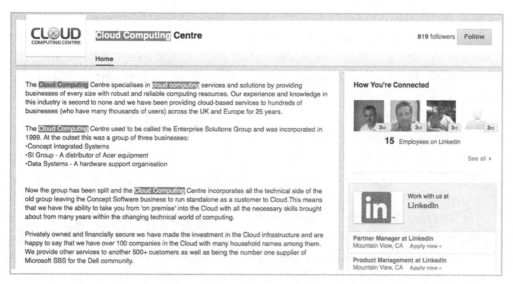

FIGURE 8–3. Checking Keyword Density

Followers

To rank well in LinkedIn search results, you must have a significant number of followers. I've seen companies with literally no summary or company information other than their Company page title and over 800 followers rank number one for their search terms. Obviously, I recommend providing a comprehensive summary in your Company page profile. My assumption is the company that ranks number one without a summary has hired offshore workers to follow their company just to receive the high ranking.

TAKING ADVANTAGE OF THE SAVE OPTION

Once you find a set of search options that provides the best results, you can save that search by clicking the Save Search link in the upper-right-hand corner of the page. Saving the search criteria will let you run this exact search query automatically on a weekly or monthly basis. LinkedIn sends you an email every time the Saved Search is run so you can see the latest search results without having to manually run the query.

ADVANCED LINKEDIN SEARCH

Okay, you've had a couple of tastes of the basic LinkedIn Search, and now it's time to dig into the main course: Advanced LinkedIn Search. This is the skill you need to master to become a top-tier LinkedIn user. Whether you are in sales hunting for prospects, a recruiter looking for top talent, or just a regular LinkedIn member, becoming an expert at searching on LinkedIn will take your career to the next level.

Advanced Search has changed dramatically since the first edition of *Ultimate Guide to LinkedIn for Business*. You used to be able to sort the search results by Relevance, Relationship, Relationship + Recommendations, Connections, or Keywords. This was so confusing, and very few people knew what these categories meant. Today, it's much easier to sort your search results based on Keywords, First Name, Last Name, Title, Company, School, Location, Country, and Postal Code. When you subscribe to a LinkedIn Premium account, you will have access to more data fields like LinkedIn Groups, Years of Experience, Function, Seniority Level, Interested In, Company Size, Fortune 500 level, and When Joined LinkedIn. The higher level of subscription you purchase, the more data you will see.

At your fingertips, you have access to more than 330 million business professionals from around the world. Obviously you don't need to connect with all of them, but you can build a strong professional network of 150 colleagues that you can carry with you for the rest of your career. No longer will you have to worry about recessions and high unemployment. When you surround yourself with a strong international professional network, recessions will have little or no impact on your career.

Think about this. When we entered the new millennium, everyone was worried that the Y2K date problem in older computers would bring businesses to their knees. We survived Y2K without a hitch, but the dotcom collapse crushed our economy and changed the high-tech world forever. Thousands lost their jobs, but eventually most people found new jobs or careers. In 2008, the banking crisis collapsed the world economy, with millions of people around the world losing their jobs. Not only did they lose their jobs, many lost their homes and their life savings. The past ten years have been a wild roller-coaster ride for many middle-class citizens around the world.

While the economy and unemployment were bouncing up and down over the past ten years, the number of millionaires and billionaires around the world increased significantly. According to a finding in *The Wall Street Journal* in the year 2000, there were 306 billionaires in the world. In 2011 there were 1,210 billionaires—a fourfold increase.

How did so many people become billionaires during the worst economic conditions in our lifetime? They built a strong personal network around themselves, so they could withstand the recession and actually make a significant amount of money during the past few years.

I know it seems like I'm drifting a bit off track, and you're probably wondering how this relates to LinkedIn Search. It's directly related to LinkedIn Search because you have the opportunity to build a powerful personal network from the LinkedIn database. Everyone you need to know is on LinkedIn. If for some reason you need to connect with someone who is not on LinkedIn, a LinkedIn connection can lead you to that person. Remember, success in business is about who you know, not what you know.

The better you get at LinkedIn Search, the closer you come to putting your personal dream network together. Mining through the LinkedIn database, looking for the nuggets of gold, will put you in a position where you will never have to worry about earning money again. When you need a new project, one of your connections will know someone who needs your expertise. Looking for some new sales prospects? A few of your second- and third-degree connections are sure to need your product. It's all about leveraging the power of the rapidly growing LinkedIn network. Since I started writing the first edition of this book two years ago, LinkedIn grew from 130 million members to 330 million members. By the time this book hits the bookstores, LinkedIn will likely be well over 350 million members, since statistically they are adding two members every second.

The following sections offer just a few examples how you can use Advanced LinkedIn Search.

SALES REP SELLING CUSTOMER RELATIONSHIP MANAGEMENT SOFTWARE

You are a sales rep who sells customer relationship management (CRM) software to enterprise-level clients. Your key decision-maker is usually at the CXO level, and your target companies are in the Fortune 500. Your software has a 6- to 12-month buying cycle, and there are many departments involved in the decision-making process, including sales, information technology, and sometimes marketing. There are also project managers from these departments involved in the purchase decision.

Your initial contact is usually with a manager in the IT or sales department who does the initial evaluation of your product. After she does the initial evaluation, an IT or sales director gets involved. You want to use LinkedIn Advanced Search to find managers who are doing the initial evaluation or directors who are involved in the second phase of the project.

In the past, an easy way to find managers or directors who were shopping for CRM systems was to search LinkedIn Answers for phrases like:

- What is the best CRM software?
- I am looking for insight . . .
- Looking for advice . . .
- I want a GREAT CRM system. What is the best?
- What is your current CRM?

Now that LinkedIn Answers has been discontinued because the conversations were turning spammy and self-promotional, we have to take another approach to finding our prospects. One way to search for discussions is to join groups related to CRMs. Most of the CRM-related groups are managed by vendors who are probably your competitors so it's a great idea to join those groups if they let you. This will give you access to people who are evaluating your competitor's CRM product and to their current customers who may be having problems with their CRM. Figure 8-4 shows you how to start with a broad search to find groups, companies, and people in the CRM business; this is a great example of how to become a LinkedIn detective to track down hot prospects!

This is where you'll find the groups of CRM consultants and CRM providers, including your competitors. Also join groups where your decision-makers would hang

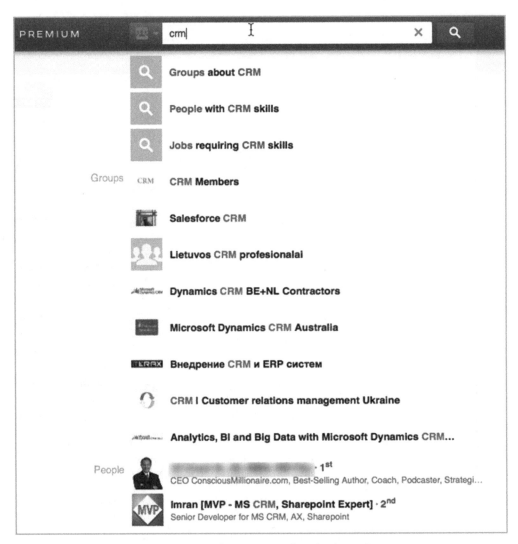

FIGURE 8–4. Finding CRM-Related Discussions

out like CMO Network, Inbound Marketers, Marketing Profs Pro, and other sales and marketing-related groups.

I use my competitors' groups and groups related to the products to find out what people are saying about the products, both good and bad. It's a great way to gain competitive intelligence about your competitors' products. People will be discussing what they love about your competitors' products and, even more importantly, what they don't like about them. When you're doing a sales presentation to a prospect, you can let them know the weaknesses of your competitors' product and show them how your product excels in that area.

To find this competitive intelligence, you have to search each group individually. Unfortunately there isn't a way to search for keywords in all groups at once. In Figure 8–5, I show you how to search for keyword phrases in your groups.

Next, you want to view the person's profile to see if he is a potential prospect. Is he a decision maker who can purchase your product or service? Is he connected to anyone in your network who can give you feedback about this person or can introduce you to this person?

If you think this person is a good prospect, click the Get Introduced link and ask one of your first-degree connections to introduce you. I find this is more effective than reaching out to the person directly because that is the equivalent of cold-calling. When I'm introduced to someone, he has a level of trust immediately because we have a connection in common who is recommending me.

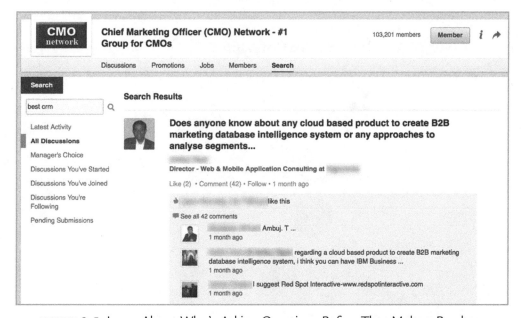

FIGURE 8–5. Learn About Who's Asking Questions Before They Make a Purchase

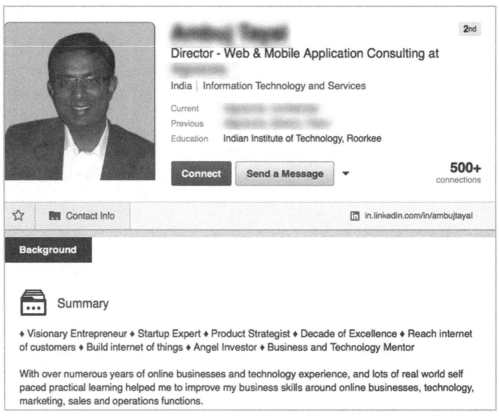

FIGURE 8–6. View the Full Profile

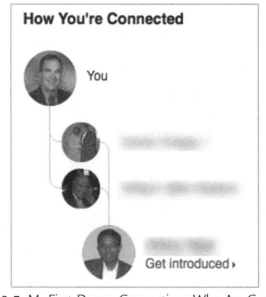

FIGURE 8–7. My First-Degree Connections Who Are Connected

A MORE DIRECT ROUTE TO HOT PROSPECTS

While it was relatively easy to look for prospects in the LinkedIn Groups section, you saw the obvious drawback. There is no easy way to prequalify the potential leads you find in LinkedIn Groups. You have to take that extra step of reviewing the profile of the person asking the questions to find out if she works for a company that meets your demographic target. Unfortunately, there isn't an Advanced Search capability for LinkedIn Groups that lets you filter by anything other than keywords. It would be nice to be able to filter group discussions by the same fields as the People Search provides—but LinkedIn can't do that yet.

From my experience, it's rare to see high-level executives asking questions about products in the LinkedIn Groups section, since they enter the buying process toward the end after much due diligence by the managers and directors. You can target managers and directors in the LinkedIn Groups section, but you have to use a different approach to connect with the C-level executives who are the final decision-makers.

I prefer to use the Advanced Search under People when I'm looking for very specific information about a person or company. In this example, you could do an Advanced Search to find C-level execs or managers and directors in Fortune 500 companies located in your territory.

To do an Advanced Search for specific people, make sure the Search is set to People and click the Advanced link next to the magnifying glass. The Advanced People Search tab will appear with a slew of options.

Let's keep it simple and search for C-level executives who work for Fortune 500 companies within a 100-mile radius of your office. Leave all of the fields empty except for your postal code and change the "Within:" to 100 mi. On the Seniority Level check the CXO box. This will search for all C-level executives. Check the appropriate boxes under Fortune 1000 to select only the Fortune 500. Figures 8–8 and 8–9 on page 62 show you what your search criteria should look like.

Click Search and you will see a list of all C-level executives who work for Fortune 500 companies within 100 miles of your office. You can sort your results using the same options I described earlier to organize your search results. Sort your results by Relevance, Relationship, Relationship + Recommendations, Connections, or Keywords.

If you notice a manager or director from a certain company researching CRM options in LinkedIn Groups, you can use the Advanced Search to find other managers, directors, and C-level execs so you will know who will probably be involved in the decision-making process.

You can see your relationship to them and ask for introductions from your first-level connections when the time is right. You can also modify your search to specific companies once you know which companies are researching new CRM systems.

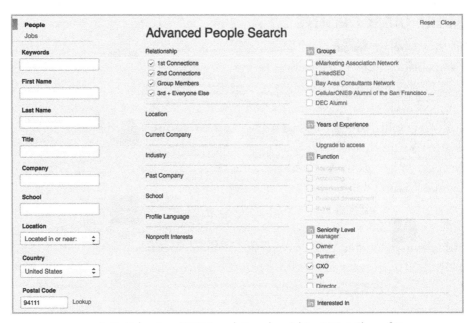

FIGURE 8–8. Selecting CXO-Level People within 100 Miles of You

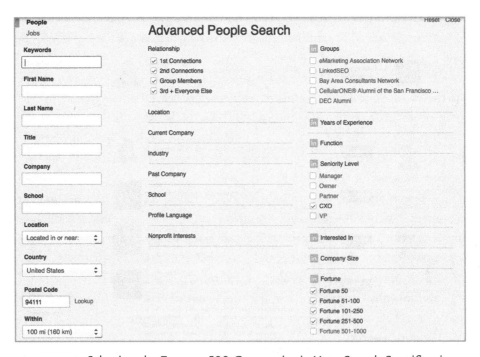

FIGURE 8–9. Selecting the Fortune 500 Companies in Your Search Specifications

There are hundreds of ways you can slice and dice your searches using the Advanced People Search. I can't get into every combination of searches you can do, but here are the high-level categories offered in the Advanced People Search:

- Keywords
- First name
- Last name
- Title
- Current company
- Past company
- School
- Location
- Industries
- Seniority Level (only if you are a LinkedIn Premium Member)
- LinkedIn Groups (only if you are a LinkedIn Premium Member)
- Relationship
- Interested In (only if you are a LinkedIn Premium Member)
- Language
- Fortune 1000 (only if you are a LinkedIn Premium Member)
- Company Size (only if you are a LinkedIn Premium Member)
- When Joined (only if you are a LinkedIn Premium Member)

Within each of these high-level categories, you can select many subcategories, making your filtering options almost limitless. With more than 330 million LinkedIn members, you have access to the world's largest—and highest quality—business intelligence data anywhere.

LINKEDIN REFERENCE SEARCH

If the Advanced People Search didn't provide what you were looking for (though if this is the case, it may mean you haven't tried hard enough!), then you can click on the Interested In tab and you will have access to the Reference Search. The Reference Search is for LinkedIn Premium Members only.

The LinkedIn Reference Search lets you find references who can give you feedback on candidates before you hire them. You can reach out to past employers and colleagues via Introductions or InMail to get honest feedback on job applicants. You can also keep track of your references in your Profile Organizer, which comes with your LinkedIn Premium subscription.

SAVED SEARCHES

Over time you will create custom Advanced People Searches that return great results. With your free LinkedIn account you can save up to three searches per week, up to ten daily searches with the Executive LinkedIn Premium subscription, and you can retain your search criteria in the Saved Searches tab. This is very handy and timesaving because it can take a lot of time to refine your Advanced People Search and get your desired results. New leads are delivered to your inbox automatically when you use Saved Searches.

ADVANCED JOB SEARCH

You can search for jobs using Job Title, Keywords, or Company Name in the basic Jobs Search box. LinkedIn also provides advanced search capabilities in Jobs. The filters work the same way as the Advanced People Search filters, but they are tailored to help you narrow down your search results when looking for a new job. A great trick is to use the Advanced Job Search when you are looking to hire new employees. Search for jobs similar to the job you want to fill, and see how other companies describe the job, what skills and keywords they are using, and how they position the job. You can learn a lot by "spying" on your competitors.

You can filter your job search by the following categories:

1. Keywords
2. Job Title
3. Location
4. Company
5. Job Function
6. Experience Level
7. Industry
8. Date Posted
9. Salary (this is accessible if you upgrade to the Job Seeker or Job Seeker Plus subscription levels)

Each of these categories has numerous subcategories to help you zero in on jobs compatible for you that will pay the salary you're targeting. The Advanced Job Search is a great tool, considering LinkedIn is becoming the top place for companies to post jobs and for people to find new jobs.

LinkedIn Jobs also lets you save your favorite searches in the Saved Searches tab. When you find jobs you are interested in, you can save them in the Saved Jobs tab.

THE DARK SIDE OF LINKEDIN SEARCH

The LinkedIn search algorithm gives relevant results when you search for People, Companies, and LinkedIn Groups, but it's still relatively easy to trick the algorithm so you can rank highly for your target skills or keywords. It's like the old days when you could add some HTML metatags to your web page and rank highly in Google for many search terms by overstuffing the meta keyword tag.

I don't recommend abusing the system to gain a high rank because eventually the LinkedIn algorithm will mature and you will lose your high ranking. Also, it's pretty easy to see who's tricking the system when you look at certain LinkedIn profiles.

Let me show you how you can easily trick the LinkedIn search algorithm to gain a high ranking. Before I demonstrate it, I want you to know that I do not recommend these "black hat" search engine optimization techniques—whether it's on LinkedIn or any other search engine—as they are considered unethical. Eventually you will get caught, your website can be banned from Google, and you can be removed from LinkedIn for violating their terms of service. Being ranked at the top of the search results for a short period of time is not worth the risk of being banned from the largest professional networking website. Also, you will see that modifying your profile to rank highly will not bring you more business because of the overuse of certain keywords.

Okay, here we go. Again, don't try this at home without adult supervision!

Go to the LinkedIn Search box and do a People search for "SEO," which is the acronym for search engine optimization. You would think this is one of the most difficult phrases to rank highly for because you are competing against the best search engine optimization specialists in the world. The competition on Google is fierce for the top ranking of SEO and SEO-related keywords because SEO experts take pride in beating their competitors for their industry keywords. If you rank on the first page of Google for SEO-related keywords, you are considered among the "best of the best" SEO experts in the world.

So what happens when you search on LinkedIn for "SEO"? Take a look at Figure 8–10 on page 66.

I blurred the name of the top search result because he does not deserve any recognition in this book. He used black-hat SEO techniques, which may have included one or more of the following:

- Violated search engine terms of service
- Created a poor user experience by overusing keywords or creating low quality content that is optimized for search engine ranking instead of creating high quality content that is beneficial to the web visitor

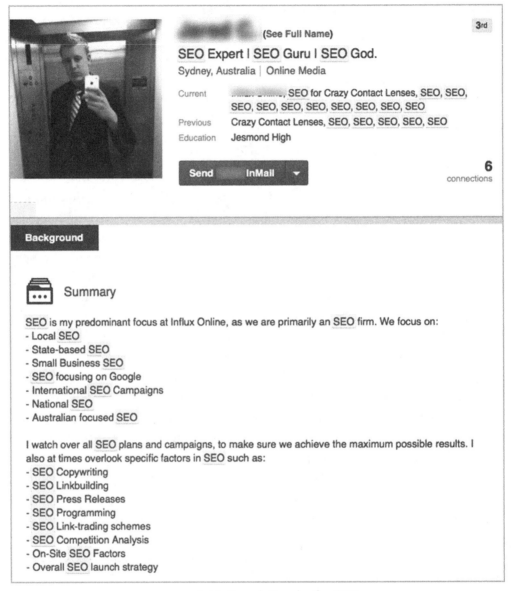

FIGURE 8–10. Search Results for SEO

- Unethically presented content to search engine bots and search engine users. This includes creating invisible text, which is seen only by the search engine bots. This is not a problem on LinkedIn because we don't have the ability to modify the website code.

Again, I strongly recommend against using black-hat SEO techniques. You would be deceiving the search engines for the benefit of you or your business. When you practice black-hat SEO techniques, it is no different than practicing unethical business practices in any profession—except you won't go to jail when you get caught. However, if Google catches you practicing black-hat SEO or violating their terms of service, it can ban your company URL from their search rankings. How would you explain that to your boss if you were the in-house SEO at your company? Whether you are practicing black-hat SEO or any other unethical business method, your reputation will be permanently damaged when you get caught—so don't do it.

Well, enough ranting about people taking shortcuts for short-term gain and permanent pain. Let's get back to our SEO "experts" who are gaming the LinkedIn search algorithm. Figure 8–11 shows us the profile of the top-ranking SEO expert on LinkedIn.

I'm assuming the gentleman in the figure is a Facebook marketing, internet marketing, and SEO "expert" and social media manager. His current and past employment consists solely of fake jobs using only his target keywords. He has 16 Recommendations, but they look very suspicious and are very light on details. He is smart enough not to let us see his 500+ Connections because I would guess many of them are fake LinkedIn members. When I look at the profiles of some of his Recommendations, their profiles are very light in content and substance, and every person is from a different country.

Red flags are flying everywhere. This is a classic example of keyword stuffing and a violation of the LinkedIn terms of service. In case you are wondering, I did report this

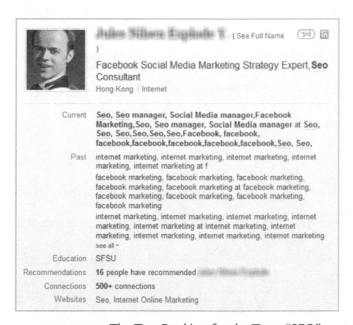

FIGURE 8–11. The Top Ranking for the Term "SEO"

profile to LinkedIn, and you should report profiles like this to maintain the quality and integrity of the LinkedIn community.

You get the point. These guys are promoting themselves as SEO experts by gaming the system. Sure they know how to get the top ranking for their target keywords, but would you want to hire them to do this to your LinkedIn profile? This is a completely unprofessional approach, and you should run the other way if an SEO "expert" with a profile like this approaches you. These guys are the equivalent of ambulance chasers in the legal world, willing to do anything to make a buck. Unfortunately, there are many people who would hire these guys to do SEO work for them because they don't know any better.

CONCLUSION

You now know more about LinkedIn Search and Advanced Search than 90 percent of all LinkedIn members. We just scratched the surface of what you can do with these advanced search capabilities and a database of more than 330 million business professionals. Play around with LinkedIn Search and see what you can uncover in the treasure trove of business intelligence.

I'll show you some more advanced tricks later in the book when I teach you how to use LinkedIn as different user types like students, sales reps, recruiters, and job seekers. For now, take a short break and practice your LinkedIn searching while it's still fresh in your mind. See you in the next chapter, where I will show you how to get found on LinkedIn.

For additional updates and how-to videos, visit
www.tedprodromou.com/chapter8

Getting Found on LinkedIn

What do you do when you want to learn more about a product or service? I bet the first thing you do is go to Google and search the internet. With so much data available to us today, search engines are an integral part of our life. When you search Google, you can find information about literally anything in seconds.

The problem with Google is you get a broad search result. If you search for "web marketing consultant," Google doesn't know if you're looking to hire a web marketing consultant or if you're trying to find information on how to become a web marketing consultant. Google isn't smart enough to read our minds yet—but it continues to get better!

When you search LinkedIn for "web marketing consultant," chances are your search result will show you a list of web marketing consultants. By narrowing your search, such as by a location like "web marketing consultant New York," you can generate a targeted list that may give you the result you need.

LinkedIn is a vertical search engine. A vertical search engine shows you very focused results based on the keywords you search for. This is why it's so important to use your target keywords when creating your LinkedIn personal and company profiles.

What are target keywords, you ask? Target keywords are the phrases you enter into a search engine to find targeted results. The more specific your keyword phrases are, the better your search results will be. If someone did a Google search to find you or your business, what keywords would they have to enter?

Optimizing your LinkedIn profile is similar to optimizing your website or blog so you can rank highly in Google. Optimizing your LinkedIn profile not only helps people find your profile through the search function, it helps LinkedIn recommend people to connect with, companies you may be interested in, or your perfect job. LinkedIn scans your profile and uses your keyword phrases to make targeted recommendations for you. The more targeted your profile is, the more targeted the LinkedIn suggestions will be. Once your LinkedIn profile is fine-tuned, you will see targeted recommendations in your sidebar every time you log in. The LinkedIn algorithm is a very powerful artificial intelligence tool.

KEYWORD SELECTION

The most important component of search engine optimization is keyword selection. Search engines use keywords and phrases to find and rank websites. The crawler or spider-based search engines—so called because they sift through websites and add keywords to their databases—sort through millions of websites by following an algorithm, or set of rules.

The algorithms for the various search engines are not exactly the same, which is why a search of the same keyword brings different results. However, they follow very similar processes. Most of the search engines rank websites based on where and how often a particular keyword is used on the website. They will rank a website higher if, for example, the keyword is used in the title, placed near the top of the page, and if it is used often.

LinkedIn has its own search algorithm, which ranks user profiles on a number of factors, including your keywords.

Take time now to use the questionnaire in Figure 9–1 on page 71 to create a list of at least ten keyword phrases that best describe you and your expertise. The more focused your keyword phrases are, the more your profile will stand out.

If you are like most people, you have a hard time describing your skills and areas of expertise, so you're struggling to come up with your keyword list. If you're struggling

LINKEDIN SEO TIP

To increase your chances of having your LinkedIn profile rank highly, use your keywords in these sections of your profile:

- Profile Headline
- Current Work Experience
- Past Work Experience
- Summary
- Specialties

Think about these questions while creating your list of keyword phrases:

1. What are your skills? _____

   _____

2. What is your expertise? _____

   _____

3. What job titles best describe you or the job you are looking for? _____

   _____

4. What makes you different from your competitors? _____

   _____

5. What makes you better than your competitors? _____

   _____

FIGURE 9–1. Keyword Worksheet

to come up with a list of what you're really good at, ask your friends or colleagues. They'll be glad to tell you what you're good at (and what you're not so good at, if you're brave enough to ask!).

COMPETITIVE ANALYSIS

One of my favorite ways to compile keyword lists is to look at my competitors' and colleagues' profiles to see what keywords they use to make their profiles stand out.

Let's say you're a certified public accountant in San Francisco, and you want to see which keywords are being used in the profiles of the top search results. Start by doing an Advanced Search in LinkedIn, then entering CPA as your keyword, and your ZIP code in the Location field. Start with 25 miles in the "Within" box, so you get a variety of profiles to view. Leave the rest of the search boxes empty, and click on Search, as shown in Figure 9–2 on page 72.

When your search is complete, you'll see the top rankings for LinkedIn members who have CPA in their profile. In the past you used to be able to sort by Relevance,

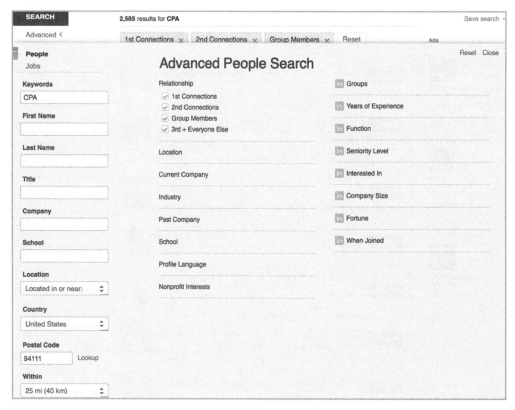

FIGURE 9–2. Advanced People Search for a CPA Located within 25 Miles of the ZIP Code 94111

Keywords, and other options, but LinkedIn discontinued the sort feature because it was rarely used. The LinkedIn Advanced Search will rank the search results based on your search criteria, as you see in Figure 9-3 on page 73.

As you see, the top search results have a few things in common. All of the top results contain CPA at or near the beginning of their professional headline or in the last name field.

You can search for people you are connected to using the Relationship sort. The Relationship search results will be displayed by first-degree, second-degree, and third-degree connections, and then groups. To see only people you are connected to, uncheck Second Connections, Group Members, and Third + Everyone Else, as shown in Figure 9-4 on page 73.

LINKEDIN RANKING FACTORS

My clients and students frequently ask me what determines the search rankings on LinkedIn. Some of the ranking factors are obvious as I've shown in previous examples.

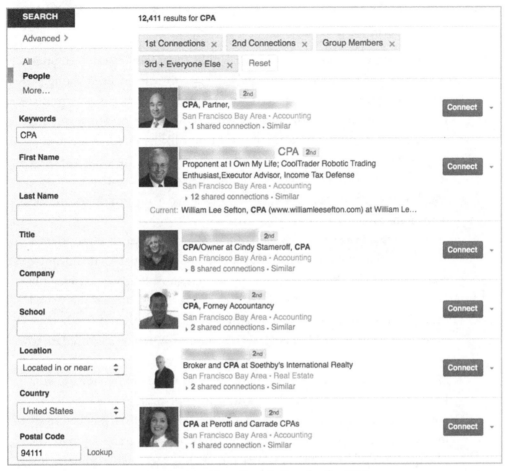

FIGURE 9–3. Your Search Results for CPA

FIGURE 9–4. Sort by Connections Search Result

Use your target keywords as your last name field, in your professional headline, and in your profile summary. As obvious as these seem, LinkedIn doesn't officially tell us what determines our search rank. Here is what LinkedIn officially tells us. This can be found at http://help.linkedin.com/app/answers/detail/a_id/4447/~/linkedin-search-relevance-people-search.

LinkedIn uses proprietary algorithms to rank and order the results you get when you search for people on the site.

1. *There's no single rank for LinkedIn search.* Unlike the standard search engines, we generate relevance scores uniquely for each member. Even though a query will return the same results for everyone, the order is determined in part by the profile, activity, and connections of the person searching. Testing a query from a handful of users is not likely to reflect the overall rank any profile has across the millions of queries that LinkedIn has every day. A closer measure would be the number of views your profile gets, which you can learn about in the Who's Viewed Your Profile section on your homepage.

2. *Searcher relevance is based on a variety of factors.* Relevance is a proprietary algorithm that we are constantly improving. Our goal is to optimize search results for the searcher. Before we return results, we consider the searcher's activity on LinkedIn, the profiles returned by the query, and other members who have run similar searches in determining the sort order. These, along with other factors, combine to provide us with data to improve the overall quality of our members' search results.

3. *More keywords aren't always better.* Our advice would be to include only the keywords, including repeated keywords, in your profile that best reflect your expertise and experience. If you integrate an extended list of keywords into your profile, you're likely showing up in a high number of searches. The question you need to ask yourself, however, is whether members consider your profile relevant to their search. If not, their behavior as a collective group may be influencing the algorithm used to rank you in search results.

THE GOOGLE KEYWORD PLANNER

Another great way to find keywords for your profile is to use the Google Keyword Planner, which is located at https://adwords.google.com/KeywordPlanner. The Keyword Planner replaced the Google Keyword Tool, which was retired in March 2013.

You may be wondering why I'm teaching you how to research the most popular keyword phrases on Google in a book about LinkedIn. First of all, if a search term is popular on Google, it's usually a popular search term on Yahoo!, Bing, and LinkedIn because people tend to use the same thought process when using search engines. Second, LinkedIn profile information—including keyword phrases—frequently appears on Google search results, often near the top. That means if you use keyword phrases that are popular on Google in your LinkedIn profile, there is a good chance your profile will appear on the first page of Google searches for that keyword phrase. This is because Google considers LinkedIn to be a reputable authority site so profile information from LinkedIn can rank higher than other website content that isn't as highly regarded by Google. It's another case of "who you know," not "what you know."

Keyword research has always been a frustrating task because there is no source that provides the actual search data. Every keyword tool, including the Google Keyword Planner, provides only estimated values, which are "guesstimates" at best. I'm sure Google knows the exact numbers, but it is infamous for not sharing these for competitive reasons.

While the Google Keyword Planner is meant for pay-per-click advertising research, it's also a vital tool when performing keyword research for search engine optimization. The Google Keyword Planner provides a ballpark estimate of the number of searches for specific words or key phrases, which is still valuable information. Knowing which keywords or keyword phrases are most popular can give you a huge advantage over your competition.

You need to have a Google AdWords account to access the Keyword Planner. You don't have to actually run ads, but you'll need to set up a free AdWords account which you will be prompted to do when you try to access the Keyword Planner. If you already have a Google AdWords account, you can access the Keyword Planner under the Tools tab in your account.

Let's try some keyword searches, so you can see how to use the Google Keyword Planner effectively. If you go to the keyword tool and search for "web developer," "website design," and "web design," you'll receive a listing similar to the one shown in Figure 9–5 on page 76.

The first column lists your target search terms. The next column, Avg. monthly searches, tells you approximately how many times those keyword phrases were searched based on the date range and targeting settings you've selected. The Competition column tells you how competitive your keyword phrases are, High, Medium, or Low. The next column is your Suggested bid, which is calculated by taking into account the costs-per-click (CPCs) that advertisers are paying for this keyword for the location and Search Network settings you've selected. The amount is only an estimate, and your actual cost-per-click may vary. If you are doing Google AdWords pay-per-click advertising, the last column, ad impression share, is the number of impressions you've received divided by the total number of searches for the location and network you're targeting that matched the keyword exactly in the last calendar month.

Now let me show you a little trick that will give you more accurate results from the Google Keyword Planner. By default, Google gives you the number of searches based on an exact match type, and they will display broadly related keyword ideas.

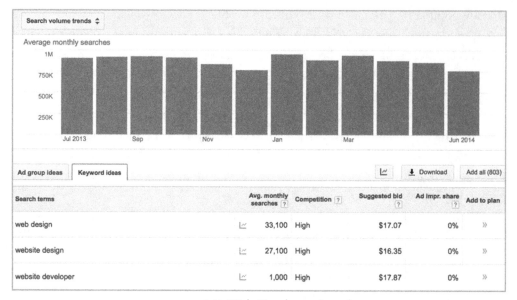

FIGURE 9–5. Web Developer Search

When you change the keyword filter option to "Only show ideas closely related to my search terms," you will see more accurate keyword recommendations. I like to start broad (Figuer 9-6) to get "out of the box" keyword ideas, then tighten up my targeting to display the closely related keywords.

As you see in Figure 9-7 on page 77, these results are much more accurate than the broadly related match results.

The Google Keyword Planner is powerful and can provide a lot of great information about the best keywords to use in your LinkedIn profile. We don't need

Keyword (by relevance)		Avg. monthly searches [?]	Competition [?]	Suggested bid [?]
web design inspiration	📈	3,600	Medium	$10.32
freelance web design	📈	1,000	High	$9.20
web design firm	📈	590	High	$19.53
website design and development	📈	260	High	$15.81
custom web design	📈	720	High	$20.89

FIGURE 9–6. Broadly Related Match Search Results

Keyword (by relevance)		Avg. monthly searches [?]	Competition [?]	Suggested bid [?]
website design and development	⌇	260	High	$15.81
custom web design	⌇	720	High	$20.89
web design websites	⌇	320	High	$20.36
website design development	⌇	70	High	$24.73
custom website design	⌇	1,000	High	$15.26

FIGURE 9–7. Closely Related Match Search Results Are More Accurate

to go into the advanced features of the Google Keyword Planner, since you are just trying to get a high level overview of the most popular keyword phrases to use in your LinkedIn profile.

Some tips for finding the best keyword phrases to use:

- Try to find keyword phrases that have a fair number of monthly searches, especially local searches, if you are a local business or service provider. The more searches per month, the higher the competition. Your best keyword phrases are medium competition with a fair amount of monthly searches, so you have a good chance of appearing near the top of the Google search results.
- You can add the highly competitive keywords from Google as Skills in your LinkedIn profile, so they appear in LinkedIn searches. It's much easier to rank well in LinkedIn right now because very few people know how to optimize their LinkedIn profile. Since you are reading this book, you are among the 10 percent of LinkedIn users who do know how to optimize their profile, so you have a huge advantage.

CONCLUSION

Use your target keyword phrases frequently when you fill out your LinkedIn profile, but don't overdo it. Figure 9–8 on page 78 shows us the search results for the term "Search Engine Optimization." This person, who will remain anonymous because she's gaming the LinkedIn search algorithm, ranks on the first page of a LinkedIn People Search for "Search Engine Optimization." Would you hire this person to do SEO for your website?

In the next chapter, I'll show you the best way to give and receive LinkedIn Recommendations, which are an essential part of your LinkedIn profile.

SEO Training★SEO Trainer★SEO Solution★**Search Engine Optimization** Expert★**Search Engine Optimization** Solution★SEO Strategy

Toronto, Canada Area | Information Technology and Services

Current	**SEO,Search Engine Optimization,Training,Trainer,Expert,Specialist,Strategy** at **SEO,Search Engine Optimization,Training,Trainer,Expert,Specialist,Strategy**
	SEO,Search Engine Optimization,Training,Trainer,Expert,Specialist,Strategy at **SEO,Search Engine Optimization,Training,Trainer,Expert,Specialist,Strategy**
	SEO,Search Engine Optimization,Training,Trainer,Expert,Specialist,Strategy at **SEO,Search Engine Optimization,Training,Trainer,Expert,Specialist,Strategy**
	see all ▾
Past	**SEO,Search Engine Optimization,Training,Trainer,Expert,Specialist,Strategy** at **SEO,Search Engine Optimization,Training,Trainer,Expert,Specialist,Strategy**
Education	Michigan State University - The Eli Broad Graduate School of Management
Connections	**500+** connections
Websites	Search Engine Optimization
	SEO Training
	SEO Trainer

FIGURE 9–8. A Profile Optimized for "Search Engine Optimization"

**For additional updates and how-to videos, visit
www.tedprodromou.com/chapter9**

Giving and Receiving LinkedIn Recommendations

The evolution of the internet and social media has changed the way we make decisions. Social proof existed long before the internet, but the ability to submit and view online reviews for products and services has revolutionized our purchasing behavior. In a matter of minutes, we can tap into the collective opinions of hundreds—even thousands—of people who have already purchased a product or service and know exactly how they feel about their purchase. You can see how many raving fans are gushing about the product or how many disgruntled customers want their money back. With the evolution of mobile apps, we can scan a barcode on a product with our mobile phone to receive comparative pricing as well as product reviews while standing next to the product in the store.

Today, there's no hiding if you're offering an inferior product or service. If you read a lot of negative reviews, you probably won't complete the purchase. On the other hand, when you read a lot of positive reviews, you feel comfortable purchasing that product or service and won't hesitate to spend more for the more advanced version of the product if others recommend it. Also, your chances of buyer's remorse diminish significantly because social proof justified the purchase in your mind.

In case you're not familiar with social proof, it's when we make decisions based on what others recommend, whether it's really the best option or not. What happens when you drive by a new restaurant and see a long line out the door? You assume the food is great, so you quickly park your car and jump in line. The food may be no better than your favorite restaurant, but the fact that so many others are waiting to get into this new restaurant makes you have to join the crowd. You will probably love the food, even if it's only average, because you're caught up in the moment and the excitement of the crowd. If the crowd loves the restaurant, you love it, too, so you can be part of the "in" crowd.

In the past, social proof was primarily word-of-mouth or through print media, so word spread slowly. Today, a good or bad review can be seen or heard by millions of people around the world instantly. The internet spawned many new forms of social proof that I'll get into in a minute. First, I'll offer some background about the evolution of social proof.

Let's go back a few years, so I can show you an example of social proof before the era of online reviews. Your best friend went to a movie last night, and she can't stop raving about it. She's gushing with enthusiasm and wants to tell you every detail of the movie, but she resists because she doesn't want to ruin the movie for you. You can tell from her actions that it was one of the best movies she's seen in years. She's so excited she can't sit still, and she's champing at the bit to tell you more.

Based on your best friend's actions and opinion of the movie, will you go? Of course you will—probably tonight! This is classic old-school social proof.

When someone you trust tells you she likes a movie, you want to see it as soon as possible. If your trusted friend tells you the movie sucks, you won't see it, and you'll probably tell your other friends to avoid it as well—even though you haven't seen it. Negative social proof spreads exponentially based on what people say, even if they didn't have a negative experience themselves.

The key to social proof is that you act on someone's advice—without question—if you trust that person. If you don't know the person well enough or don't trust her, you'll probably take the advice with a grain of salt and seek advice from a trusted source. We all have our trusted circle of friends and colleagues that we depend on when we need to make decisions. The bigger the decision, the more trusted opinions we will seek. We all want to feel comfortable that we are making the right decision. So we like to bounce ideas off of people we trust. Discussing the issues with others makes us feel confident, even if they just listen to our concerns.

Today, online social proof has evolved from online forums to popular websites like Yelp, where you can post reviews about local businesses. On Yelp, the business owner doesn't have control over the reviews posted by customers. A few positive reviews can send your sales through the roof. An angry customer can write a scathing review about a business and damage the reputation of that business. The business owner can respond to that criticism online, but the negative comments remain. These unmoderated comments make social proof more credible because everyone knows that every business has unsatisfied customers occasionally. When you see a series of negative reviews, a red flag should go up in your head telling you to avoid that business. Chances are, the business won't survive if the company doesn't address the negative comments head-on and change its business practices.

Facebook created its own form of social proof with the "Like" button. You "vote" for comments, pictures, and companies that you like on Facebook. Unlike Yelp, which posts positive and negative comments, Facebook registers only positive votes. Facebook "Likes" have taken off, and it has become a significant measurement of success if your Facebook Company Page receives a lot of likes. It has the same effect as great reviews on Yelp.

Google implemented its +1 button, which is the equivalent of the Facebook Like. You click the +1 button when you like something on Google-related pages. The +1 button isn't as popular as the Facebook Like, but you can be sure Google is doing everything in its power to increase its popularity.

So what does social proof have to do with LinkedIn, anyway? Well, actually social proof has a lot to do with LinkedIn. Essentially you are marketing and selling yourself on LinkedIn. Your profile, job experience, skills, the expertise you demonstrate in your posts, and Recommendations are your marketing collateral that people read to get to know your product—which is you!

HOW CAN SOCIAL PROOF GET YOU HIRED IN TODAY'S ECONOMY?

You and a few million other people are looking for jobs these days. You can spend hours every day on Craigslist and hope you can be one of the first to submit your resume when a new job listing is posted. If you don't submit your resume within a few minutes, your resume will go unnoticed because often hundreds of people apply in the first hour.

You can spend the rest of your day searching Monster.com or other job websites and pray that your resume will be noticed. You can apply for hundreds of jobs and rarely will you receive any acknowledgment that they even received your resume.

It's so frustrating, especially when you know you are qualified for these positions, but you can't cut through the noise and get noticed. You have to resort to making one of those crazy YouTube videos to catch their attention, but still, your chances of getting the job are minimal.

Finding a job online is very similar to cold calling. You are a complete stranger to each company, so getting past the gatekeepers is a huge challenge. You need to get very creative to get your resume in front of the hiring manager, which seems nearly impossible.

Now let's look at the other side of the coin. You work in the human resources department, and you've posted some jobs online. Within minutes, you have more than 100 resumes for one open position. You scan through a few of the resumes, and very few people are qualified for the position, even though you clearly spelled out the job qualifications in the job posting.

People are so desperate that they're applying for any job—even if they aren't qualified. They hope to catch the attention of the human resources department or the hiring manager, so maybe they can get hired for a more appropriate position. The human resources department is overwhelmed and spends hours digging through the hundreds of resumes to find a handful of people to interview. There has to be a better way!

So how do you find good candidates in today's economy with millions of qualified workers looking for a job?

Most jobs are filled through word-of-mouth recommendations, not by sifting through hundreds of resumes. When a job is posted online, hundreds of resumes are submitted, which makes finding your perfect candidate like finding the proverbial needle in a haystack. It's much easier and more reliable to hire someone who comes highly recommended by one of your trusted colleagues. The old adage "it's not what you know, it's who you know" is more powerful than ever today, and you can get to know the "right" people by leveraging social proof.

Again, the key is building your network of trusted resources and keeping in touch with them on a regular basis so they are there when you need them. Once you establish your network of 100 to 150 trusted people, you can reach out to them and tap into their expertise or into their network of resources to solve your problem, or, if they can't, they'll introduce you to someone else who can. If you don't have a stable professional network and you suddenly lose your job, you have to spend months building up your professional network and gaining their trust before you can reach out to them for help.

You build a strong professional network by creating a strong online reputation with a lot of social proof. When someone searches Google for your name, you want a lot of very positive social proof to appear. When people see pages and pages of positive social proof about you, they will be pursuing you to join their professional network. You will be the one in demand, and your professional network will be full of A-list players.

WHAT ARE LINKEDIN RECOMMENDATIONS?

LinkedIn created its own version of social proof called LinkedIn Recommendations, which is a reputation manager for professionals. When people write LinkedIn

Recommendations for you, it's the online version of the written recommendations you used to receive from your instructors and former employers. The good news is that you have control over the recommendations that are posted on your LinkedIn profile, so you won't see negative comments.

Recommendations are not just for the person receiving the recommendation. The person writing the recommendation can display the recommendations they write on their own profile. This adds value to your credibility when you write strong recommendations for others because it shows LinkedIn members that you have strong people in your professional network.

You can think of LinkedIn as a reputation engine for business professionals. Your LinkedIn activity builds a complete picture of you and your business. Your LinkedIn profile is more than an online resume with a list of your past and present jobs, your education, and your accomplishments. Your professional reputation includes whom you associate with, the groups you belong to, the associations and clubs you belong to, and how much you interact with your network. I like to combine all of these things and think of them as your LinkedIn image.

If you are a small-business owner looking to hire new employees, recommendations can help you determine if a potential employee will be a good fit for your business. Recruiters and hiring managers at large companies do read recommendations and take them into account, but it's unlikely that a recommendation would make or break a LinkedIn member's chance of getting hired. Recommendations add value to your overall LinkedIn profile, but usually they are not evaluative since most recommendations are solicited. Later in this chapter, I will show you some sample recommendations that are so powerful they can influence a manager's decision to hire a person. These are the type of recommendations you want to look for when you are searching for new employees.

Savvy LinkedIn members can tell if you are actively networking and reaching out to others or if you are a passive LinkedIn member with a static profile and no networking activity. If you are not active on LinkedIn, it doesn't mean you are not good at what you do. It just means you are not actively building your professional network as well as you could be. In today's economy, no one's job is safe, given the constant corporate mergers, reorganizations, and restructuring. You need to spend a few hours every week networking on LinkedIn so you can quickly land on your feet if you're unfortunate enough to lose your job.

The way the market has been and how industries and positions seem to come and go, chances are you will have to change jobs or careers in the next few years. The 20-year career I had as a network engineer in the 1990s doesn't exist today, and I had to learn new skills. Now I manage Google AdWords, social media, and do search engine optimization for a living. None of these jobs existed in their current form ten years ago. A few years from now, Google AdWords will evolve into some other form of online advertising, social media will have a new name, and who knows if search engines will even exist in 2020.

When you keep your LinkedIn profile current, participate in LinkedIn Groups, and publish and share great content, potential employers can learn more about you than they ever could by just reading your resume. The icing on the cake is the LinkedIn Recommendations, which provide third-party verification of your skills. Each online activity is like a piece of a puzzle, and recommendations are the glue that holds the puzzle together. When you are using LinkedIn to find new employees for your company, you want to look for LinkedIn members who have a complete, updated profile with lots of great recommendations.

LinkedIn Recommendations are a huge part of your LinkedIn image. Obviously, it's good to have a lot of recommendations, but it's much better if they are quality recommendations. In this age of online deception, it's possible to hire offshore workers to write fake recommendations for you. You can have hundreds of hollow recommendations in a matter of days for less than a hundred bucks. It's better to have a dozen high-quality reviews instead of hundreds of low-quality, suspicious reviews.

WHY DO I NEED LINKEDIN RECOMMENDATIONS?

Great question! People rarely provide written recommendations when they apply for jobs these days, so why bother getting recommendations on LinkedIn?

First of all, your LinkedIn profile will not be complete until you have at least three recommendations. Getting to the All Star level on your profile is a huge accomplishment and adds a lot of credibility to your LinkedIn profile.

The second reason you want LinkedIn Recommendations is because they are the only way you can verify your LinkedIn profile and accomplishments. You enter your LinkedIn profile information, including your education, work history, and accomplishments. There is no way for others to verify this information by reading your profile. When people recommend you on LinkedIn, it's a written testimonial of your work history, education, or accomplishments. It's very important to have that third-party verification of your LinkedIn profile, especially if you are a consultant or independent service provider.

Did you know the keywords in your LinkedIn recommendations show up in search results and help your LinkedIn search ranking? Many factors determine your search ranking on LinkedIn, and every little bit helps.

While we are on the subject of LinkedIn search rankings, did you know the more recommendations you have, the higher you can rank in LinkedIn searches? If your recommendations contain the same keywords you want to rank for, your search ranking should rise as your recommendations increase. You don't want to get recommendations full of your keywords just to increase your search ranking. Be genuine and nurture good recommendations, and your search results will take care of themselves.

If you are a small-business owner, a consultant, or service provider, your potential customers expect to see recommendations in your profile. Recommendations and your complete LinkedIn profile are the way they judge you to determine the quality of your work and your expertise before they'll hire you or trust your product.

HOW MANY LINKEDIN RECOMMENDATIONS SHOULD I HAVE?

There is no right or wrong answer for this question. I see some LinkedIn profiles with a few excellent recommendations that go a long way highlighting a person's expertise. I see other profiles with page after page of recommendations, but they don't convince me that this person is an A-lister who is worthy of being part of my professional network or someone I would hire. The recommendations seem hollow, and they're not convincing.

How many recommendations are right for you? I would recommend at least one recommendation for every year you work at a job. If you've been at your current company for five years, I think you should have at least five recommendations for that company. I have no scientific proof that you should have one recommendation per year of work, but don't you think you have at least one great accomplishment at work every year?

When you accomplish something great at work, you need to have someone who benefited from that accomplishment write you a recommendation. When you benefit from someone else's accomplishment, write that person a LinkedIn recommendation, and don't wait for them to ask you. Just do it!

WHAT MAKES A LINKEDIN RECOMMENDATION GREAT?

People want to read relevant recommendations that are clear, concise, and add value to their assessment of a person's professional skills and capabilities. Recommendations are a form of social proof that expresses your personal and/or professional opinion of the person you are recommending.

Recommendations should go beyond letting people know you are a whiz at Excel or a social media aficionado. Every recommendation should be personalized and detail why you think this person is worthy of your recommendation. When you recommend a person, it impacts your reputation as much as hers. If you create a bunch of meaningless recommendations for people who are not worthy of your recommendation, it negatively affects you and your reputation.

Say your friend Joe calls you up one day asking if you know a good plumber who can quickly fix a leaking pipe. The last time you hired a plumber he didn't do a very good job for you, but he's the only plumber you know. You give Joe the plumber's name, and the plumber goes out to Joe's house to fix the leaking pipe. Instead of stopping the leak, the plumber breaks the pipe, causing a huge flood at Joe's house. Joe is furious at the plumber, and he wonders why you recommended this inadequate person. Your reputation has taken a huge hit with Joe, and it could end your friendship.

Recommending people on a professional level is no different. If for any reason you don't feel comfortable recommending someone, then you shouldn't write a recommendation. Remember, your reputation is at stake here, too. If one of your connections hires someone based on your written recommendation and it doesn't turn out well, then your connection is going to lose faith in you and your credibility suffers.

You need to carefully craft your recommendations so you are always telling the truth and not exaggerating. If they are the "best of the best" in their field, you can say that. If they are not the best, then you shouldn't "highly recommend" them. You can phrase your recommendation in a different way, so you are not stretching the truth but you are highlighting their strengths and giving them a positive recommendation.

WHAT TO SAY IN YOUR RECOMMENDATIONS

Here's a sample recommendation I found underneath a profile of one of my connections:

Joe is always a pleasure to work with! He is extremely knowledgeable, personable, communicative, and highly effective.

So what do you think about that recommendation? Are you going to hire Joe? Do you even know what Joe does for a living or what he is extremely knowledgeable at? Since Joe is my friend and I know that he is very good at what he does, I know this recommendation is completely true.

If you don't know Joe, this recommendation isn't going to help you decide if Joe is the right person to hire for your project. You know Joe is a pleasure to work with, which is always a good trait if you are looking to hire some help. What did Joe do for this person when they worked together? What skills did he use? Was it a big project or a small project? How many times did Joe work with this person? What challenges did he overcome while working on the project? These are the things you need to mention when writing a review for someone, so you can paint a complete picture for the person reading the recommendation.

Unfortunately, the above recommendation doesn't help Joe nor does it help the person who wrote it. If you are going to take the time to write a recommendation, make sure you write a thoughtful, thorough summary so others will know exactly what kind of person you are recommending.

Now, take a look at this recommendation.

Melanie has been one of the biggest influencers on me in my career. I knew the first time I saw her speak at a conference that she was someone I needed to meet and model myself after. She's incredible at seeing the big picture in order to make the necessary changes needed to create a well-oiled machine out of an organization, program, or process, while still understanding the details of the minutia involved.

We were at different enterprise-level companies with the same challenges when I met Melanie, and the things I learned from her about how the organization needs to be set up for success, properly measuring success, creating accountability, getting the right pieces in place for all moving parts to work together to get to an end goal, and getting around the bullshit were fundamental insights for me, that truthfully, I just didn't hear from other people in the industry.

She's a born leader, she's bright, she's quick, she's motivated, and she's fun to be around. One of the true top players in the entire industry, who I will always intend to continue to learn from.—April 17, 2011

—Laura Lippay, Director of Technical Marketing, Yahoo!

Wow! Now, that is an incredible recommendation. What do we learn about Melanie from just one recommendation? She had a big influence on Laura's career, and Laura wanted to meet her because Melanie is her role model. (My guess is that Melanie has a big influence on many careers!) We know that Melanie has the unique skill of being able to see the big picture while understanding the details of minutia. It's rare to see one person with both skills.

Laura was encountering the same problems in her organization as Melanie was in hers, so they had a lot in common. By connecting with Melanie, Laura learned how to change the direction of her organization by modeling what Melanie did.

The last paragraph sums up Laura's opinion of Melanie: a born leader, bright, motivated, and fun. With all those attributes, it's no wonder Melanie is one of the top players in her industry. From my personal experience, I would second what Laura said about Melanie, and she definitely is one of the top players in the search marketing industry.

Laura's entire recommendation was only 186 words, but look at what we learned about Melanie in just three short paragraphs. Wouldn't you love to have a powerful recommendation like this in your LinkedIn profile? Melanie has dozens of other recommendations in her LinkedIn profile just like this, which provides a ton of social proof that Melanie is an

A-list player in the search marketing industry. There's nothing more powerful than your peers writing glowing recommendations about you to build up your reputation and let others know you are a true leader in your field.

WHO SHOULD I RECOMMEND?

The best way to get started with LinkedIn Recommendations is to recommend others. If you work for a company, recommend co-workers whom you respect and appreciate. You can also write recommendations for your boss if you want to score some brownie points—just kidding! Don't ever write a recommendation for your boss just to suck up. Write one only if she is a mentor to you and if you really respect the work she does.

If you own your own business, you can write recommendations for your customers or the vendors you do business with. When your IT consultant comes in and fixes your server that was down and affecting your entire business operation, take a few minutes and write him a glowing recommendation on LinkedIn. Tell the story how he responded to your call for help in minutes, isolated the problem in no time, and had your business up and running in less than an hour. Highlight his responsiveness, troubleshooting skills, and beaming personality in the recommendation. He will appreciate your thoughtfulness in taking the time to do this, as it will do wonders for his business. Someday, he may do a favor for you when you least expect it.

If you are a consultant, write favorable recommendations about other consultants you work with. Let's say you're a web designer and you work with a graphic designer who creates the beautiful graphics you turn into a website. You can talk about the different projects you've collaborated on and highlight her design skills, creativity, timeliness for completion, and passion for the work. Provide as many details as you can in the project, so you can fully demonstrate the range of her talents and expertise.

The best time to write a recommendation for someone is right after you've completed a successful project that you worked on together. You know that fantastic feeling of accomplishment that you have after you've finished a long project. You and your co-workers work long days for many months, riding the emotional highs and lows of a difficult project. Some days you don't think the project will ever end, and then you suddenly have a breakthrough that takes you to the next stage. The breakthroughs come when you work together, combining all your strengths to create a powerful team.

It's easy to write a recommendation for someone after struggling through a long project together. You know their strengths, emotions, leadership ability, and motivation. As we saw with Melanie's recommendation from Laura, you can write a very

FIGURE 10-1. Make a Recommendation

powerful recommendation in fewer than 200 words. If you write the recommendation while you're still riding the high of the project completion, it will be authentic and very meaningful, which has a powerful effect on the reader. I don't know this for sure, but I would guess that Laura wrote Melanie's recommendation shortly after seeing her speak at an event while she was still feeling the emotional impact of the speech.

When you are ready to write a recommendation for a colleague, you can simply click on the Recommend link next to her profile. You must be connected to a person before you can recommend her. Once you click the Recommend button, you will see the screen shown in Figure 10-1.

Choose the appropriate option and you will be prompted with a few questions to help customize your recommendation. The first prompt, "Recommend this person as a:," gives you a list of choices where you identify whether they were a Colleague, Service Provider, Business Partner, or Student. This shows up in the recommendation, so the reader will know the professional relationship between you and the person you are recommending. If you choose "Service Provider," "Business Partner," or "Student" from the list shown in Figure 10-2 on page 90, you will need to select from a different set of relationship options, which are tailored to each category. Again, this relationship will appear in the recommendation when it's posted on the LinkedIn profile.

On the next screen, as shown in Figure 10-2, you select the Position at the time of the recommendation. The dropdown list will display all the titles she has listed in her LinkedIn Profile. You'll need to select the Service category (if she was a service provider) and the year she was first hired.

FIGURE 10–2. Create Your Recommendation

Next you'll select the top three attributes that best describe this service provider. This is a relatively new addition to recommendations that makes it easier to let others know the strengths of the person you are recommending.

Below the Relationship section of the form is the actual Recommendation area, where you can enter your formal recommendation. Remember to make your recommendation clear and concise. Don't make it too short—as in Joe's example—and don't make your recommendation too long or people will stop reading it and miss some key points.

After you enter the recommendation, click Send and the person you are recommending will be notified that you have written a recommendation for her. The recommendation will not be posted in her profile until she approves it. A few things can occur at this point, all of them fairly common: She can send it back to you for revision if she would like you to change it; she can approve it as is; or she can reject it, if she doesn't want a recommendation from you for some reason. Remember: Your professional reputation is at stake here, so you don't need to accept recommendations just for the sake of having a lot of recommendations. If you were feeling as if you should reject a recommendation from someone, then it's probably a sign that you shouldn't be connected with that person on LinkedIn.

After you recommend someone, LinkedIn will ask that individual if she wants to recommend you. There's an ongoing debate about reciprocal recommendations by many LinkedIn experts. Some contend that reciprocal recommendations have less value than one-way recommendations. They compare it to sharing website links on the internet. To rank highly in Google, you need a lot of links from high-quality websites to your website. In the past, webmasters would trade links so both websites benefited. Eventually Google learned people were sharing links to improve their search rankings and lowered the value of the links on both sites because they worked out a deal to share the links.

Some LinkedIn experts say sharing recommendations has the same effect on your LinkedIn reputation. Since LinkedIn automatically prompts you to reciprocate the recommendation, they feel you can get a lot of recommendations by writing a lot of recommendations. They feel this isn't natural to have one-to-one recommendations and devalues them. Sometimes I feel like someone recommended me just so I would write a recommendation for him. Most of the time I know if the person is sincere and writing a recommendation for me because he values the work I do for him. I do know some people who are not sincere and are just looking for recommendations for themselves. After working with people, you get to know them, and you know who is sincere and who isn't.

Other LinkedIn experts feel that a good recommendation is a good thing whether there is a reciprocal recommendation or not. If someone feels you are worthy of a recommendation and they take the time to write it, then that adds value to your LinkedIn reputation.

I'll leave it up to you whether you want recommendations only from people who you haven't recommended or if you want to do reciprocal recommendations. Personally, I write recommendations for people I feel are worthy of my recommendation. It doesn't matter to me if they ask me to write a recommendation for them or if it's a reciprocal recommendation.

I frequently receive requests from former employees to write a letter of recommendation for them, and I gladly write a letter for them. With the evolution of LinkedIn Recommendations, people don't ask for written letters of recommendation as often as they used to. I will write them a recommendation on LinkedIn, which appears in their profile under the company we worked for at the time. Again, if I don't feel they were a good employee or not worthy of a recommendation for the work they did for me, I politely decline the invitation.

HOW TO ASK FOR RECOMMENDATIONS

Personally, I don't ask people for recommendations very often. It's not that I'm afraid to ask for them. If I were going to ask someone for a recommendation, it would be from someone I worked closely with and respected a great deal. I would have a close professional relationship with this person, and she would be among the 150 people in my network with whom I keep in touch on a regular basis. I would write a strong recommendation for this person not because I want a recommendation from her, but because I strongly respect her professional ability. Most of the time I receive a strong recommendation in return. If the individual doesn't reciprocate, I don't take it personally; I just assume she doesn't have time to write recommendations on LinkedIn.

If you want to ask someone for a recommendation, you need to ask in a professional way. Don't use a standard request message in LinkedIn; instead, write a thoughtful message and explain why you are asking for a recommendation at this time. You can say you are looking for a new job and would appreciate a recommendation. Don't ask for a recommendation from someone you don't know well or haven't worked with in a long time. A recommendation about your technical skills from a co-worker from 1990 isn't going to be relevant today and will have very little impact on your LinkedIn Profile. If that coworker is now a chief technology officer at a large company, you could ask them to write a recommendation for you that is focused on your customer service skills or your work ethic. That type of recommendation would carry a lot of weight in your profile.

When you ask for the recommendation, mention a specific project or job you worked on together. Explain why you think that project succeeded and how well you worked together. Tell the connection what you think her strengths were on the project and ask her what she thinks you did well. Also ask her to mention the specific skills or traits you demonstrated on that project and others on which you worked together.

You need to be very clear when you ask someone for a recommendation. Tell him or her exactly what position you are applying for and what skill set and experience it requires. You can even include a link to the job description if you don't think she may be interested in the job, so she can write a recommendation that fits the requirements of the position you are pursuing.

For example, if you are applying for a position as a software project manager that requires Scrum experience and knowledge of LAMP, ask the person writing your recommendation to include those skills and knowledge in the recommendation if she is familiar with your skill set. Obviously you should not ask someone to write a recommendation for you if she isn't familiar with your specific skills. Have her focus the recommendation on the skills she knows you excel at.

Here is an example of a recommendation for a director of development for an internet business. Notice how the person writing the recommendation highlighted Michael's project management skills, software development skills, and technical programming language skills. This recommendation clearly demonstrates Michael's well-rounded skill set.

> *I worked with Michael at GS1 Canada. Michael is an excellent development director with in-depth knowledge of current software development technologies and a keen sense of how to apply technology to maximize business applications. I worked with Michael on several projects. Michael is very capable at any level of software development: analysis, design, development, and support. Michael has excellent knowledge of .Net and Java development environments. At GS1 Canada, Michael made significant contribution to several strategic projects, including GDSN integration with 1SYNC. I would highly recommend Michael for any development director role.*

See how the person writing the recommendation focused on two skills: his knowledge of the products in his industry and the ability to form partnerships to develop new streams of revenue. It's clear this person worked with Michael and knows his strengths and skills.

If you want great recommendations like this, don't be afraid to reach out and ask for what you want. When you ask for a recommendation, you have more control over what the person will write when you specify what you are looking for in the recommendation. Unsolicited recommendations are usually thin in content and are written in very general terms. I think I just convinced myself to change my personal policy of not asking for recommendations and start asking for great recommendations!

LINKEDIN ENDORSEMENTS

In 2013, LinkedIn added a new feature called Endorsements, which are often confused with Recommendations. The primary difference is Endorsements come from the keywords you used when you added Skills to your profile. Recommendations are manually written testimonials while Endorsements can be done by simply clicking on a popup message that appears when you view a profile.

Figure 10–3 shows you the Endorsement popup message. If you feel Melanie deserves an Endorsement for all of the skills on her list, you can click on the Endorse button. If you feel Melanie isn't worthy of an Endorsement of any of the suggested skills, click the Skip button. If you want to endorse Melanie for some of the suggested skills, deselect the inappropriate skills by clicking on the X in each box, and then click Endorse.

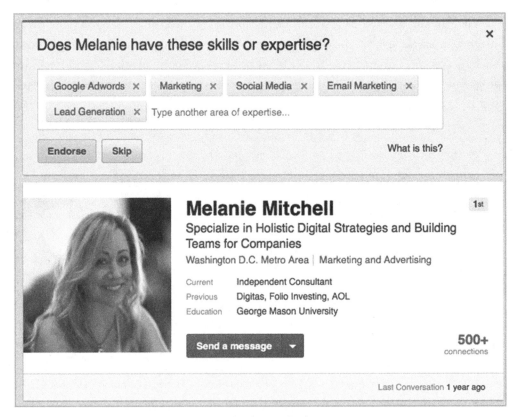

FIGURE 10–3. Make an Endorsement

What happens next? In Melanie's profile, her list of Skills will have one more vote for each one you selected in her Endorsement. The more votes you have for each Skill, the higher it ranks in your profile list.

In Figure 10–4 on page 95, you see Melanie's colleagues feel she's very skilled in SEM and Digital Marketing. She has over 99 votes in these Skills. If Melanie no longer does SEM or Digital Marketing as her primary job focus, she can rearrange the list of Skills in her profile by dragging them to change the order. I did this in my personal profile when I stopped doing SEO, which was my top-ranked skill. I moved it near the bottom of my

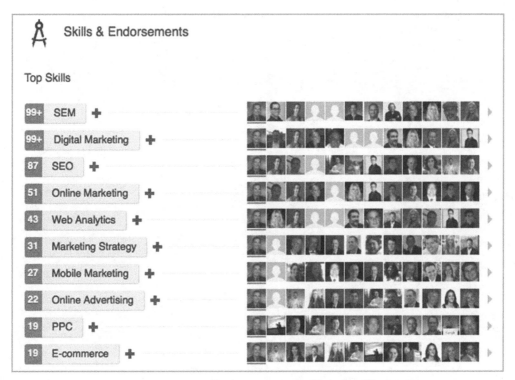

FIGURE 10–4. Endorsements in Your Profile

Skills list because I wanted to show I was knowledgeable in SEO, but it was no longer my job focus.

CONCLUSION

As you see, LinkedIn Recommendations can be a very powerful addition to your LinkedIn profile. I strongly suggest you focus on a smaller number of quality recommendations instead of large quantity of lower quality recommendations. Get at least three quality recommendations for each position you've held. Take time to recommend co-workers and colleagues, too, which adds credibility to your LinkedIn profile. Recommendations are a form of social proof, validating your work history and expertise.

People will endorse you for skills in your profile because LinkedIn automatically prompts them to do it when they visit your profile. Make sure to keep your Skills list updated and ordered properly so you receive appropriate endorsements.

In the next chapter, I'll show you how to connect with others on LinkedIn so you can build a powerful professional network.

For additional updates and how-to videos, visit
www.tedprodromou.com/chapter10

Connecting with Others

How many connections should you have on LinkedIn? I'm asked that question frequently, and there isn't a magic number that works for everyone. LinkedIn isn't a popularity contest where the person with the most connections wins. LinkedIn is not like Twitter, where Lady Gaga has more than 41 million followers but has no idea who those followers are. LinkedIn is about building relationships and connecting with others, which is very different than the monologue communication of Twitter.

There are two distinct approaches to networking on LinkedIn. The first, which is used by most LinkedIn members, is called strategic networking, where you focus on quality, not quantity. Strategic networkers usually have fewer than 500 people in their network and keep in touch with about 100 to 150 people in their network. They have deep connections with a small number of people.

The other approach, which is often used by sales representatives and recruiters, is called open networking; this is where you cast a very wide net. Open networkers often have thousands of connections in their network because their business is a numbers game. The more people in your network, the easier it is to find someone to fill an open position or outreach customers for a sale. As an open networker, you have a limited connection with a lot of people.

STRATEGIC NETWORKING

How many people do you think are in your professional network now? Most people know hundreds of people and often have more than 500 contacts in their online address book. The question is: How many of those contacts do you correspond with on a regular basis? Some people apply the 80/20 rule and think they correspond with about 20 percent of their professional network on a regular basis. The reality is that you don't have time to correspond with 20 percent of your professional network on a regular basis if you have more than 500 people in your network.

A number of studies—such as "Psychology, Ideology, Utopia and the Commons," by Dennis R. Fox, and "Sorry You May Have Gone Over Your Limit of Network Friends," by Carl Bialik—have been conducted over the years trying to determine the optimal size of a professional network. The studies vary dramatically, with some concluding we can maintain a stable social network of only 100 people, while others suggest we can maintain stable social networks of up to 300.

Maintaining a stable social network means we know everyone in our network and maintain regular contact with each and every individual. To maintain a larger social network requires more restrictive rules, laws, and enforced norms, so essentially you are almost being forced to maintain these relationships, which is not natural.

A widely accepted study by Robin Dunbar in 1992 resulted in Dunbar's Number, which suggests the theoretical cognitive limit to the number of people with whom one can maintain stable relationships is between 100 and 230. Dunbar does not specify an exact number because there are so many variables, but the generally accepted number is 150. Dunbar concluded, "This limit is a direct function of relative neocortex size, and that this in turn limits group size . . . the limit imposed by neocortical processing capacity is simply on the number of individuals with whom a stable interpersonal relationship can be maintained."

Do you maintain a regular relationship with 150 people? If you work for a medium to large-sized company and count your co-workers, you probably do maintain a regular relationship with that many people. If you work for a small company, you may not have regular communication with 150 people in your network. If you own your own business, you should be communicating with 150 people on a regular basis to generate leads or find opportunities.

The average number of connections for LinkedIn members is around 60 people, according to a Nielsen study. While many LinkedIn members have fewer than 60 connections, I see many members with more than 500 connections. When you view their profile you will only see 500+ connections. Once you are connected with that person, you will be able to view a list of their connections and can connect with anyone on the list because you have a second-degree relationship with them. A great way to expand your network is by connecting with appropriate second-degree relationships. Use your invitations wisely because LinkedIn gives you 3,000 invitations, after which you have to request more. It shouldn't be a problem, since you're trying to keep your network manageable.

OPEN NETWORKING

Open networkers on LinkedIn are often called LIONs (an acronym for "LinkedIn Open Networkers"). LIONs seek to actively increase their connections by sending out and accepting connection invitations. LIONs, in general, accept invites from anyone, so it's relatively risk-free to invite a LION into your network.

Most LIONs take pride in touting their specific number of connections; it's similar to the way celebrities compete to have the most Twitter followers. The majority of LIONs believe bigger is better and that large networks lead to more opportunity.

How Do I Become a LION?

There is no official LinkedIn designation for a LinkedIn open networker. It's an unofficial designation coined by people willing to connect with anyone to grow their network as large as possible. The official LinkedIn response in the LinkedIn Help Center is:

> *LION is a designation used by several user-created groups and individual LinkedIn members to indicate a high level of interconnectivity to other LinkedIn members. This term is not endorsed by LinkedIn. As a reminder, only connect to people you know and trust and only join groups you want your name associated with. If you need additional information regarding any group's purpose and/or philosophy, contact the identified group owner in the LinkedIn Groups Directory.*

If you want to be recognized as a LinkedIn LION, you can add LION to the end of your name in your profile or in your profile headline, as you see in Figure 11–1 on page 100.

Being a LION can have its drawbacks. Unfortunately, with any website or online tool that gets popular, people start abusing its popularity. We're seeing it on Twitter with people automating their tweets, so they send an endless stream of tweets 24/7. We're also starting to see a steady stream of tweet spam where people are creating thousands of fake Twitter profiles that automatically re-tweet tweets from popular tweeters. These automated programs begin with the legitimate tweet, but then re-tweet it thousands of times through fake profiles and fake links that lead to automated blogs, which in actuality are intended to sell affiliate products. You can see this tweet spam when you follow a popular celebrity tweeter because you will see a hundred re-tweets in a few seconds from hundreds of fake profiles that are all using the same profile picture.

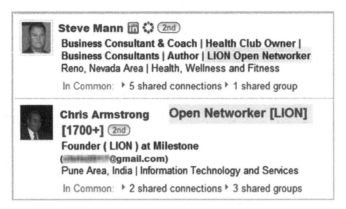

FIGURE 11–1. How to Identify a LION

We're now seeing similar tricks on LinkedIn with fake LinkedIn profiles. Be careful if you receive an invitation from:

- Someone who has no LinkedIn connections; LinkedIn now warns those who don't have connections or if they are new to LinkedIn
- Profiles with no profile picture—one of my pet peeves, the incomplete profile
- Profiles with company logos as their profile picture, which is a violation of the LinkedIn Terms of Service
- Profiles with company names instead of a person's name; we connect with people, not companies, on LinkedIn!
- Profiles that use partial names or symbols in their names so it looks machine generated
- Profiles that have an SEO-optimized name, a phone number, email address, or their website URL
- Keyword-stuffed title or summary

Do not connect with these people because it's probably a machine-generated profile or someone who is not on LinkedIn for the right reasons. If someone is not willing to provide a complete name and fill out a complete profile properly, he is not fit for your network.

POP QUIZ

Let's say you are into social media and you connect with a lot of social media managers on LinkedIn. It's always good to network with others who share the same type of job so you can bounce ideas off each other.

One day you receive an invitation from this person, who has internet marketing, social media marketing, and community manager in his job title; this looks inviting to you because you are in the same field. The person owns his own business just like you do and has 206 connections. On first glance, this looks like a good fit for your network, and connecting to this person will get you closer to 206 other people who are probably in the same field as you.

Should you connect with this person, after reading the Profile Headline in Figure 11–2?

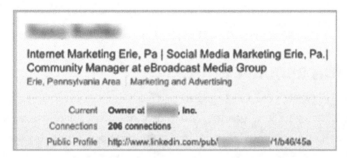

FIGURE 11–2. The Profile Headline of an Internet Marketing Person

This Profile Headline gives you the impression that the individual is an expert in internet marketing, social media marketing, and community management. If you said "no," good for you! Let's take a closer look at this person's profile, shown in Figure 11–3, and I'll show you why she probably isn't a good fit for your network.

FIGURE 11–3. There Is No Experience Listed in the LinkedIn Profile

This is an example of a SEO-optimized profile that contains very little information about the individual. It's clear this person is an internet marketing and social media marketing consultant in Erie, Pennsylvania, and she created this LinkedIn profile to help her Google and LinkedIn search results. There are no recommendations, no summary, no education, and nothing that would make me want to hire this person to help me with my internet or social media marketing. If the person were a legitimate internet marketing consultant, she would claim her LinkedIn personal URL, add a summary with keywords, add her skills, and get at least a dozen recommendations.

This person is gaming the system. I highly recommend ignoring or declining requests like this. Better yet, you should report them as spam so we can keep LinkedIn as professional as possible.

CONNECTION REQUEST ETIQUETTE

As your network grows, you will begin to receive connection requests from people you don't know. When you join groups and participate in conversations in that group, people will reach out to you with an invitation to connect. What should you do?

You have six options when you receive an invitation request. Your options are:

1. *Accept*. The person will immediately become a first-degree connection in your network.
2. *Reply*. You can reply to the person who invited you to connect if you are not sure you want him to become a first-degree connection with you at this time. If you just met someone at a networking event or in a LinkedIn Group but you don't know much about him, you can reply to the invitation and set up a meeting or phone call to get to know each other. I also review the profile in detail to see if he will add value to my network. After reviewing his profile and speaking with him, I will know if I want to add him to my network as a first-degree connection.
3. *Delete*. If I don't know this person, never corresponded with him in a group, and have no mutual connection with our networks, I delete the invitation—unless he will somehow add value to my network. I vet each thoroughly before accepting the invitation to connect. If I recognize the person and he recently joined LinkedIn but hasn't connected with anyone yet, I will accept his invitation if I know he will add value to my network.
4. *Archive*. If I receive an invitation from someone I don't know, I will review the profile to see if he is a fit for my network. If I don't think he is right at this time but may be a fit at some time in the future, I will add the invitation to the Archive. This lets me review the invitation at a later date and accept the invitation when I believe he will add value to my network.
5. *Ignore*. This is similar to adding the invitation to the Archive, but you have two options: You can select "I don't know them" or "Report as spam." This sends a message to LinkedIn flagging the person as being a spammer or as someone not using LinkedIn appropriately.

6. *Forward.* Sometimes I receive an invitation from a high-quality person who may not be a fit for my network but is a great fit for one of my connections. I will forward the invitation to my connection, suggesting that she connect with the high-quality person. This is kind of a blind recommendation since I don't know the person and I'm referring him, but I can get a sense from the profile that he is an A-list player and worthwhile for my connection.

REMOVING A CONNECTION

Sometimes you can connect with a person thinking, She would be perfect for my network! but it turns out she's not a good fit. Sometimes your connections will be overzealous with constant invitations to webinars or live events they're conducting. Don't get me wrong. I love to see people actively promoting their business and events. I don't mind occasional invitations, if the events are interesting and related to my current position. I do mind people inviting me to events weekly and sometimes every day—especially if the events are not related to my current job.

If you are connected with someone who you feel is taking advantage of your LinkedIn relationship and sending too many invitations, contact her and ask her to slow down or even remove you from her invitation list. Most of the time these individuals get the message and stop sending frequent event invitations. Unfortunately, there are those who won't get the message and keep spamming you with invitations, so you have to remove them as a connection.

You can remove a connection by going to the Connections tab, browse to the person you want to remove, hover over the bottom of her listing and when the More link appears, click on Remove Connection. This will remove the connection from your network, and it will not notify her.

CONCLUSION

You now know the essentials to connecting with others on LinkedIn. It's up to you to decide if you will build a smaller, high-quality network or become a LION and build a massive professional network. You have the ability to vet your connection requests so you can build a professional network that best suits your business needs.

In the next chapter, you're going to learn about LinkedIn InMail, a powerful tool that will help you connect with people who are not in your first- or second-degree networks.

For additional updates and how-to videos, visit
www.tedprodromou.com/chapter11

Using LinkedIn InMail to Reach Out

There are several ways to contact people through LinkedIn, and each has its nuances, depending on whether the individuals are in or out of your network. LinkedIn is built to respect users' professional privacy, so you can pick and choose who becomes part of your network and avoid being barraged by spam or people who will disrupt you or your business. Of course, the site does want to encourage positive connections and has devised a number of tools, such as InMail and Introductions, which allow users to communicate without invading anyone's privacy.

LINKEDIN INMAIL VS. INTRODUCTIONS

Introductions are free to all users. If you want to contact someone who is two or three degrees away from you, you can request an introduction through one of your connections who is a first-degree connection with that person.

You get a total of five introductions per month with a Basic (free) account and no more. If you need more introductions, you can upgrade to the Business account where you will be allowed to have up to 15 outstanding introduction requests at a time. The Business Plus account allows you to have up to 25 outstanding introduction requests, and the Executive account gives you up to 35 outstanding introduction requests at a time. This means you can use as many introduction requests as you want, as long as you don't exceed the maximum number of outstanding introduction requests. There is no monthly maximum number of introduction requests for paid accounts.

LinkedIn has a number of features to help you connect with people outside of your network. The best way to connect with someone outside of your network is via an introduction by someone already in your network. A virtual introduction increases your chances of connecting with that person because there is a level of trust between you and your connection and a level of trust between your connection and the person you want to meet. The trust is essentially passed from connection to connection.

WHAT IS INMAIL?

When you send email to someone you don't know, it can be perceived as spam or inappropriate if you aren't careful. Reaching out to people who don't know you through normal email channels usually has a very high failure rate. How do you respond when you receive an unsolicited email from a stranger who wants to meet with you? I rarely respond to unsolicited emails, unless I see something in the subject line or first sentence that catches my eye. There has to be some benefit to me to make me respond to that unsolicited email.

Reaching out to someone you don't know in a trusted community like LinkedIn is a different story. LinkedIn is a trusted network where most members are reputable business professionals. You don't expect people to bother you with unsolicited emails unless they can provide value to you. Even though LinkedIn is a trusted network, LinkedIn understands not all members will respect others' privacy and may abuse the privilege of being able to reach out to each other. They created InMail so members can reach out to each other while protecting their privacy.

It's not always possible to have one of your contacts broker an introduction for you, but there are other ways for you to connect with a person. One option is to use InMail: These are private messages that enable you to contact—or be directly contacted by—another LinkedIn user, while protecting the recipient's privacy. InMail is a paid feature that can be purchased individually or as a part of a premium account.

If you have a Basic (free) account, you don't receive any InMail credits, but you can purchase up to ten InMail credits. If you have a premium account, you receive a certain number of InMail credits available based on your premium package. The Business account gives you three InMail credits per month, the Business Plus account gives you ten InMail credits per month, and the Executive plan gives you 25 InMail credits every month. If you want more credits than the number you've been allotted, you can always purchase up to ten more.

What Are the Benefits of InMail?

In addition to helping you outreach and connect with people while respecting privacy, InMail offers several valuable benefits:

- *It helps you reach out to passive job candidates.* For example, let's say you're looking for a new network engineer for your company, and you read some great updates from a really sharp network engineer in the Pulse section of LinkedIn. You want to contact this guy because he'd be a perfect fit for your company. He's not actively looking for a new job, but you see that he has Career Opportunities listed in the Contact Settings section at the bottom of his member Profile. He's not in your network and you don't have any connections in common, so you can't connect with him. You can still reach out to him with a personal message using InMail to see if he'd be interested in your network engineer position. The personal message can compliment him on some accomplishments that you found in his profile, so he'll feel honored that you know so much about him. This will make him more responsive to your InMail.

- *You can reach out to active candidates who listed Career Opportunities in the Contact Settings section at the bottom of the member Profile or have written that they are actively looking for a new opportunity.* If they have Premium Job Seeker accounts, this will be noted by badges in their profiles so you know to reach out to them using InMail.

- *You are writing an article about social media, and you were looking for social media experts to interview.* You search for social media experts on LinkedIn and find a few who seem to fit your criteria. You have no connections in your network to make introductions, and they are not in any groups with you. Even if you were in a group with them, they don't allow emails from other group members unless you are already connected with them because they value their privacy. You can use InMail to reach out to them even though you have not actually had a "face-to-face" relationship with them.

- *You have a huge project starting tomorrow, and your front-end developer is unavailable because of a family emergency.* You need to find a great front-end developer who can start on the project immediately. You find the right developer, but she's not in your network; however, she is connected with your friend Joe. You email Joe and ask him for a LinkedIn Introduction, but he doesn't respond because he's out of the country. You can use InMail to reach out to the front-end developer so you don't have to wait for Joe to respond or rely on a long chain of contacts using LinkedIn Introductions.

- *You don't have to be a premium member to receive or respond to InMails.* A few times people have reached out to me using InMail to see if I was interested in an opportunity. I didn't know the people contacting me, but it didn't feel intrusive because they had included some personal details like "I see you actively participate in the Social Media Managers group." It's important to break the ice in the subject line or in the first line of the email to create a level of trust or familiarity.

■ *There is a seven-day guaranteed response*. If the person doesn't respond to you within seven days, your account will be credited with an InMail on the eighth day. It's like a "no-questions-asked money-back guarantee," so you don't lose your InMail if there is no response from the person you send the message to.

Purchasing and Sending an InMail

You can send an InMail by clicking the Send InMail link in the upper right of a member's profile page or from search results. If you have a Basic (free) account and you don't have any InMail credits, you will be prompted to upgrade your account when you try to send an InMail. If you don't want to upgrade to a Premium account, you can purchase InMail credits from within your profile under Settings. You can also check to see how many InMail credits you have remaining from this screen, as shown in Figure 12–1.

FIGURE 12–1. Available InMails

InMail credits can be used up to 90 days after they are issued. Once they expire they are not renewable, so make sure you don't purchase too many at once.

Remember, you don't need to use InMail to send messages to your first-degree connections. Just click Send a Message in the upper right of your connection's profile, and you can send them a message for free. You can also send free messages to other group members, even if they aren't a connection, as long as they accept messages from other group members. If you do not want to receive messages from other group members with whom you are not connected, see how to modify your preferences in Chapter 5, "LinkedIn Privacy Settings." I don't recommend preventing people from contacting you on LinkedIn because the purpose of being on LinkedIn is to connect with others, and you never know why someone will want to reach you; it could be an opportunity that would lead to additional revenue.

Here are some InMail facts for Premium account holders:

■ *InMail credits are issued on the monthly anniversary of your subscription start date.* (The number of credits you get each month varies by type of Premium account you have.) For example, if you signed up for a Business Plus account on July 3, you will receive ten new InMail credits on the third day of every month, as long as your Business Plus account is active.

■ *You can accumulate InMail credits from month to month, but they will expire after 90 days.* For Business Plus members, you could accumulate up to 30 InMail credits over a three-month period, but the initial ten credits expire on the 91st day if you don't use them. To be safe, you would have to use ten of your InMail credits before the 90th day.

■ *You can purchase up to ten more InMails than your account type allows or upgrade your account if you need even more.* Let's say you are a Business level account holder where you receive three InMail credits every month, and you're paying $24.95 per month for your account. You're looking for a new accountant for your company so you use up your three InMails reaching out to candidates. You could upgrade your account to Business Plus for $49.95 per month and receive ten additional InMail credits. Once you fill the position, you won't need ten InMail credits every month, and you don't want to spend that amount when you won't be using all the features of the Business Plus account. Instead of upgrading your account, you could purchase up to 10 additional InMail credits at $10 each. You could even purchase the additional InMail credits one at a time until you fill the position, saving you even more money.

If you have a Basic (free) account you can purchase up to ten InMail credits on your account at once or one at a time.

The guarantee is the same for Basic accounts as it is for Premium accounts. InMails are guaranteed a response by the recipient within seven days. If the recipient doesn't open the InMail within seven days, on the eighth day you receive another InMail to send. If the recipient responds after your account is credited, LinkedIn won't take the InMail credit back. If you send an InMail then withdraw it, you will not receive credit for it—even if the recipient doesn't respond.

What's an InMail Feedback Score?

LinkedIn rates your InMails to prevent overuse and spamming by members. Without the rating system, companies could abuse the InMail system by sending too many InMails, which would degrade the quality of the system and community. Everyone hates being spammed, so LinkedIn created the Feedback Score as a mechanism to monitor the effectiveness of the InMail system.

An InMail Feedback Score shows the acceptance rate of the sender's most recent InMails. Senders are rated on a five-star scale that appears at the top of the InMail message. You can see your own feedback score at the bottom of an InMail before you send it.

INMAIL FEEDBACK SCORE RATINGS

Five Stars   =   At least nine positive responses*

Four Stars   =   At least eight positive responses

Three Stars   =   At least seven positive responses

Two Stars   =   At least six positive responses

One Star   =   At least five positive responses

Zero Stars   =   Fewer than five positive responses

New   =   The sender has received InMail Feedback fewer than five times

*Positive response = InMail was accepted by recipient

InMail Rules If You Don't Like Spam

LinkedIn created delivery rules for InMail to minimize the amount of unsolicited emails you receive and to ensure that emails sent only from reputable LinkedIn members will be delivered to you. You can also customize your profile settings to control which InMails will be delivered to you and which will be blocked. The basic InMail rules include:

- InMails will come to your email address only if the sender has three stars or more. This means the InMail will be delivered to the email address you used when you signed up for LinkedIn in addition to your LinkedIn Inbox.
- InMails from someone with a rating of "New" or lower than three stars will be seen only when you sign in to LinkedIn. The InMail will not be delivered to the email address you used when you signed up for LinkedIn. The InMail will be delivered only to your LinkedIn Inbox.
- You can always select the types of messages you're willing to receive or set the frequency of emails from your Settings page. If you do not want to receive InMail

Types of messages you're willing to receive   ×

MESSAGES
- ◉ Introductions, InMail and Open Profile messages (Recommended)
- ○ Introductions and InMail only
- ○ Introductions only

OPPORTUNITIES
- ☑ Career opportunities   ☑ New ventures
- ☑ Expertise requests   ☑ Personal reference requests
- ☑ Consulting offers   ☑ Job inquiries
- ☑ Business deals   ☑ Requests to reconnect

ADVICE TO PEOPLE WHO ARE CONTACTING YOU

The best way to contact me is email at ted@tedprodromou.com or call 415 233-7234

Include advice on your availability, types of projects or opportunities that interest you, and what information you'd like to see included in a request. See examples.

Save changes   or Cancel

FIGURE 12–2. Types of InMail

messages, simply uncheck the Introductions and InMail radio button under your Settings, Email Preferences page, as you see in Figure 12–2.

TIPS FOR WRITING INMAILS TO INCREASE YOUR RESPONSE RATES

It's important for you to carefully structure your InMail so the receiving person will open it and respond. If she doesn't open your InMail, you get penalized in two ways. First, you're wasting $10 if you purchased the InMail outside of your LinkedIn membership. Second, your InMail Feedback Score decreases, making it harder for you to send InMail.

If you are familiar with email marketing, you understand what I'm talking about, except that in email marketing you don't receive a "double penalty" as with InMail. In traditional email marketing, if she doesn't open your email message, there is no penalty except your open rate decreases.

According to a study by Epsilon, the world's largest email marketing firm, and the Email Experience Council, the email marketing division of the Direct Marketing Association (www.thedma.org), the average open rate of direct marketing emails is around 31 percent and has been steadily increasing since 2011, as you see in Figure 12–3. The open rates vary by industry, but the overall average has been increasing, which is surprising to many email marketing experts.

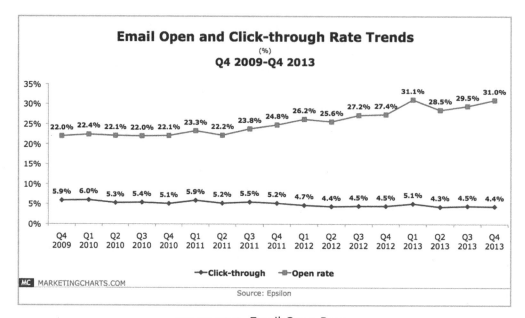

FIGURE 12–3. Email Open Rates

The good news is that LinkedIn InMail open rates are much higher if you structure your message properly. If the open rate of InMails were only 31 percent, it would be a very expensive way for you to reach out to others in LinkedIn. You would have to spend around $40 to get one person to just open your InMail, and opening the message does not guarantee anyone will respond to your request; it is easily possible to spend more than $100 just to get one person to respond.

LinkedIn doesn't provide template options for InMail, which is a good thing. If they did, InMail messages would start to look the same and people would stop paying attention. It's hard enough to get someone's attention these days when everyone is constantly being bombarded with messages and marketing promotions.

As with email marketing, your subject line is the most important part of your message. Some email marketing experts claim that the subject line is 90 percent of your message. If you don't catch their attention in the subject line, they'll never open the email and they'll never see your compelling message. Many copywriters spend more time crafting a powerful subject line than they do writing the email message.

Here are some tips for creating a powerful subject line for your InMail:

- Create curiosity by asking a provocative question.
- Promise answers to a question or solutions to a problem.
- Include a key benefit for the recipient.
- Ask them for advice or their opinion.

You want your subject line to be brief and to the point, catching their attention without giving away your message details. On TV, news programs have mastered the technique of piquing our attention about upcoming stories so we don't change the channel. Many times, the actual story is nowhere near as exciting as the teasers they used to pique our interest. The teasers are like subject lines in an email or headlines in sales copy. Their sole purpose is to grab our attention to make us want to learn more.

Remember your goal is to get the recipient to open your InMail so she'll read your message and start a dialogue with you. You want the recipient of your InMail to be so curious she finds herself unable to resist opening your message. You don't want to overhype your subject line or deceive her into opening your InMail, but you want to grab her attention enough to want to open it.

Here are some basic guidelines when composing your InMail to increase your response rates:

- *Design your InMail as a conversation starter.* You don't ask someone out on a date the second you meet her. You start a conversation first and get to know her before moving to the next level. The same holds true when you're establishing new business relationships. If you are too aggressive, she will naturally back away.
- *The goal of sending the InMail is to discuss and explore an opportunity—not seal the deal immediately.* Again, don't be too aggressive. Your goal is to get her to open your InMail and reply to you to establish a channel of communication.
- *Mention the profile content that prompted you to write.* If you were impressed by her education or a specific project she worked on, mention it in the first sentence or paragraph of your message.
- *Adopt a conversational, enthusiastic tone.* Don't use a form-letter approach with boring, scripted text. Be friendly and inviting so she'll want to get to know you.
- *Choose words that reflect your personal voice.* Write your message in a natural tone like you're speaking with your colleagues. Don't use words you wouldn't use in your everyday conversation because it will sound unnatural.

- *Express interest in helping her achieve her goals, rather than your need to fill a position if you're looking to hire her.* People are always thinking, "What's in it for me?" so you have to speak to her from that perspective.
- *Be brief and to the point so you don't waste anyone's time.* If you write a long, drawn out message, she'll lose interest and not want to connect with you.
- *Don't share too much.* If you do, she may not feel the need to reply. Your only goal is to get a response.
- *Focus on finding out her availability and interest in a job or networking opportunity.* Express your objective clearly in your InMail so she knows exactly why you reached out to her.
- *Give her a reason to reply by asking for advice, opinions, or referrals.*
- *Don't send a message with something like "Look at the job and tell me if you're interested" in the subject line.* Your message will be ignored 99 percent of the time, wasting your valuable InMail credits. A better subject line may be, "Are you interested in joining the number-one consulting company in the world?"

Every InMail you send should be a very personal message to each recipient with a unique subject line. Don't cut and paste subject lines and email content; it's too impersonal, and it won't grab her attention. If you are recruiting for a position, it's best to write a personal message mentioning skills or accomplishments you read in her profile and include a link to the job description. Do not include the entire job description in the InMail message.

The same holds true if you are using InMail for networking. Each message and subject line should be unique and let the recipient know your objective in the first sentence or paragraph. Explain what you read in their profile that made you want to reach out to this person. People love it when others notice their accomplishments and bring it to their attention. Play to a person's ego, and you'll have a friend for life!

Personally I don't use InMail to network with others. I prefer to use LinkedIn Groups, or LinkedIn's new publishing platform, to connect with others. When I notice an outstanding person, I reach out to him in a group we have in common instead of blindly sending him an InMail. Most of the time, he is very responsive to connecting if we are in a common group.

CONCLUSION

InMail is a great, unobtrusive way for you to reach out to people who are not part of your immediate network. InMail has a very high success rate because LinkedIn's ranking process ensures that people don't abuse the system. If you have a low response rate, your InMails will not be delivered, so it's imperative that you take the time to craft meaningful messages to your recipients. InMail is a unique tool that makes it relatively easy for you to connect with key decision-makers who are out of your network.

In the next chapter, we're going to learn about LinkedIn Groups, which are niche communities within the LinkedIn community. I'll show you how to effectively connect with subject-matter experts in your industry and how you can become a recognized thought leader in your field.

For additional updates and how-to videos, visit
www.tedprodromou.com/chapter12

LinkedIn Groups

When used properly, LinkedIn Groups can be a powerful tool to help you grow your business or professional network. LinkedIn Groups can provide you with the connections you need to reach new industries or regions. In order to create an effective LinkedIn Group, you need to understand how LinkedIn Groups work and determine the purpose for your group. Some companies use LinkedIn Groups to support their products, while others use groups to build a relationship with prospects or to solidify relationships with existing customers.

WHAT ARE LINKEDIN GROUPS?

LinkedIn Groups are forums or discussion boards where LinkedIn members can converse with each other to find solutions to their problems or share relevant information about a product, service, or topic related to your industry or niche.

LinkedIn Groups can be open, allowing anyone to join without approval, or closed, meaning you have to be approved by the group manager before you can participate.

Keeping your group closed keeps the discussions focused on specific topics and cuts down on the unwanted comments that plague many open social networking sites. This allows your LinkedIn Group discussions to be higher quality and more relevant to group members, since a group manager must approve all members. The group manager can moderate discussions and remove inappropriate posts or comments, as well as remove people from the group if they are disruptive or out of line.

How Many Groups Should I Join?

This is one of the most common questions I hear about LinkedIn. There are more than two million groups on LinkedIn at the time of this writing, and you are allowed to join up to 50 groups and 50 subgroups. Interesting new groups appear every day, and you're prompted by the "Groups You May Like" widget in your sidebar, so it's very easy to join a large number of groups without realizing it. The problem with joining numerous groups is that you just don't have time to be an active participant in all of them. Another issue with joining a lot of groups is that you may receive daily or weekly email updates from each group. If you belong to 30 groups, your inbox will be full of LinkedIn group updates that you won't have time to read. You can turn off email notifications from groups, but then you would have to visit each group manually to see new discussions.

It's best to join a few groups and be an active participant instead of joining 50 groups and barely participating. People can see if you are actively participating in a group, which helps build your reputation and searchability in LinkedIn. If you are a member of numerous groups and not participating, it could hurt your reputation because people may perceive you as unfocused or unorganized.

I have to be honest and tell you I belong to at least 40 groups at any given time, but I'm active in only a handful. I belong to the other groups to expand the reach of my network and give me access to people who are third-degree connections. Remember, when you are in a group, you can contact other group members via LinkedIn mail even if you aren't first-degree connections.

You can join a group if you want to learn about a specific subject and leave the group once you receive the information you need. For example, if you're looking for a new social media monitoring tool, you can join a social media group and see which products the attendees are recommending. Ask a few questions about the different products so you can make an informed decision when it's time to buy. Once you

> **LINKEDIN SEARCH TIP**
>
> To find the most popular groups on LinkedIn, select Groups from the Smart Search dropdown menu, then search with no query in the search box. This will display the most popular LinkedIn groups, and you have the option of seeing similar groups by clicking on Similar Groups in the search result.

make the purchase and get the software running properly, leave the group since you're unlikely to need to visit it again.

Finding LinkedIn Groups

You can search for groups using the search box in the top toolbar, by switching the search option from All to Groups. You can also look under Advanced search and select Groups to find groups related to your niche.

It's easy to find groups related to your job, position, industry, or skill set. If your LinkedIn profile is complete and optimized with your target keyword phrases, LinkedIn will recommend related groups for you in the Groups You May Like section. To see Groups You May Like, locate the widget at the bottom of the right sidebar on your LinkedIn homepage. LinkedIn will display a list of recommended groups based on the data in your profile, including keywords, job titles of your present and past jobs, industry, company name, and the groups your connections belong to.

If you don't see an appropriate group in the Groups You May Like recommendations, you can do an advanced group search. LinkedIn lets you search for groups by keyword, category, and country, so you can find a very specialized group that may not show up in your recommendations, as you see in Figure 13–1 on page 120. To do an advanced group search, go to Advanced on the top toolbar and select Groups.

Simply enter your keywords, select a relationship, and choose a category if you're looking for a specific type of group, like an open or members-only group, then select your language.

Evaluating LinkedIn Groups

LinkedIn Groups are a very effective way to grow your professional network and demonstrate your expertise. To be effective in your use of groups, you shouldn't just join the first one that looks interesting. When it comes to professional groups on LinkedIn, there will usually be several options to choose from, and you need to research the available groups to find the top three to five in a particular area.

First you want to make sure the group is active before joining. See how many members are in the group, and check out some of their profiles to see if there are people you know and some you would want to add to your network. It's better to join a small group with the right members than a very large group with people you wouldn't want to add to your professional network.

How often are new discussions started in the group? Do people comment on discussions to continue the conversation, or do discussions sit idle with no response? Another pet peeve for me is people starting discussions that turn out to be self-promotions.

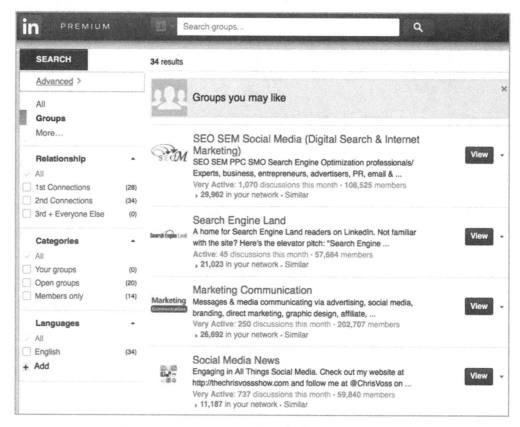

FIGURE 13–1. Search Groups

They aren't trying to add value to the group. They just want to promote their product or service. If most of the discussions are self-promotions, I avoid the group.

If you see a lot of discussions like these in a group, you may not want to join the group:

> *Tonight I will teach you the simple way to generate tons of leads. Are any of you interested in taking a very inexpensive (about $27) "how to" or "101" class on LinkedIn (and/or Facebook)? If so, contact me. . . Thanks!*

If you see discussions like these, it's probably OK to join the group because people are doing market research or gathering information without obviously promoting their business:

> *Knowing what you know now about Starbucks, ten years ago would you have invested in the company? Yes or No*

> *Hey everyone, I just opened Nothing Bundt Cakes in Corte Madera! I wanted to get some feedback, so if you have tried my cakes let me know what you think.*

There can be a fine line between self-promotion and fact finding so you have to decide for yourself if the group is right for you. If you notice the quality of the discussions isn't up to your expectations, you can always leave the group.

Read some of the discussions so you can get a sense of the group. If you're looking for a group of senior-level web analytics professionals but the discussions are very basic, like how to install Google Analytics, the group isn't right for you. You can search for groups using specific keywords that you know will result in deeper conversations. You could search the analytics groups for questions like "How do you effectively measure customer engagement?" which should result in finding discussions by senior web analysts.

Another way you can assess the quality of a group is to review the Group Statistics, which is located at the right side of the header when you're viewing the group. Click on the "I" next to the Join button. You will see tabs labeled Discussions, Members, and Search, with another row of tabs below including Summary, Demographics, Growth, and Activity, as shown in Figure 13–2.

The Discussions tab lets you view the current group discussions. I like to make sure there are vibrant discussions in a group, not just blog posts by group members. I look at the number of new discussions and the number of comments, shares, and likes for each discussion. If you don't see a lot of comments on the discussions, then you can assume

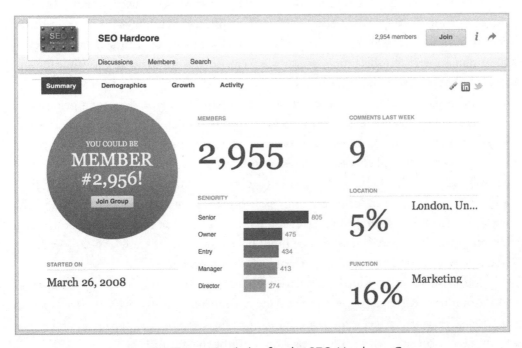

FIGURE 13–2. Group Statistics for the SEO Hardcore Group

most of the posts are just low quality blog posts and articles that are being auto-posted by group members.

The next tab I look at is the Members tab. I like to view the profiles of the most active members of the group to see if they are my target audience. If they are, then I'll usually join the group to get to know them.

The Search tab lets me search this specific group for keyword phrases, job titles, company names, and products or services. This lets me quickly vet the group to see if it's worth joining.

The Summary tab shows you a snapshot of the group, including when the group started, the number of members, comments last week, seniority, location, and function.

The Demographics tab provides detailed demographics of the group. This screen shows you the seniority of the group, its function, location, and industry. This is very valuable information when you're evaluating a group. If you're looking to connect with network engineers in London but the group comprises IT executives located in Japan, you know immediately this isn't the right one for you.

The Growth tab shows you New Members, Total Members, New Members Last Week, and Week Over Week Growth Rate. It's best to join a group that is growing, but the growth rate doesn't have to be significant if there are dynamic discussions between existing members. A fast-growing group doesn't mean it's a quality group, so you have to consider many factors before determining if it's worth joining.

The Activity tab summarizes the number of comments, discussions, jobs, and promotions in a group. You'll also see a graph displaying trend lines for the number of comments and discussions over time. This tab will help you determine if the activity in the group is increasing, declining, or stagnant. You don't want to waste your time joining a group that has stagnant or declining activity; your time is too precious to waste.

As you see, there are a number of factors to consider before joining a group, and there is no magic formula. The key is to join a group only if it will benefit you in some way. If you're looking to connect with other network engineers in your local area so you can get together and talk about the latest trends, the group may not have a lot of online activity but could be a fantastic in-person resource. If you work in a very specialized field and don't have access to local resources, you can connect with colleagues around the world in a LinkedIn group, so you can share information and insights. The group may be small, but the expertise level will be high. It's comforting to know you can reach out to a group of trusted experts for assistance when you need it.

You can also join groups to receive tech support on products. Large companies like Computer Associates (www.ca.com) have multiple groups dedicated to specific products, so you can get expert assistance instantly from other group members or Computer Associate tech support reps who monitor the group.

Joining a LinkedIn Group

When you find a group you want to join, simply click on the Join Group button located in the group listing. A message like you see in Figure 13–3 will appear, acknowledging your request to join the group and offering you a chance to adjust your settings.

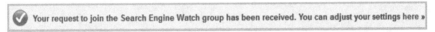

FIGURE 13–3. Search Engine Watch Group Automated Response Message

This is where you can control where email notifications will be sent, how often you will receive updates, and which notifications will be sent to you.

Posts: Send Me an Email for Each New Discussion

Sometimes you will want to be notified immediately whenever a new discussion is started, so you can contribute quickly. If you are a consultant and want to demonstrate your expertise by answering questions posted by other members, you should select this option. When a new discussion is started you can respond quickly, and your comment will appear right after the question, which will give you more exposure. If you are the 20th person to comment on a question, chances are most people will not take the time to read all of the comments, and your brilliant response will go unnoticed.

Don't use this option if you are a member of a very popular group, unless you want to receive an extra 500 emails a week for every new discussion.

Digest Email: Send Me a Digest of All Activity in This Group

Delivery Frequency

- *No email.* You will not receive email updates from this group
- *Weekly digest email.* You will receive one weekly email update
- *Daily digest email.* You will receive one daily email update

I usually set my email updates to daily digest email for most of my groups and use the weekly digest email updates for groups with less activity. You can always change the frequency of your group updates in your profile settings under Settings, Group, Companies & Applications, and set the frequency of group digest emails as you see in Figure 13–4 on page 124.

Choose if you want to receive group announcements and if you want to allow other members of the group to send you messages. Once you Save Changes, you will be ready to participate in the group (and receive approval from the group manager, if it's a closed group).

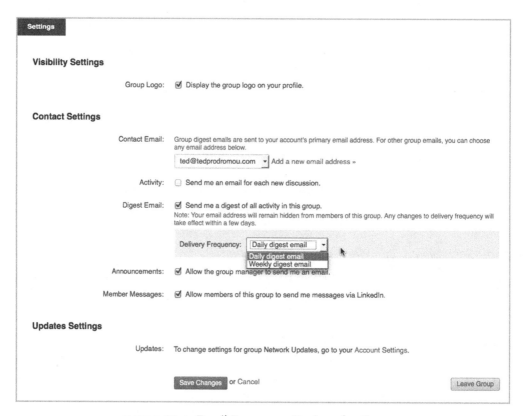

FIGURE 13–4. Email Frequency Settings for Groups

WHAT IS THE BEST WAY TO USE LINKEDIN GROUPS?

Visiting and following up on the groups regularly is the only way to effectively use LinkedIn to build up your professional network. You need to make frequent and regular appearances within your group in order to maximize your exposure. One of the best ways to make sure that you are seen within the group is to target the most popular discussions and then be a regular and beneficial contributor to that discussion.

Once you feel comfortable with how groups work, the next step is to start your own discussion. Start with a topic that you are knowledgeable about so you can keep the conversation going. When you start a new discussion you want it to be as engaging as possible. You can look at a few of the extended conversations in your group and see how the discussion started. Starting a discussion isn't always just asking a question. You can ask for advice about a particular scenario or post information that would be useful to the target market you are looking to attract. Once you get the conversation started and others join in, be sure to reply in a timely fashion. You can subscribe to conversations, so you are notified by email when comments are posted.

You want to visit your LinkedIn groups regularly and participate whenever you can add value to a discussion and keep the conversation going. You can follow people in your group if you find them interesting and may want to add them to your network. After following them for a while, you can invite them to join your network if they are a good fit.

If you are interested in a particular discussion, you can "Like" it, which lets people know you are interested in that topic. Your profile picture will appear below the discussion, showing people you are interested in the topic. Your profile will also appear in the group's latest update widget in the sidebar, giving you more exposure to the group.

A WORD OF CAUTION

In 2013, LinkedIn implemented new rules for groups intended to cut down on self-promotion and spam within the group discussions. Many LinkedIn members were queuing content in programs like Hootsuite so every day thousands of articles and blog posts were automatically posted in groups. The content's purpose was to promote a product or service and added very little to the group discussions.

Up to 90 percent of the content being posted in groups received no likes, shares, or comments because it was so self-promotional. Group moderators are supposed to flag this content and remove it so the group discussions remain interesting, but most moderators ignored the content. The result is many LinkedIn groups have thousands of members but very little discussion. Most LinkedIn members stopped participating in groups because there were no thoughtful discussions.

LinkedIn implemented new group rules in 2013 that allow the group moderator to flag people who post too much self-promotional content. When you are flagged in one group, every post you submit in any LinkedIn group needs to be moderated before it's posted. This is a very severe penalty and has cut down on some spam, but most group moderators don't take the time to flag the spammers.

I have heard from some people who were flagged that it's very difficult to get the restriction removed. You have to determine which group moderator flagged you and have him remove the restriction. The group moderator doesn't always remove the restriction in a timely manner, limiting your group activity. I agree with the new penalty because most groups are not well moderated and very spammy. If LinkedIn required the moderators to better police their groups, the problem would go away, but at this time the moderators are not held accountable by LinkedIn.

CONCLUSION

LinkedIn Groups are a great way for you to connect with other colleagues in your industry to keep up with the latest trends and to share information. The discussions in

LinkedIn Groups are usually more focused than the discussions in comment threads on long-form posts because the group members are subject matter experts and industry leaders. LinkedIn Groups is also the perfect place to demonstrate your expertise by participating in the group discussions.

In the next chapter, we are going to learn how to manage your LinkedIn connections and remain top of mind with key decision-makers.

For additional updates and how-to videos, visit
www.tedprodromou.com/chapter13

Managing Your LinkedIn Connections

As your LinkedIn network grows, you will want to keep track of the new people being added. LinkedIn provides some great tools that help you monitor your LinkedIn network and activity. You see a snapshot of Your LinkedIn Network, which includes the total number of Your Connections and connections two and three degrees away. With two people joining LinkedIn every second, your network two and three degrees away can grow very quickly. You'll also see the Total users you can contact through introductions.

As you see in Figure 14–1 on page 128, I have 2,834 first-degree connections and 22,677,835 potential connections in my network. I can reach these professionals through an introduction or an InMail, which is unbelievable. Where else do you have access to so many targeted resources?

Each time I add one new person as a first-degree connection, my network grows exponentially. After I took the screenshot in Figure 14–1, I added five more people to my network, so I now have 2,839 connections. My entire network increased to 22,720,924 people. The famous book and movie *The Secret* talks about the Law of Attraction and learning how to attract new clients. LinkedIn is like the Law of Attraction on steroids, automatically adding new prospects to your network while you sleep.

Your LinkedIn Network

2,834 Connections

22,677,835 Professionals in your Network

Your LinkedIn Network

2,839 Connections

22,720,924 Professionals in your Network

FIGURE 14–1. Your Network Connections

When you click on Connections, you'll be redirected to your Connections page as shown in Figure 14–2 on page 129. It's important to understand LinkedIn considers a connection as being someone you are directly connected with on LinkedIn. The lower portion of your Connections page displays your Contacts, which you may have imported from your email address book. A contact isn't always a LinkedIn connection, which can make this page a bit confusing.

To increase engagement, LinkedIn added a feature where you can congratulate people when they have a new job or when it's their birthday. I log into LinkedIn every morning and spend five to ten minutes congratulating people or saying happy birthday. This may seem trivial, but when you do this, the person is notified that you reached out to her, and it puts you top of mind with her. I've had students land big deals with people they "ping" after not communicating with them for years. You can easily access this feature by navigating to Connections, then Keep in Touch on your main menu.

If you import your contacts from your email address book, LinkedIn will let you know when you communicate with your contacts in the Contacts section. I imported my contacts from my Gmail and iPhone address books so you see the icons in Figure 14–2.

In Figure 14–3 on page 129 you see the email communication log between me and my friend Bruce Burtch. I'm subscribed to Bruce's email newsletter with my Gmail account, and you see the messages he sent me. I can also create a Note, which is kept in Bruce's profile for me; I can set a Reminder to contact Bruce; I can add a note in How You Met; and I can tag Bruce's contact record (explained further in the section, "Using Tags" on page 130). There are very handy tools that make LinkedIn Connections like a mini-CRM.

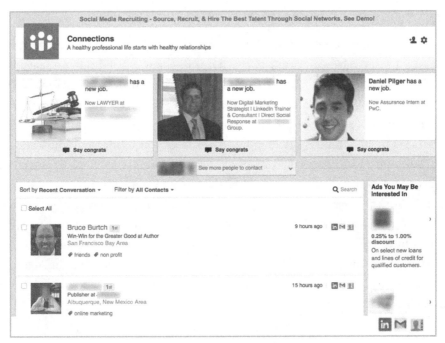

FIGURE 14–2. Your Connections Page

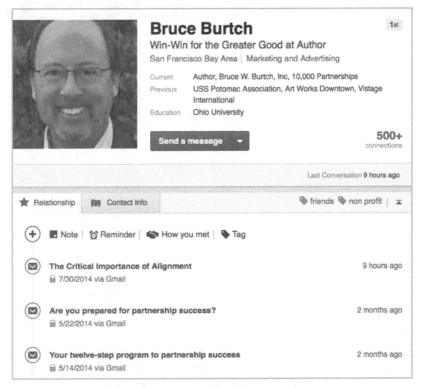

FIGURE 14–3. Tracking Conversations

USING TAGS

As you add new connections to your network, you want to keep them organized so they're easy to find when you want to reach out to them. LinkedIn has a feature called Tags, which is located within each contact record. LinkedIn describes Tags as "simple keywords that you can create to organize your connections for quick filtering on LinkedIn. You can use this window to create new tags or delete old ones. Note that you can create up to 200 unique tags." Figure 14–4 shows how to manage your tags.

LinkedIn predefines some tags, such as colleagues, friends, partners, group members, and classmates. You can create custom tags that are appropriate for your network. Some of the tags I use are search marketers, PPC experts, SEO experts, and programmers.

Once you tag your connections, you can easily communicate with specific segments of your connections. You could send a LinkedIn email to all of the attorneys in your contact list. To do this, change Filter by All Contacts to Tag, then select the Attorney tag. Now you can send a personalized email to up to 50 connections who have the attorney tag in their contact record.

FIGURE 14–4. Manage Tags

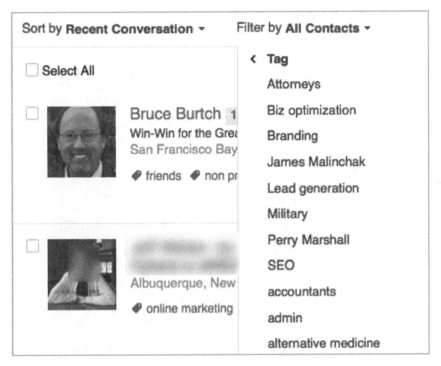

FIGURE 14–5. Filtering Contacts

CONCLUSION

LinkedIn lets you closely monitor your professional network and gives you tools that help you keep in touch with key decision-makers who hire you. The Keep in Touch feature prompts you when your connections update their profile so you can quickly reach out to and remain top of mind with them.

In the next chapter, we're going to explore LinkedIn Publishing and content marketing so you can share your expertise with your network, company followers, and all of LinkedIn.

For additional updates and how-to videos, visit
www.tedprodromou.com/chapter14

The Definitive Publishing Platform

This is the title of a blog post from LinkedIn in February 2014, when it announced the new publishing platform. The overwhelming success of the LinkedIn Influencer program and the high quality content posted in status updates by LinkedIn members demonstrated the power of LinkedIn.

Here is the official announcement from LinkedIn:

We believe in giving our members access to the business knowledge they need to be great at what they do. To put that simply, we are making a commitment to our members: the time you spend on LinkedIn will make you better at your job today.

The valuable Influencer posts and the wide range of professional content from millions of publishers that we currently aggregate on LinkedIn are powerful, but only the tip of the iceberg. Combined, our members have extremely valuable and varied experiences; however, their knowledge and expertise have not yet been captured and shared.

Starting today, LinkedIn is opening up our publishing platform to our members, giving them a powerful new way to build their professional brand. When members publish a post on LinkedIn, their original content becomes part of their professional profile, is shared with their trusted network, and has the ability to reach the largest group of professionals ever assembled. Now members have the ability to follow other members that are not in their network and build their own group of followers. Members can continue to share their expertise by posting photos, images, videos, and their original presentations on SlideShare.

LinkedIn's goal is to become the largest publishing platform on the internet, and they're off to a great start. Many business professionals have used LinkedIn to establish themselves as industry experts and thought-leaders simply by posting content on a regular basis through their status updates.

What's the difference between an Influencer, Publisher, and a status update?

STATUS UPDATE

This is the original way to share content on LinkedIn. A status update is similar to a tweet on Twitter where you have a limited number of characters and the ability to add images and links to additional content. You have 180 characters in your LinkedIn status update so the key is to write a compelling statement, very similar to a headline, which grabs readers' attention so they click on the image or link to learn more. Posting status updates is a great way to drive traffic to your website, blog, or LinkedIn company page where people can learn more about your business.

To create a status update, simply type your message in the box at the top of your LinkedIn homepage. Figure 15–1 shows the Status Update box.

FIGURE 15–1. Status Update

If you want to add a file or an image to your status update, click the paper clip icon, and you will be prompted to upload the file that will appear in your status update.

Various file types can be uploaded, as shown in Figure 15–2 on page 135.

PUBLISHER

The Publisher feature started rolling out to all LinkedIn users in February 2014. This feature lets you publish full articles just like you publish on your website or blog. To create a new post, click on the pencil icon you see in Figure 15-1. This opens a full-featured web editor where you add text, images, and even embed YouTube or iFrame-based videos. Once you complete your post, it appears in your LinkedIn Newsfeed, and you can choose to share the post on Twitter. Figure 15-3 on page 135 shows the full-featured editor.

FIGURE 15–2. Supported File Types for Status Updates

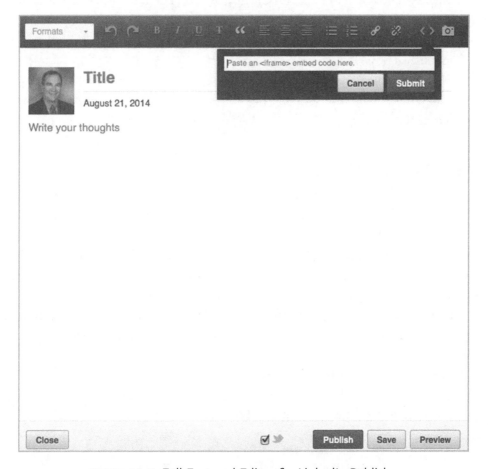

FIGURE 15–3. Full-Featured Editor for LinkedIn Publisher

TIPS FOR GETTING PEOPLE TO NOTICE YOUR CONTENT

Posting status updates and publishing on LinkedIn is a huge opportunity, but how do you get people to read your content? We've all written outstanding content we were proud to publish on our blog, and nobody knew it existed so only a handful of people read it.

Here are some keys to getting your content noticed:

- Publish new content at least once a week. Consistency is the key to success.
- Let your network know when you post content because they may not notice it in their Newsfeed. You can send them a message through LinkedIn letting them know you have an interesting article that may benefit them.
- Tweet your content, post it on your Facebook page, and share it on social bookmarking websites like reddit. Social bookmarking sites still generate a lot of web traffic.
- Share your content in LinkedIn Groups, but don't do it in a self-promotional way or you could be flagged by the moderator.
- Create status updates on your LinkedIn Company page that link to your full published post.
- Create a sponsored update where you pay to promote your content to a targeted audience. This is an affordable way to get your content in front of millions of LinkedIn users.

LINKEDIN INFLUENCERS

LinkedIn Influencer started in fall of 2012 and features top voices in business like Richard Branson, Martha Stewart, and Bill Gates. The expertise they have shared through their Influencer posts has resonated in a meaningful way with LinkedIn members and is fueling business conversations. The average Influencer post drives more than 31,000 views and receives more than 250 likes and 80 comments. By any measure, this is a remarkably high level of engagement for digital content.

You have to be invited by LinkedIn to be an Influencer. If you know an Influencer, you can ask them to recommend you to LinkedIn, and you may be lucky enough to be invited.

Becoming a LinkedIn Influencer is a career-changing event because most of the Influencers are already considered industry leaders. You'll be in the same circles as Jack Welch, Warren Buffett, Guy Kawasaki, and many more business success stories.

CONCLUSION

LinkedIn wants to become the definitive publishing platform network on the internet, and it is well on their way to achieving that goal. Sharing your content via status updates, company page updates, and the publishing tool helps demonstrate your expertise and establish you as an industry thought-leader. As LinkedIn grows, more professionals are creating and sharing content at an incredible rate.

In the next chapter, I'm going to show you LinkedIn's tools that help you monitor the effectiveness of your networking and content marketing efforts.

For additional updates and how-to videos, visit
www.tedprodromou.com/chapter15

Measuring Your LinkedIn Engagement

The LinkedIn networking site has a collection of powerful analytics tools that let you measure your effectiveness on LinkedIn. Some of these tools are included with your free LinkedIn account while others are offered only to Premium account holders. These tools are a great addition to LinkedIn because now you have the ability to see how many people view, like, comment, and share your status updates and published content. You can also see detailed demographics of who views your profile so you can see what kind of people your profile is attracting.

WHO'S VIEWED YOUR PROFILE

LinkedIn has been letting us see who's been viewing our profile for a few years, but they've dramatically enhanced this tool for Premium members. This feature alone is worth the investment in a Premium LinkedIn account. Figure 16–1 on page 140 shows you how many people viewed your profile in the past day and also where your profile ranks compared to your industry and to your LinkedIn network.

Let's dig deeper into who's been viewing your LinkedIn profile and how you can use this to your advantage.

To see the detailed information, I click on the link that says "12 Your profile has been viewed by 12 people in the past day." The next screen

Who's Viewed Your Profile

12 Your profile has been viewed by 12 people in the past day.

▲**13** Your rank for profile views improved by 13% in the past 15 days.

FIGURE 16–1. Who's Viewed Your Profile

shows a graph with the total number of profile views in the past 90 days, the number of viewers from specific industries, the number of viewers from various regions, and the number of viewers found by the People Similar to You sidebar widget on LinkedIn.

This is why the way you fill out your profile is so important. The LinkedIn algorithm takes into account your industry, your region, your education, and the keywords you use in your profile, including your professional headline, job titles, keywords in your summary, and the rest of your profile. Knowing how people found you on LinkedIn helps you customize your profile so you attract the right profile viewers. Figure 16-2 shows the first layer of Who's Viewed Your Profile.

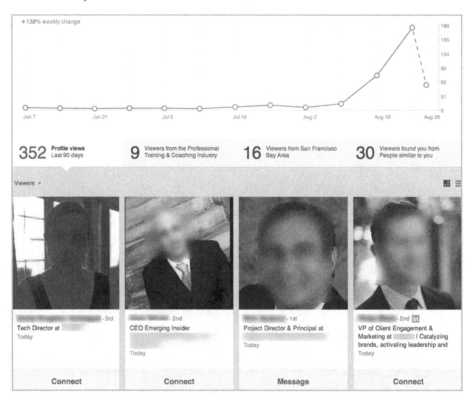

FIGURE 16–2. Detailed Who's Viewed My Profile Data

Below the graph, you see profiles of the people who viewed your profile. If you are connected to that person on LinkedIn you will see the Message link so you can easily send him or her a message. If you see the Connect button, you can quickly connect with him or her if he or she is right for your network. I like to view profiles to see if they are a match for my professional network before inviting them to connect with me. If you are a LinkedIn LION, you will connect with everyone who views your profile no matter what. I consider a person who viewed my profile as a "warm" lead because something compelled him to view my profile. I find that at least 80 percent of the people who viewed my profile will connect with me if I reach out to them.

Let's dig even deeper into the data provided by the graph. When you hover over the dots in the graph you see how many profile views you drew each week. The highest point of the graph in August shows 181 profile views for that week. When you click on the dot, you will see the people who viewed your profile that week, as shown in Figure 16–3.

Now the fun begins. Click on Viewers from the Professional Training & Coaching Industry, and you'll see the people from that industry who viewed your profile, plus some very valuable information, as shown in Figure 16–4 on page 142.

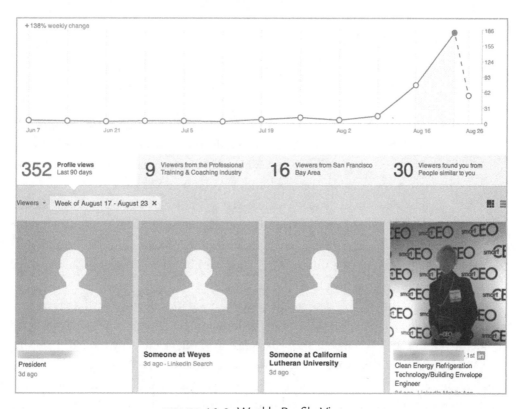

FIGURE 16–3. Weekly Profile Viewers

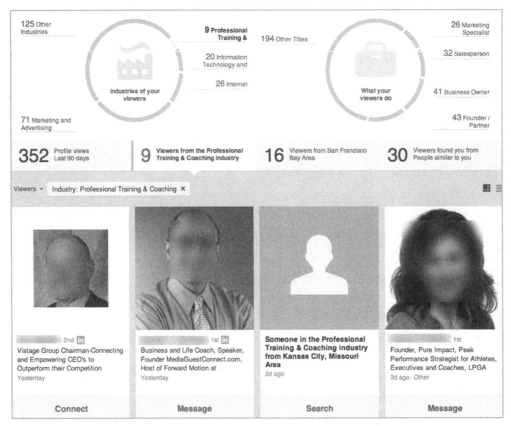

FIGURE 16–4. Detailed Profile Viewer Demographics

You'll see all of the industries that attracted your profile viewers. In this example, 20 viewers were from the Information Technology industry, 26 from the Internet industry, and 71 from Marketing and Advertising. When you click on each industry, you'll see exactly who viewed your profile from each industry. How cool is that?

On the right side of the graph, you use the job titles of the people who viewed your profile. If you are trying to attract C-level executives and most of your profile views come from lower-level management, you need to update your profile and start distributing your content to a different audience on LinkedIn. This alone is worth the small investment in a Premium LinkedIn account.

As you explore all of the tabs in the chart, more data categories will appear. As a marketer, this data gives me the keys to the kingdom as I target my ideal clients on LinkedIn. I know what's working and what's not working in my daily LinkedIn activity.

My favorite data comes from the Viewers Found You from People Similar to You tab. As you see in Figure 16–5 on page 143, LinkedIn tells you how people found your LinkedIn profile and which keywords they used to find you. This data shows you if they

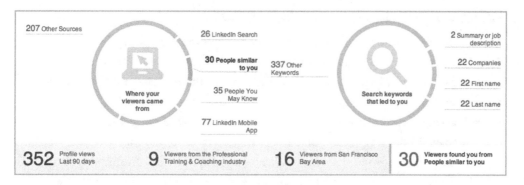

FIGURE 16–5. Viewers Found You from People Similar to You

found you on the LinkedIn homepage, LinkedIn Groups, from LinkedIn InMail you sent them, and even if they found you from a Google search.

This again helps you fine-tune your profile so you include the right keywords in the right sections of your LinkedIn profile. This is like receiving the answers to the test before you take it.

Below the first row of people who viewed your profile, LinkedIn shows you groups, LinkedIn Influencers, and people you may want to connect with to increase your profile views. Again, these recommendations are based on the LinkedIn algorithm so your profile views will probably increase if you follow LinkedIn's advice. I like to let the LinkedIn algorithm do the work whenever possible. Figure 16-6 shows you LinkedIn's recommendations.

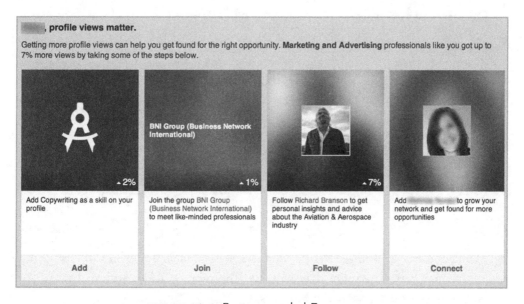

FIGURE 16–6. Recommended Engagement

HOW YOU RANK FOR PROFILE VIEWS

The tab next to Who's Viewed Your Profile is the How You Rank for Profile Views. This lets you compare your profile views with professionals similar to you and to your network. I find the more active I am on LinkedIn, the more profile views I receive, and I can move up (or down) in the rankings quickly. Figure 16–7 shows Perry Marshall's ranking among his peers and the increase or decrease in his ranking over the past 15 days. LinkedIn also provides tips to help you improve your ranking. In this case, LinkedIn is recommending Perry update his Summary to increase profile views.

This information lets me know how active I have to be on LinkedIn to keep my profile in front of the right people. It also keeps me active on LinkedIn because when I'm not consistent, my rankings drop quickly, prompting me to get back on track. It's like an unofficial competition among peers, which is always fun.

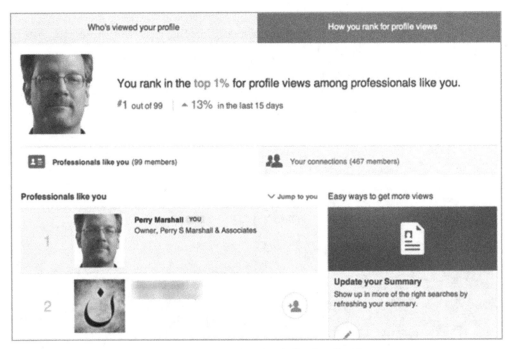

FIGURE 16–7. How You Rank for Profile Views

LinkedIn has committed to providing more valuable tools like these to their Premium members. The more data we have, the more efficient we can be with our LinkedIn usage while growing our business.

WHO'S VIEWED YOUR UPDATES

In the past, we posted status updates, but we had no idea how many people viewed them or if the updates were engaging. With the new analytics, we can see how many people Viewed, Liked, Shared and Commented on our updates. I love this new feature because it lets me know exactly what content my network is interested in.

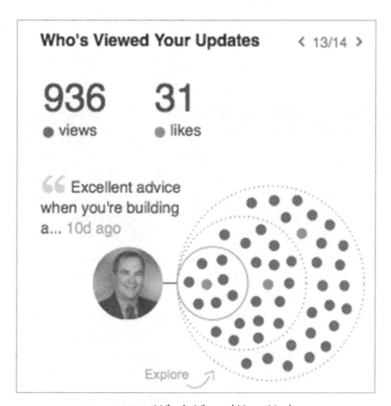

FIGURE 16–8. Who's Viewed Your Updates

In Figure 16–8, you see the statistics for a status update I shared with my network. This was an article I found on LinkedIn Pulse and shared it with my network, which took about ten seconds. In one day, 936 people viewed my status update, and 31 people liked it. Over the next week, a total of 2,498 people viewed the update, and I received 98 likes.

When you hover over each purple dot on your screen, you see who viewed the update. Hovering over the green dots shows you who liked the update. I often reach out to people who like my updates and personally thank them for liking my update, which they always appreciate.

Notice there are three circles in the diagram. The circle closest to my profile picture is my first-degree network. The next circle is my second-degree network, and the largest circle is my third-degree network. This means many people in my first-degree network shared the update with their network, and the second-degree network members shared the update with their networks.

Your goal is to create status updates that go viral and are shared to every level of your network. Monitor the statistics of every status update to see which messages and headlines resonate with your audience. Treat status updates like ads with the intent of enticing people to click on your update, like it, share it, and comment on it.

I like to look at status updates from my network to see which messages receive the most likes, shares, and comments. This helps me identify the content which engages our networks.

MEASURING THE ENGAGEMENT OF YOUR PUBLISHED ARTICLES

When you publish content using LinkedIn Publisher, you measure your engagement differently. Figure 16–9 on page 147 shows a LinkedIn Publisher article posted by Dave Kerpen on January 28, 2013. This was the most popular post on LinkedIn for over a year, and at the time of this writing, it's the second most popular post ever.

If you look at the bottom of Figure 16–9, you see the engagement statistics. This article has been viewed over 2.7 million times since it was published and still receives numerous views every day. Over 26,800 people have liked the article, and over 7500 people have commented on the article. That is serious engagement for one article.

What makes an article engaging? From this screenshot, you see three factors that could entice people to read the article. First, Dave Kerpen is an established LinkedIn Influencer with almost 500,000 followers. When Dave published this article he had a fraction of those followers, so I'm assuming a lot of his followers shared this with their LinkedIn networks, causing the article to go viral. The second factor that encourages engagement is the image you use with your content. Articles with good images receive more clicks. This image gives you a hint of what the article will be about, which may get you to click to read more. The biggest factor, in my opinion, is the headline. Just like ads, a great article headline gets people to want to read the article to learn more. This headline is perfect to grab the attention of a busy business professional. The number 11 tells me there isn't an overwhelming number of things I have to learn or do to be successful. The word "simple" tells me these concepts are easy to understand. We all love easy! Every business professional wants to be a better leader, so why wouldn't I click on this article to learn more?

FINDING POPULAR PUBLISHED ARTICLES

Before I write an article and headline, I like to see what's popular on LinkedIn today and for the past week. To find the most popular posts, go to LinkedIn Pulse, which is

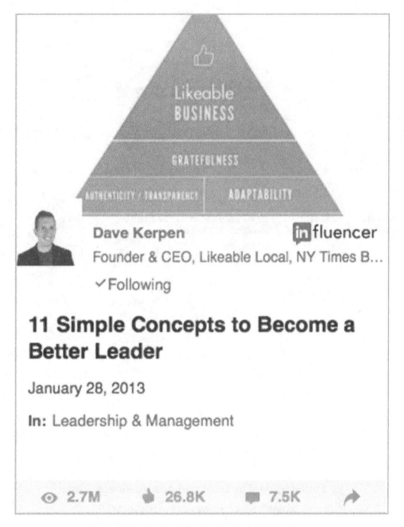

FIGURE 16–9. Measuring LinkedIn Publisher Engagement

under the Interests tab in the main LinkedIn menu. Select the Top Posts tab, as shown in Figure 16-10 on page 148, and you can filter the top posts on the right side of the page. Your options are Top Posts Today, Top Posts This Week, Top Posts All Time, and Recent Posts. This gives me an idea of what content and headlines are popular right now and which content has longevity. While it's great to have a Top Post that lasts a few weeks, wouldn't it be even greater to have a post that engages people for years?

CONCLUSION

LinkedIn Publisher gives you a golden opportunity to establish yourself as an authority among over 330 million business professionals. Publisher levels the playing field and

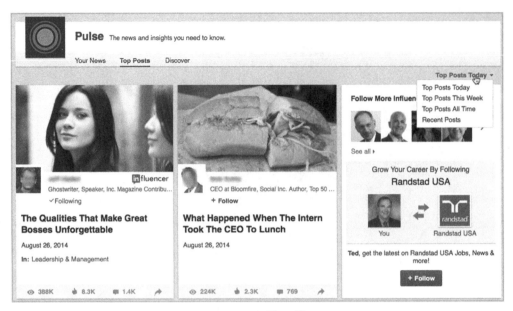

FIGURE 16–10. Top Posts

lets a complete unknown become famous in a very short period of time. Using LinkedIn analytics you can see what's popular and create similar content you know your audience desires. LinkedIn is making it very easy for everyone to establish themselves as an industry expert.

In the next chapter, we'll explore the LinkedIn mobile apps, which help us keep in touch with our network from anywhere.

For additional updates and how-to videos, visit

www.tedprodromou.com/chapter16

LinkedIn on the Go

A s the world migrates to mobile computing, LinkedIn has been developing mobile apps to meet the demand. Instead of creating one massive app that performs many functions, LinkedIn has chosen to create numerous apps for specific purposes. I love the LinkedIn mobile apps because they are very easy to use and keep you focused on the task at hand.

LinkedIn makes it easy for developers to create new apps and tools that extend LinkedIn, and you can learn more at http://developer. linkedin.com.

In this chapter, I'll introduce you to a few of the most popular LinkedIn tools. All of these tools are free to download and will enhance your LinkedIn experience.

LINKEDIN MOBILE

LinkedIn developed mobile applications for the iPhone, Android, BlackBerry, and Windows smartphones. The apps are free to download and connect you seamlessly to your LinkedIn account from your phone. See Figure 17–1 on page 150 to see what LinkedIn Mobile will look like on your smartphone and iPad.

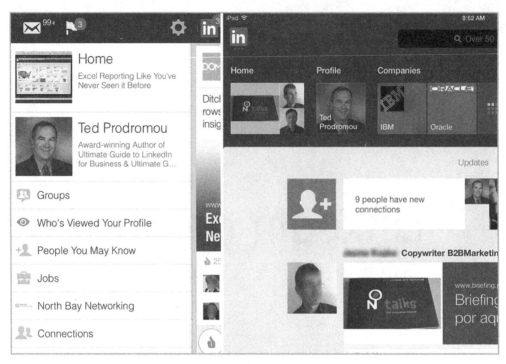

FIGURE 17–1. LinkedIn Mobile on the iPhone and iPad

The apps are well-designed, fast, and easy to use. They let you check messages in your inbox, invite people to connect, review updates, and send messages to your connections.

They are simplified so you can easily navigate by swiping your screen. The smartphone version of the LinkedIn apps lets you see and interact with your newsfeed. When you swipe to the right, you see the screen shown on the left side of Figure 17–1. On this screen you have access to messages, notifications, one rotating item from your newsfeed, your profile, Groups, Who's Viewed Your Profile, People You May Know, Jobs, one of the groups you belong to, your Connections, Companies, Pulse, and the ability to add a shortcut to your most frequently used application.

The iPad version of the LinkedIn app is shown on the right side of Figure 17–1. With the larger display, the menu bar is displayed across the upper section of the display and gives you access to the same items you see in the smartphone version. Your messages, notifications, and access to your profile is at the top of the screen next to the Search box. The lower portion of the display shows your newsfeed with the latest updates from your LinkedIn connections.

CONNECTED

Connected was released in 2014 (FIgure 17–2) and lets you quickly see what's happening with your LinkedIn network. From your desktop version of LinkedIn, you can use Keep

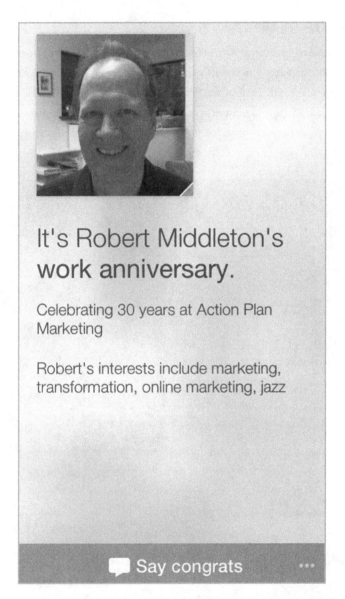

FIGURE 17–2. Connected

in Touch, which shows you the same information as the Connected app. LinkedIn will prompt you to congratulate people when they start a new job, have a job anniversary, when it's their birthday, or when they make any other changes to their LinkedIn profile. You may think it's trivial or a waste of time to congratulate people on LinkedIn, but it's a very effective way to remain top of mind with your network. Congratulating someone you haven't spoken with in a few years puts you back on her radar and often results in a "catch up" call or email exchange that results in a business transaction.

LINKEDIN JOB SEARCH

When you are looking for a job on LinkedIn, the Job Search app is a must-have tool so you can respond quickly to new job postings. Figure 17–3 shows you the screen for a job seeker. If my son, Mike, were interested in this position, he could easily submit his application from the app. The majority of LinkedIn users are now accessing LinkedIn via mobile devices, and with most of LinkedIn's revenue comes from job postings, the LinkedIn Job Search app is one of the most popular.

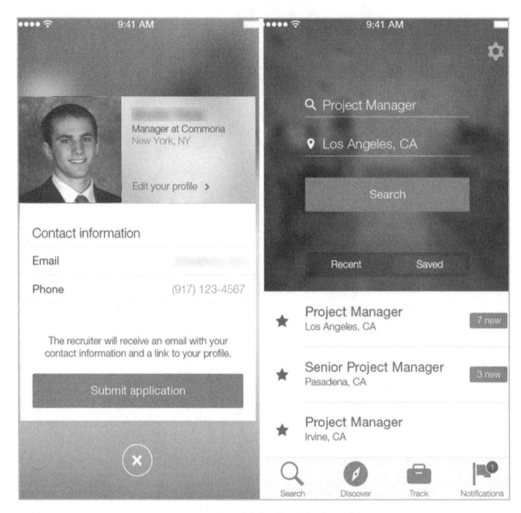

FIGURE 17–3. LinkedIn Job Search

LINKEDIN PULSE

Get up to speed in one newsfeed. This award-winning app lets you create your custom news feed from thousands of top sources, including popular media outlets and LinkedIn

Influencers. From there, explore content that's trending worldwide, gain indispensable insight, and share with your network.

LinkedIn Pulse lets you find popular and relevant content you can comment on, like, and share with your LinkedIn network. Sharing great content is the best way to keep in touch with your network without being intrusive. Figure 17–4 shows how you can create custom Lists of content within the Pulse app.

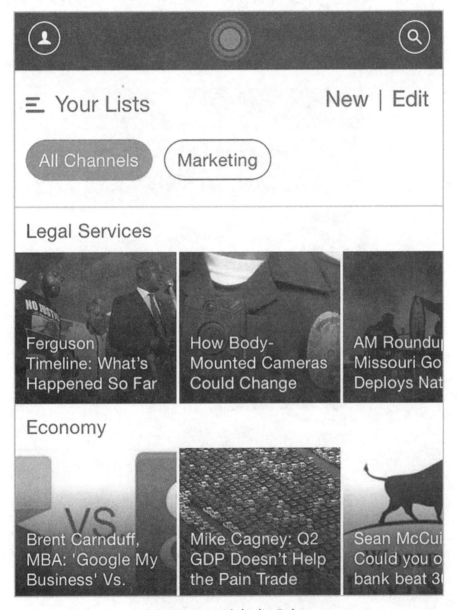

FIGURE 17–4. LinkedIn Pulse

LINKEDIN RECRUITER

The LinkedIn Recruiter app is a handy tool that helps you manage your LinkedIn job postings. After logging in, you're taken to the Recruiter Mobile homepage, where the updates stream provides you with the latest information on candidates you follow. For example, if a candidate edits his profile or if someone on your recruiting team takes an action on a candidate follow, you'll see it in your updates stream. Updates will also highlight new applicants for jobs you posted, new results for saved searches, and new hiring manager reviews.

As you see in Figure 17–5, viewing candidate profiles in Recruiter can help you evaluate a candidate's fit for a job you posted. The top card gives you a quick summary

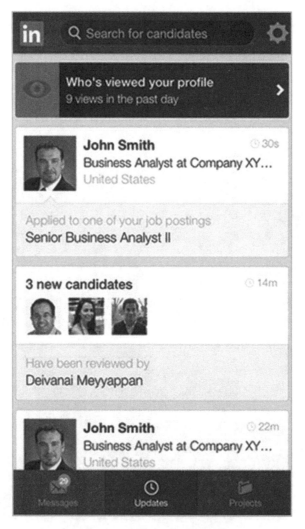

FIGURE 17–5. LinkedIn Recruiter

of his or her current role: name, headline, location and industry. The Team Activity tab lets you know if anyone on your recruiting team has already evaluated the candidate for another job. You can see the LinkedIn profile sections, optimally ordered for your recruiting needs.

From the profile, there are four actions you can take:

1. The left button is for messaging a candidate directly.
2. The middle button is for saving him to a project for future action.
3. The right button allows to you add notes to the candidate's profile and qualifications.
4. The top "share" button lets you email the candidate profile to the hiring manager or a team member.

The Recruiter mobile app makes it easy to call, text, InMail, or email the candidates when you want to connect with them. You can also organize candidates in project folders so you can follow up with them at a later time or when you have a position that is a better fit. The Recruiter mobile app also has a comprehensive search function, which makes it easy to find relevant prospects. As you find qualified candidates, you can forward the candidates to the hiring manager with a single click.

CONCLUSION

LinkedIn mobile apps are powerful extensions to the LinkedIn platform. As LinkedIn expands its API (application program interface), developers will be able to build even more powerful tools and applications, extending the LinkedIn platform further. This will be beneficial to all LinkedIn members as the community grows larger and larger.

In the next chapter, I'll show you how to set up your LinkedIn Groups and optimize it to give your company a strong presence on LinkedIn.

For additional updates and how-to videos, visit
www.tedprodromou.com/chapter17

Creating and Managing LinkedIn Groups

LinkedIn Groups are an easy way for you to start an online community for your company. If you already have a lot of customers and prospects who are members of LinkedIn, starting a LinkedIn Group for them is a smart thing to do.

HOW TO START A LINKEDIN GROUP

Before you start your own group, you need to determine if you are willing to make the time commitment to make the group a success. Starting a group is easy, but growing it and keeping it active can take a lot of work, especially in the beginning. I highly recommend you create a team of people who can share in the management and promotion of your group. As your group grows, you can invite a few of the most active people in the group to become facilitators. Most of the time, they will feel honored if you invite them to facilitate the group.

The topics you choose to be the focus of group discussions will determine how appealing your group is to others and how many members will be willing to join. Before starting your group you should research topics within your niche that generate interest and choose the top two or three as the basis for your group.

When you start a new group you will need to fill out a profile. You need to create a description of the group, which includes keywords that will help to generate interest in the group. Look at some popular LinkedIn groups, and see how they worded their descriptions, so you know what to say in your group description.

Here is the group description for The Recruiter.com Network:

Recruiter: #1 LinkedIn Recruitment & Career Networking Social Media Group. Network with recruiters, find a job or headhunter. Read recruiting, HR, staffing, & employment news. Recruit talent, find jobs, careers, executive, alumni, and professional connection. Members in US, UK, Europe, Canada, India, USA.

The Recruiter.com group is managed by Recruiter.com, the global recruitment platform. Join Recruiter.com to network, find jobs, and connect with both corporate recruiters and recruitment agencies.

As you see, they clearly state they are the top LinkedIn recruitment group, which catches your attention immediately. They go on to describe the benefits of joining the group whether you are looking for a job, looking to get to know recruiters, or looking to hire new employees. They capture the essence of the group in a just a few sentences.

GROUP SETTINGS

LinkedIn offers many options for configuring how your group will function in the Group Settings section under Manage. It's important you consider all of these when configuring the Group Settings.

First you'll want to make sure you check the Enable the Discussions and News features, which is on by default. You have the option to display promotions and jobs. You have to determine if you want to allow your group members to move discussions to the Promotions area and post jobs. There are pros and cons of each option, so I recommend allowing only moderators and managers to use these functions until you get to know the group members. Many group managers disable the promotions, jobs, and subgroups initially to help members focus on creating quality discussions and not be distracted by the other options. You want to enable your group members as much as possible, but I believe it's best to start slow and add features as the group matures. Your Group Settings options are shown in Figure 18–1 on page 159.

Permissions

The Permissions section allows you to control how group members can post new content. I recommend setting the Permissions to the first setting, Free to post

🔒 This group is restricted to members only.   [Learn About Open Groups]

☑ Enable the Discussions and News features.

　　☑ Enable the Promotions Feature.

　　　　☐ Allow only moderators and managers to move discussions to the Promotions area.

　　☑ Enable the Jobs Feature.

　　　　☐ Allow only moderators and managers to move discussions to the Jobs area.

　　☐ Allow LinkedIn to move jobs automatically out of the Discussions area to the Jobs area.

　　☐ Allow LinkedIn to move promotions automatically out of the Discussions area to the Promotions area.

　　☑ Automatically remove content flagged as inappropriate by group members.

　　　　Number of flags: [10]   ⓘ Discussions and comments cannot be retrieved once removed.

FIGURE 18–1. Group Settings

Permissions:

Members of this group:

◉ Free to post (discussions, promotions, jobs and comments).

○ Free to post promotions, jobs, comments only, and submit everything else.

○ Free to post jobs, comments only, and submit everything else.

○ Free to post comments only and submit everything else.

○ Submit everything for approval.

FIGURE 18–2. Group Permissions

(discussions, promotions, jobs and comments), as you can see in Figure 18-2. When the group is just starting, you don't want to frustrate users by limiting their access. If they create a new discussion or want to comment on a current discussion, they want to see their content immediately. If they have to wait for the group manager to approve discussions or comments, they will get frustrated and limit their participation.

I see no reason to ever change this setting because everyone in your group is a professional. If someone is posting inappropriate discussions or comments, the group manager should address the offending member and remove him from the group if he continues violating the group rules.

Restrictions

You have the ability to temporarily moderate new group members, new LinkedIn members, and members with few or no connections, who are usually spammers. Figure 18-3 shows your options as a moderator.

If someone is new to LinkedIn or has few or no LinkedIn connections, I wouldn't approve her membership to the group because she wouldn't be able to provide much value. Once she becomes established on LinkedIn, she would understand how groups work and be able to contribute. The only time I would admit a person who just joined LinkedIn to my group is if I knew the person or if that person was recommended by someone I trusted.

FIGURE 18-3. Group Restrictions

Membership

You have two membership options with your group. You can automatically approve all members if you want your group open to everyone, or you can keep your group closed so everyone has to be approved.

From my experience, open groups that serve large audiences can become unfocused if the group manager or moderator doesn't participate actively. Even when the group manager is an active participant, it can be hard to keep thousands of group members focused on the group topics. A good group manager can keep the group focused on her topic by starting new discussions, featuring popular discussions that are relevant to the group, and privately contacting members who are posting discussions that are off topic. It also helps to have multiple moderators for a large, open group.

If you are starting a group that you know will be large, it's much easier to keep the group open so you don't have to manually approve every member. If you are starting a group for a popular product such as Adobe Photoshop, you know the group will be large, active, and focused. Products like Photoshop have many highly engaged online communities where users ask questions and get support from other Photoshop users and moderators from Adobe.

Currently, the Adobe Photoshop group on LinkedIn has more than 40,000 members. It adds almost 500 new members every week and averages more than ten new discussions and 100 comments per week, making it a fairly active community. Since it's an open group, the group manager can focus on moderating discussions and promoting the group, instead of manually approving new members.

GROUP MEMBERSHIP OPTIONS

The discussions in product-related communities are amazingly focused and on topic. You don't see many people asking questions about other Adobe products or competitors' products in the Photoshop communities because the members are knowledgeable enough to keep the discussions focused. If someone does start a discussion that is not relevant to the group, a group member or moderator will often respond to that member and suggest a better place to post that question. These communities are often self-policing and self-supporting, which makes the community much stronger and more vibrant.

Closed groups by nature will be smaller and more focused, since every member is manually approved by the group manager or moderator. You usually don't have as many new discussions or comments, but the discussions are very focused. You also have a small community of experts who are very knowledgeable about specific products or topics.

Not all closed groups are small and focused. For example, the Media Professionals Worldwide group is closed, but it has more than 161,000 very active members. The group averages almost 600 new discussions and more than 300 comments every week. The group also adds almost 2,500 new members every week.

It's up to you to decide if your group will be open or closed. You can start your group open and close it anytime you want or vice versa. Groups often start out open or closed and later decide to switch. Here are some questions that may help you decide how to structure your group:

- What is your group's purpose (i.e., building loyalty, providing support, networking)?
- Is your product or service mainstream or is it a niche product/service?
- How many members do you estimate your group will have? If your company has 2,000 current customers, you wouldn't expect your group to have 10,000 members.

Membership:

○ **Auto-Join:** Any member of LinkedIn may join this group without requiring approval from a manager.

◉ **Request to Join:** Users must request to join the group and be approved by a manager.

ⓘ Users with few or no connections will require approval from a manager to join the group.

☐ Display this group in the Groups Directory.

☑ Allow members to display the logo on their profiles.

Auto-approve users with these email domains (e.g. linkedin.com, cardmunch.com):

FIGURE 18–4. Group Membership

- How many group managers or moderators will you have?
- How many new discussions and comments per week do you expect?
- How fast do you expect your group to grow?
- How are you promoting your group?

There are a lot of factors that come into play when deciding how to structure your group, and it's imperative that you have a plan and a goal before you begin. The reputation of you and your company are on the line when you create a group; if it's unfocused or unmanaged, it will reflect poorly on you.

Identify the purpose of your group, allocate resources, and create a detailed plan, so your group will thrive and provide value to your company. Your membership options are displayed in Figure 18–4.

STARTING THE DISCUSSIONS

When creating your group, you always want it to be listed in the Groups Directory unless you are creating an exclusive, private group for your customers. Also, to help promote your group in LinkedIn, allow members to display your group logo in their profiles.

After you configure your group settings, make sure you add some valuable content and information before you promote the group. Get some co-workers and a few of your better customers to join the group, and ask them to start some discussions and comment on each other's discussions. You want to show some activity and quality content before you start promoting your group. If you invite people to join your group and there are no active discussions, they probably will not join.

Using an RSS feed, you can automatically populate your group with a steady stream of content from your blog or an industry news blog. Using a tool like Hootsuite, you can automatically post content to your group, so new posts will become available to the members of your group for reading and discussion. Once you are getting enough content from your members, you may want to remove the feed and manually update the news section with a variety of content.

Once you show some activity and quality discussions, you can start promoting the group by inviting your network to join. Have your co-workers invite their network, too. If you feature some of your customers in the group discussions, they'll likely join the group and promote it to their customers.

PROMOTING THE GROUP

Once you've seeded the group with some stimulating conversations, you can start promoting the group to your network and through social media. Never, ever send group invitations using the Send Invitations tool under Manage Group. This tool looks useful—it allows you to send a mass email invitation to your entire network and to contacts outside of LinkedIn—but it's not a good idea. When you send a mass, automated invitation, recipients may not remember how you are connected and how they would benefit by joining your group. Also, the automated invitation is very impersonal, as you can see in Figure 18–5.

The best way to invite others to join your group is by sending an invitation with a personal message to let them know who you are and why you want them to join the

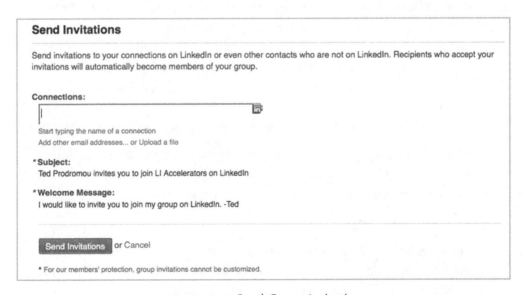

FIGURE 18–5. Send Group Invitations

group. Figure 18–5 on page 163 shows the Send Invitations Wizard with the Subject and Welcome Message, which you cannot edit.

If you turn this feature on, your group members can send automated invitations to their network, and all recipients are automatically added to the group. You can easily lose control of who is added to your group if you allow your members to invite others using the automated tool.

It is acceptable to encourage your group members to invite their friends to join the group, if they use personalized messages. You will then be able to approve or decline new invitations as you see fit.

If you want to grow your group quickly, you can start promoting it via social media. You can tweet links to your group, post an invitation on your Facebook wall, and blog about your new group. Encourage people to join your group and invite their friends. You can also run ads on LinkedIn to promote your group. I'll show you how to create effective LinkedIn ads in Chapters 21 and 22.

MANAGING THE GROUP

Consistent group management is really the key to a strong group. LinkedIn provides a powerful toolkit of resources to help managers facilitate their groups and members. A good manager will use the LinkedIn group management tools to monitor, facilitate, and grow their group.

I highly recommend creating rules for your group and posting them under Group Rules and in a Featured Discussion in your LinkedIn group. Establishing the guidelines for posting and displaying them prominently are easy ways to help new members get acquainted with your group. Such guidelines generally provide users with community contacts, encourage them to post only relevant information, and specify conduct that can get them banned. (These include items such as spamming, excessive self-promotion, verbally abusing other group members, and other rules that will keep your group safe for all members.)

Here is an example of a well-crafted group rules from the Recruiter LinkedIn Group:

The Recruiter LinkedIn group is managed by Recruiter.com, the global recruitment platform. Join Recruiter to network with recruiters, find jobs and find recruiters, and connect with both corporate recruiters and recruitment agencies.

http://www.Recruiter.com

The Recruiter LinkedIn group is the largest group on LinkedIn for recruiters. In order to maintain a quality forum and resource for the recruitment industry, we ask that you read and follow these four easy rules:

1. Share only discussions that are related to recruiting and the general recruitment industry. Linking to your own blog or articles is ok, if it's highly relevant to recruiting and HR.

2. Post jobs in the jobs area only—please make sure they are "real" jobs.

3. Promotions are fine, as long as they are placed in the promotions area and are highly relevant to the Recruiter group.

4. Lastly, be kind to one another and don't get personal, even when involved in a heated debate.

Members that violate these rules will have their Recruiter membership revoked without notice.

Thank you and enjoy the group!

Recruiter.com

As you see, the rules of the group are clear and simple. If you violate the rules, you will be removed from the group. This is a great example you can use to create the rules for your LinkedIn Group.

When a new member is added to your group, LinkedIn automatically emails him the group rules. If someone violates those of a group I'm running, I send the person a copy of the group rules and point out how he is violating them. If he continues to commit violations, I remove him from the group and block him from being able to reapply for membership.

As a group manager, you also have the responsibility of getting discussions started and helping to keep them going. This requires that you actively follow the conversations within your group, so you can promote the popular discussions using the Manager's Choice feature if you feel they are stimulating conversations.

A great way to encourage group discussions is to feature members who are top contributors. When group members see others being recognized as top contributors, they'll want to be recognized as well and will start participating more. LinkedIn also shows a graph in the sidebar, showing who is contributing the most. The graph is like a public scoreboard so everyone knows the top contributors at all times.

LinkedIn has a new moderation toolkit that helps you moderate the group discussions in the following ways:

- Managers and moderators can now receive posts right in their email box using the new option "Send me an email for each new discussion" in More, My Settings.
- Managers and moderators can now delete inappropriate comments right from their email box by clicking "Delete" within any followed-discussion email alert.

- Members can also flag items as inappropriate, which will then enter the moderation queue; or, if you choose, as manager you can delete the content outright after members have created a number of flags. You can adjust the number of flags required to move an item to the moderation queue; do this in your Group Settings, under Manage, Group Settings in the Enable the Discussions and News features section.

- The moderation queue will allow group managers to decide how many member flags can delete a thread or a comment.

- Managers can now restrict the Move-to-Jobs capability to themselves. Users will still be able to "Flag-as-job" to move an item into the moderation queue.

- Very-low-connection users will now be flagged as such in groups' request-to-join queues.

- Very-low-connection users will no longer be admitted directly to open-access groups but routed to the groups' request-to-join queues.

Excessive Self-Promotion

One of the biggest complaints about LinkedIn Groups is when members join simply to promote themselves or their business. Every discussion they start or comment on comes off as a self-promotion. They aren't showing an interest in engaging with others, which can have a negative impact on your community.

One way to manage self-promoters is by creating a Subgroup for group members to promote their service offerings. Members are allowed to post self-promotions and service offerings only in this subgroup. This keeps the low-quality content away from the main discussion area, ensuring that your group discussions are useful to your members.

If a group member continues to self-promote in the group, the moderator now has the ability to flag that member so every post submitted needs to be approved by the moderator. LinkedIn has taken this one step further to reduce self-promotion and spam in groups. If you are flagged by the moderator in one group, you are flagged in every LinkedIn group. This means every post in any LinkedIn group needs to be approved by the moderator of that group.

Group Etiquette

Most LinkedIn members joined to expand their professional network, and gain social influence and increased visibility for their business. For this reason, people generally follow group rules in order to present a professional image to their peers and prospects. As group manager, you are empowered to resolve difficulties with any members who decide they do not want to follow the rules. You need to act quickly to resolve issues and ensure that your members have an enjoyable experience as a part of your LinkedIn group.

As group manager, you set the tone for the discussions on your group. If you do not want to see a certain kind of language used in the discussions, you need to make it clear in the group rules that it will not be tolerated. The ideal tone of discussions within a group—especially business-related—should be professional. Most of the time this is the case, but there will be occasional exceptions. If you see inappropriate conduct in your group, remove the post immediately and contact the offender. Explain why his post was offensive and remove him from your group if he refuses to obey the rules.

CONCLUSION

Remember: The image of your group reflects directly upon you and your company. You need to maintain a high standard and maintain a high-quality reputation for you and your company.

If you are not the group manager, it is important to respect the role of the group manager. If both group managers and members follow the rules of social etiquette, the LinkedIn group experience can be rewarding for all.

In the next chapter, I'll show you how to use LinkedIn to recruit new employees for your company.

For additional updates and how-to videos, visit
www.tedprodromou.com/chapter18

Recruiting New Employees

LinkedIn has become a gold mine for recruiting firms and in-house recruiters. Nowhere else can they find more than 330 million business professionals in one place prominently displaying their job experience, skills, education, recommendations, and expertise. A simple search on LinkedIn can give them multiple qualified candidates in seconds. As LinkedIn grows, the available talent pool multiplies, allowing companies to pick and choose from among the very best business professionals in the world. No longer is a talent search limited to your local area.

Recruiting new employees isn't limited to searching for unemployed professionals or recent graduates entering the workforce. According to a 2011 survey from The Adler Group, 15 percent of employed professionals are active candidates pursuing a new opportunity. Another 68 percent of all employed professionals are open to listening to new opportunities. That means 83 percent of all employed professionals are willing to listen to you if you have an interesting opportunity for them. Knowing that fact, you have a pretty good chance of landing some quality candidates for your open positions. Don't they call it "shooting fish in a barrel" when the odds are stacked in your favor?

If that isn't enough evidence for you, in a recent survey of Fortune 500 companies by LinkedIn, an incredible 88 percent of all Fortune 500 companies use LinkedIn as their primary recruiting tool.

Knowing that up to 83 percent of all employed professionals are willing to listen to your opportunity, how can you find these candidates? When you do find them, how can you narrow your search to approach the very best candidates?

In Chapter 8 we covered LinkedIn Search and Advanced Search in great detail. Let's take a moment to refresh your memory on LinkedIn Advanced Search, so you'll know how to find your ideal candidates in seconds.

Let's say you are an in-house recruiter at a biotech firm, and you are looking for a director of quality to create, implement, and oversee quality systems in your company. You minimum job requirements are:

1. Minimum eight years of experience in quality assurance for a human or animal drug company
2. Substantial knowledge of cGMP requirements for multiple dosage forms along with prior experience in supplier qualification
3. Additional experience in GDPs and/or GLPs (preferred)
4. Excellent communicator and team player with the ability to proactively address and lead resolution of compliance issues internally and with external partners and contractors
5. Willingness to travel

I have no idea what most of these requirements mean, but I'm sure they are key skills for a director of quality in a biotech firm.

So let's go to LinkedIn Advanced Search and find some candidates. On the right side of your LinkedIn toolbar or menu, make sure you are set to People Search. Click on the Advanced link, which is next to the magnifying glass to the right of the search box. For this search we want to modify the parameters as follows:

1. In the Title field, enter "director of quality" if you are looking for someone who currently holds that position or held that position in the past. You can change the dropdown to choose Current or Past.
2. Change the Industries from All Industries to just Biotechnology.
3. Change Seniority Level to Director. This option is available only to LinkedIn Premium members, so I highly recommend upgrading your account if you are going to use LinkedIn for recruiting.
4. Leave all the other options at their default settings.

Figure 19–1 on page 171 shows you what your Advanced Search should look like to get your first pass search results. If you want to narrow your search to your local area,

FIGURE 19–1. Advanced People Search

you can change the Location to your local area or within 50, 100, or 150 miles of your location.

Of course, you can modify your search parameters to narrow or widen your search, but take a look at these preliminary search results. As you see in Figure 19–2 on page 172, you have a list of 1,445 directors in the biotech field with just one search! Not all of these people are looking for a job, but I bet at least a few of them would be open to listening to a new opportunity if the situation sounded interesting.

Before we start reaching out to some of these directors, let's narrow our search a bit to see if we can find better-qualified candidates. Remember: Your qualifications included eight-plus years of experience and substantial knowledge of cGMP requirements for multiple dosage forms, so let's add "cGMP" to our search criteria in the Keywords field.

Now we have only 231 candidates, which is much better than digging through 1,445 candidates. The next step is to start looking at the profiles of these remaining prospects to see if they are actively looking for work, which could be displayed in the profile headline. You can also look near the bottom of their profile where it says "Contact name for:"; one of the options is Career Opportunities. You can add or remove the reasons for people to contact you in your Profile Settings. Select Edit Profile under the Profile tab on the LinkedIn menu and scroll down the page until you come to the "Contact name for:" section and Edit to change your preferences.

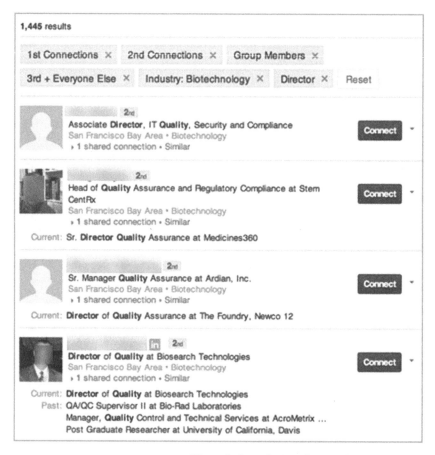

FIGURE 19-2. Biotech Search Results

If your search returns some LinkedIn members who are interested in Career Opportunities, you have a few options:

- *You can send them an InMail to introduce yourself.* Don't start out by asking them if they are looking for a new position or you may scare them away—even though their profiles say they're interested in Career Opportunities. Tell them you came across their profile on LinkedIn and saw something that caught your attention. Find something unique, like an award they won, interesting certifications, schools they attended, etc. You can ask them about these things or congratulate them. Try to establish a relationship, so you can get to know them and see if they are a fit for your organization. If you mention things you have in common they will be more apt to respond to you.

- *Find groups they belong to and join that group, so you can reach out to them by sending them a message.* At the beginning of your message state that you both belong to the same group and you thought they may be interested in an opportunity at your company. If you are a recruiter, I highly recommend joining groups related to your industry (such as in biotech) and participating frequently so people become familiar with your name. If they see your name regularly in the forum, they are more likely to respond to your messages even if they've never corresponded with you in the past. This is a very effective and inexpensive way for small businesses to recruit new employees.

■ *If they are a second-degree connection of yours, find out whom in your network is a first-degree connection between you and ask for an introduction.* You can also ask your first-degree connection what he thinks of that person to help determine if she would be a good fit for your company.

■ *If they are part of the LinkedIn OpenLink Network, you can send them a regular message without having to use an InMail.* People who are members of the OpenLink Network are open to people reaching out to them with job opportunities. As I've said many times before, you joined LinkedIn to be found, so take full advantage of all the tools available to gain more visibility. Most people join LinkedIn to be found so they can grow their professional network. Unless your company requires you to limit the visibility of your profile, I highly recommend being as visible as possible. No matter how happy you are at your current job, there are always bigger and better opportunities out there, so be open to the possibility and let LinkedIn help you!

In Chapter 9, "Getting Found on LinkedIn," we went into great detail about the importance of keywords when searching on LinkedIn and how to find the best ones. Now is a good time to review that section of the chapter and create a list of keywords that will help you find your ideal candidates. Once you create a search demographic that returns quality candidates, don't forget to save the search in Saved Searches, so you can use it over and over to fill open positions.

TIPS TO HELP YOUR RECRUITING EFFORT

For great recruiting tips, have a look at the LinkedIn recruiting blog at http://talent. linkedin.com/blog. The various LinkedIn blogs teach you more about the solutions LinkedIn provides and new features and tools as they are released. LinkedIn does a great job communicating and teaching on their blogs. Here is a summary of some recruiting tips from various blog posts:

■ If you are the recruiter looking for talent on LinkedIn, make sure your own profile is in order. Check to see that your profile is at All Star level, including your three recommendations. When you reach out to candidates, they are going to check out your profile to get to know you and your company, so you want to give a great first impression.

- Make sure the employees in your company complete their profiles, including their recommendations. When a candidate researches your organization, you want to present a professional image from top to bottom. It also makes a great impression on candidates when they see a lot of recommendations on your employees' profiles. Encourage your teams to get as many glowing recommendations as possible so your candidates see that your company hires only top-notch employees. Make sure your employees get a variety of recommendations from past and current positions, not just from current co-workers, which can look suspicious.

- Create a company page on LinkedIn and fill it out completely. Active candidates will visit your company page to get to know your company and its culture. You can set up a company page for free or invest in a Premium account in order to add additional features to your company page. Learn more about LinkedIn company pages at http://business.linkedin.com/marketing-solutions/company-pages.html.

- Join groups related to your business and industry. Be an active participant and have other employees of your company do the same. When someone sees a lot of employees from one company engaged in stimulating discussions in LinkedIn Groups, she will get a good impression of your company and the quality of your employees.

- Search LinkedIn Posts, Groups, and Profiles to find the best candidates. Use the Advanced LinkedIn Search features when you can, and save your best search templates in Saved Searches. Again, if you are recruiting new employees on a regular basis, invest in a Premium LinkedIn account so you can save your searches in the Saved Search of your profile.

All these tips are effective whether you are an in-house recruiter or work for a staffing firm. You always want to be on the lookout for quality candidates and keep your pipeline full. The key to success is consistency—whether it's searching through profiles, Groups, Posts, or Companies, or building your LinkedIn professional network—so you are always just one invitation away from a candidate or hiring manager. As a recruiter, you want to build your network as large as possible to help cast a wider net that is less focused than the network a business professional would build. It's all about quantity when you are recruiting, but you also want to build a network of quality contacts who can send you referrals or introduce you to potential candidates.

LINKEDIN RECRUITING SOLUTIONS

LinkedIn also has a number of paid solutions for companies who do a lot of recruiting and for staffing agencies. The LinkedIn Recruiting Options include:

- See full names and profiles beyond your first- and second-degree network.
- Premium talent filters help you zero in on ideal candidates.
- 50 InMail messages per month.
- See up to 1,000 profiles in search results.
- Talent Updates let you reach out to followers of your company page.
- Recruiter Mobile lets you find, engage, and manage talent from anywhere.

Now you see why LinkedIn has become the premier place to post your jobs, track down the best candidates, and find a job when you're looking for new opportunities. Let's explore these premium options in more detail, so you can see how they can help you build a premier organization with the very best employees.

LINKEDIN RECRUITER

This premium subscription is designed for corporate recruiters in large companies who are constantly searching for the best talent. Some of the benefits of the LinkedIn Recruiter Corporate Edition subscription include:

- You get unlimited access to names and full profiles of potential candidates. When you search for talent using your free LinkedIn account, you won't see the full profile of many LinkedIn members, and the number of search results is limited. With this subscription you will see the complete profile of every LinkedIn member and up to 1,000 search results, which is a huge advantage over your competitors who aren't using this premium-recruiting package.
- You receive Advanced Search Features that are not included in the free version of LinkedIn Advanced Search. With the LinkedIn Recruiter Corporate Edition subscription, you can filter your searches by Industry, Company Size, Education, Company, Years in Position, and Years of Experience. This lets you find the ideal candidates for your open positions.
- You can contact candidates directly using InMail. You receive 50 InMails per month per seat to contact any candidate you like in the trusted LinkedIn environment. When you send an InMail and it isn't answered within seven days, you get the InMail credited back to your account. In other words, this is like having 50 replies to your InMails per month guaranteed. This is a great benefit because InMails have proven to have very high response rates since LinkedIn is

such a trusted professional network. Being able to contact up to 50 prospective candidates per month is a tremendous boost to your recruiting efforts.

■ You can receive up to 50 search alerts per day when you are targeting candidates for an open position. This means you can queue up searches for specific jobs, and you will be automatically alerted when a prospective candidate is found. You can quickly reach out to this candidate before your competition, giving you a huge advantage. You can also send one-to-many InMails using saved InMail templates, enabling you to contact more candidates faster. Finding the best talent is about beating your competitors to the punch, and these LinkedIn tools help you automate many of your recruiting functions, freeing you up to personally reach out to a greater number of people.

■ You can use shared Project Folders to stay on top of each search. When you have a team of recruiters working together to source candidates, these tools help the recruiters coordinate their searches and eliminate duplicate efforts. Team members get visibility into their colleagues' projects, notes, and communication history with candidates, increasing the efficiency of your recruiting team.

■ You can set reminders on specific profiles so you can follow up with candidates of interest in a timely manner. Without these automated tools, you might forget to follow up with key candidates and lose them to another recruiter.

■ The sourcing activity and history of a recruiter does not disappear when they leave your company. You can just reassign his activity to another team member. LinkedIn Recruiting subscriptions also support your OFCCP compliance efforts.

■ You are assigned your own account manager to help you get the most from your subscription. You also receive guidance from LinkedIn training experts who will help you get the most from LinkedIn.

The LinkedIn Recruiter Dashboard, as you see in Figure 19–3 on page 177, provides a comprehensive snapshot of your recruiting activities. The easy-to-navigate menu lets you quickly access your recruiting projects, a clipboard where you create and save job postings and notes, your posted jobs, reports, and more options. In the newsfeed section you see real-time updates with new applicants, job posting status, and saved search results. In the right column, LinkedIn recommends potential candidates in the People You May Want to Hire widget. You also see Project Activity and Job Activity in separate right-column widgets.

The majority of LinkedIn's revenue comes from recruiting so they're constantly improving the dashboard and adding new features to ensure you're finding the best candidates for your company.

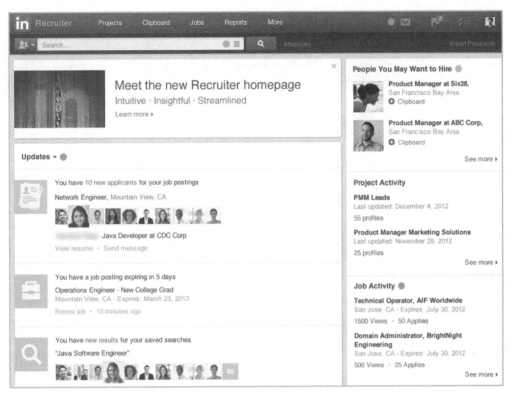

FIGURE 19–3. The LinkedIn Recruiter Dashboard

THE JOBS NETWORK

The LinkedIn Jobs Network is the fastest-growing job network on the internet. Nowhere else on the internet can recruiters find more highly qualified candidates for their open positions. For job seekers, targeted jobs are displayed on the sidebar of their LinkedIn homepage and other LinkedIn pages as they participate in Groups. LinkedIn scans your current and previous job titles, companies you've worked for, and the keywords in your profile to automatically match you up with potential jobs. These targeted jobs are displayed in your sidebar in the Jobs You May Be Interested In widget, as shown in Figure 19–4 on page 178.

As I mentioned earlier, an average of 15 percent of employed workers are actively looking for a new job. Another 68 percent of employed workers are willing to listen to new opportunities even though they aren't actively looking for a new job. By using the LinkedIn Job Board, companies can expand their search for candidates to passive candidates using the Jobs You May Be Interested In widget. Letting LinkedIn members see what other opportunities are out there in a subtle manner catches their eye so they

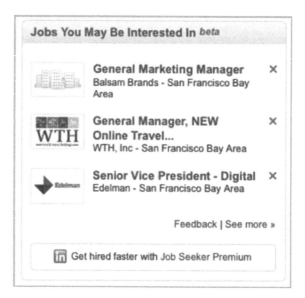

FIGURE 19–4. Jobs You May Be Interested In

explore the new opportunities. This creates a phenomenon where your job postings find the best candidates instead of putting the burden on your recruiters.

With job openings constantly but subtly being displayed on the LinkedIn sidebar, we can't help but notice and become curious when we see certain job titles or companies we may want to work for. It's sort of like subliminal advertising in a way, because the jobs don't appear in the center of our screen; however, they are just off to the side enough that we notice them out of the corner of the eye. As we see jobs that may interest us, we click on them to see if any of them are interesting enough to investigate further. If we aren't interested but we know a friend or colleague who may be interested, we can forward the job to her LinkedIn inbox—assuming she is a LinkedIn connection—or we can share the job opening on Facebook and Twitter. This gives companies a huge benefit by allowing their job openings to go viral on the internet, at no additional cost to the company who posted the job opening. Your job openings can be seen by millions of people on LinkedIn, Facebook, and Twitter, increasing the chances you will find an outstanding candidate.

Companies that post jobs in the LinkedIn Jobs Network have the ability to measure the impact of their job postings through LinkedIn's job analytics. The LinkedIn job analytics is the equivalent of Google Analytics for your websites. When you use Google Analytics to monitor your website, you learn how many visitors you have, how long they stay, what pages they visited, and what they downloaded or purchased. In addition, you can find detailed demographic information like what country, state, city, or ZIP code they live in. This information is invaluable to a website owner. LinkedIn job analytics helps you understand exactly which types of candidates your jobs are reaching and lets you see who's viewing your jobs by role, company, geography, and more to ensure you're reaching the best professionals. If you are not reaching the right people with your job postings, you can adjust the title of your open position, change the wording in the job description, or reconfigure whom you are targeting in the job search. Without these analytics, you would know you are not attracting the right candidates only because their skill sets or experience aren't right for your job, but you wouldn't know why the posting is attracting the wrong candidates. Knowing who, when, and where the candidates are coming from will save you a lot of time and help you fill your positions faster with better candidates.

Show Up in LinkedIn Career Pages

In addition to the sidebar widget, your job postings will also appear on the LinkedIn Career Pages, covered more in depth on page 180. You can purchase a recruiting program called the LinkedIn Job Slot, which allows you to do all of the following:

- Change your job posting as often as you like—even daily, if necessary.
- Easily renew and keep a position open on LinkedIn for longer than 30 days.
- Receive up to 50 real-time candidate recommendations per post.
- Streamline the job posting process with integrated third-party job distributors so your job listing gets maximum exposure on the internet.
- Pull job postings from your website into LinkedIn automatically through job wrapping, which is an additional cost. Job wrapping is a proprietary technology created by LinkedIn that automatically keeps your job postings in sync on your website and LinkedIn.
- Send applicants straight to your Applicant Tracking System from LinkedIn. LinkedIn has developed many APIs and plug-ins that let you easily connect your recruiting systems with LinkedIn. You can find out more about the LinkedIn development tools at https://developer.linkedin.com/.
- You can also add a third-party tracking URL to your job posting so you can track your results with your own analytics system. This allows you to easily track the success of your recruiting campaigns.

Jobs for You Web Ads

Jobs for You Web Ads is a LinkedIn service that automatically pushes your jobs to the most qualified candidates, wherever they go online. This lets you distribute your jobs to thousands of websites across the internet, automatically. LinkedIn doesn't provide details how this is done, but it looks like they are using a new technology called ad retargeting.

Ad retargeting is a relatively new technology, where you can place an ad on a website that will follow the web visitor for a period of time, usually 30 days. A retargeting ad contains special code that places a cookie in your web browser when the ad is displayed to you on the initial website. You don't have to click on the ad. It just has to be displayed to you in order to have the cookie placed in your browser. The ad reappears automatically on certain websites that you visit over the next 30 days. It appears that the ad is following you, which is what it's doing, but the ads will usually stop following you after 30 days. Retargeting ads will appear only on certain websites that accept banner ads from ad networks, such as DoubleClick or ReTargeter, and will only be redisplayed to you around five to ten times over the 30 days, so you aren't overwhelmed by ads from one company.

As I said earlier, LinkedIn doesn't explain the technical details about how Jobs for You Web Ads works, but here's a stab at explaining how it works:

1. You post a job on the LinkedIn Jobs Network.
2. Select the exact audience you want to target, including job title, seniority, years of experience, skills, education, or any of the other targeting options we described earlier in this chapter.
3. LinkedIn will place LinkedIn-branded ads on external websites that accept banner advertising. The headline of the 300 x 250 pixel ad will say Jobs at Your Company Name and will feature your job listings in the ad widget. Your job openings will be displayed only to those candidates who meet your targeting criteria. The ads will follow that candidate and appear periodically on other websites they visit that accept banner ads.

This is a very effective way to reach passive candidates who aren't actively searching for a new position but are open to the possibilities of changing jobs. LinkedIn uses a combination of your targeting criteria and data from a person's LinkedIn profile to display your ads to the most qualified candidates. For example, engineers will see only your engineering jobs, and sales professionals will see only your sales jobs—even if they're reading the sports section of an online newspaper.

LINKEDIN CAREER PAGES

Every organization needs a company page on LinkedIn where you can post company update messages, provide information about your products and services, post job openings, and view detailed analytics information about the people who have visited your company page.

Another important feature of company pages is the ability for people to "follow" your company. What is "follow your company," you ask? Following a company on LinkedIn is very similar to clicking the Like button on a company or personal page on Facebook. The more people who follow you on LinkedIn or like you on Facebook, the better, because it adds credibility to your company.

When someone follows your company, LinkedIn keeps him up to date on your company's job opportunities, personnel changes, and new product or services posted on your company page by automatically sending your company updates to his LinkedIn homepage. It is less intrusive than emailing to let people know about new developments at your company.

One of LinkedIn's premier recruiting packages is called the Career Page. Subscribing to the Silver or Gold Level Career Page subscription provides many enhancements to your company page that will improve your recruiting experience and build a loyal following for your company. Your Career Page, alongside your company profile, is a powerful tool to educate and inform active and passive job candidates. As potential candidates explore your company page to learn more about your company, they will see your current job openings on the same screen. You have the ability to display customized content for each visitor, based on his or her LinkedIn profile data. If a software engineer visits your Career Page, specific content related to software engineers will be displayed, including open positions that the visitor may be qualified for. This targeted content helps convince candidates that you are the right company for her.

Upgrading to the Career Page will give your more flexibility and let you customize your LinkedIn Company Page. Some of the features of the Careers Page include:

- Your messages dynamically adapt to the viewer based on information from his LinkedIn profile.
- Targeted job postings appear for each viewer.
- You can feature employees in the Employees Spotlights module so viewers can get a sense of what type of people work at your company.
- You can add a custom video to your page so viewers get to know your company better.
- You can display a list of benefits of working at your company.
- You can link to additional information on your company website.
- Viewers can contact your recruiters directly.
- You can create three additional customizable modules so viewers can learn more about the culture of your company.

You also have the ability to set up ads that run on LinkedIn to drive people to your company page to learn more about your jobs or products and services. You can also prevent ads from other companies from appearing on your company page if you choose the Gold Career Page package.

The LinkedIn Career Page can help you position your company as an "employer of choice" by providing insight into your company culture and your community of followers. Candidates are more likely to respond to your recruiting messages when they are familiar with your company and products. The Career Page enhancement also acts a mini-web portal that lets you drive traffic to other vital web destinations, such as your company website, blogs, and social media communities.

WORK WITH US

This is not only one of the simplest LinkedIn recruiting and advertising solutions, it's also one of the most effective. How do you feel when you are looking at the LinkedIn profile of one of your colleagues and you see a huge ad from one of your competitors in the sidebar? Doesn't it drive you crazy when you see your competitors invading your company's space? In the past no one had any control over this, but now we do.

The LinkedIn Work with Us ads let you display your advertising on your employees' profile pages and your company pages. Here's an example of a competitor's ad being displayed on the profile page of one of the founders of our company, in Figure 19-5. That's a very effective ad for our competitor, grabbing that much real estate on the profile page of a company founder. When people research companies, they often review

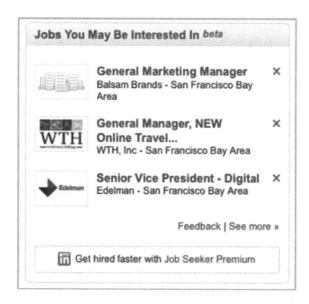

FIGURE 19–5. Competitor's Ad on Employee Profile

the profiles of the founders and executive team so it's important to protect that real estate with your own advertising.

To run Work with Us ads, just contact LinkedIn, provide them your creative material, and they will automatically place your ads on all of your employee profile pages and your company pages. If you are going to run only one marketing campaign on LinkedIn, this is the one you need to do to protect your brand.

Figure 19-6 shows you an effective Work with Us ad displaying my name and profile picture as ING Investment's newest employee. These are very effective ads because the potential candidate sees herself as an employee of your company and she can easily browse your job openings to find the job that is right for her.

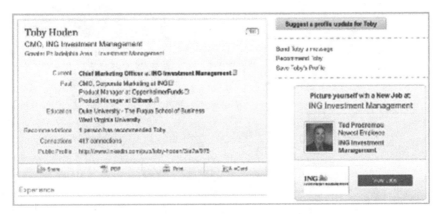

FIGURE 19-6. Work with Us Advertisement

RECRUITMENT ADS

LinkedIn Recruitment Ads are the large career ads you see in the sidebar of your LinkedIn homepage and on other pages throughout the LinkedIn website. These are 300 x 250 pixel banner ads that are primarily displayed on your homepage, since that is the page that we spend the most time on when we're visiting LinkedIn. See Figure 19-7 on page 184 for an example of a recruitment ad in from the LinkedIn website.

As you can see, your ad is prominently displayed on LinkedIn homepages, keeping your company and career opportunities top of mind for LinkedIn members actively pursuing new career opportunities. Placing your career opportunities in front of LinkedIn members also helps attract those "not actively looking but open to new opportunities" candidates. It's important to always have a full talent pipeline, so you hire the very best candidates for your company.

LinkedIn Recruitment Ads use the same proprietary ad-targeting algorithm as other LinkedIn advertising options. This ensures your ads are shown only to the appropriate potential candidates. This ability to target your ads with precision gives you a competitive advantage when you are recruiting new employees.

When you are ready to start your LinkedIn Recruitment Ad campaign, just describe your perfect hire including the targeting options you desire, send LinkedIn your ad text or banner ad, and it will set up and monitor your ad campaigns. It doesn't get any easier than that!

FIGURE 19–7. Recruitment Ad

CONCLUSION

Wow, that was a lot of information! As you see, LinkedIn gives recruiters a lot of tools to make recruiting new employees easier and more effective. No matter how big or small your organization, LinkedIn offers a premium recruiting solution to meet your needs. Of course, you could choose to search for new employees using the free search tools, but the automated solutions from LinkedIn will streamline your recruiting efforts so you can stay ahead of your competition.

In the next chapter, we'll explore LinkedIn for Sales and Marketing Professionals, a premium LinkedIn service designed to help sales professionals generate leads for their companies.

For additional updates and how-to videos, visit
www.tedprodromou.com/chapter19

Chapter 20

LinkedIn for Sales and Marketing Professionals

I f you're in sales, you have to be licking your chops at the opportunities available to you on LinkedIn. With more than 330 million members and growing at a rate of two new members per second, it's a golden opportunity for all sales professionals. Whether your product has a long or short sales cycle, LinkedIn provides the perfect networking platform that enables you to build lasting relationships with clients and prospects alike. Building and nurturing relationships keeps your sales pipeline full.

Assuming you're a seasoned sales professional, we're not going to get into Sales 101 in this chapter. If you're just getting started in sales or are starting your own business, read everything you can about sales, social networking, and social selling. The internet and social media allow sales professionals to cast a wide net to find new prospects for their products and services, if they know how to use these tools properly. The process of selling hasn't changed, but the tools used to find prospects are evolving rapidly, allowing you to reach more prospects with less effort. If you use the internet and social media to attract new leads but don't do it in a strategic manner, you'll attract lots of leads—but not the right ones that lead to relationships and closed deals.

You are probably already well aware of the importance of building a strong professional network and contact database. In the old days, sales professionals used the Rolodex as their contact "database." I use the term database loosely because the Rolodex was just a device that held specially shaped index cards that stored information about your business contacts in alphabetical order. Each contact had his or her own index card where you wrote contact information and scribbled reminder notes. If you lost that index card, you lost your contact's information. The Rolodex was bulky and sat on your desk next to your telephone, so when you traveled to visit your prospects and customers, you didn't have access to your contact database.

Obviously times have changed, and today we carry our entire contact database on our telephones. Our contact database also resides in our customer relationship system (CRM), which is accessible from any internet connection. With the evolution of LinkedIn we can now create our Rolodex on LinkedIn, which makes it accessible from anywhere. The LinkedIn Mobile app lets us add new contacts and search existing contacts right from our smartphones. Today it's easier than ever to build a large electronic database of prospects and customers. Your challenge is to build a targeted database of prospects because it's easy to fall into the trap of focusing on quantity, rather than quality.

BUILDING YOUR LINKEDIN NETWORK

In Chapter 11, "Connecting with Others," I went into great detail about building your network. Now is a good time to review the different networking strategies, so you can decide which approach is best for you—the sales professional. There is no right or wrong answer when it comes to building your professional network, as there are a lot of variables to consider. Let's review a few LinkedIn networking strategies, discuss the pros and cons of each, and help you decide which one is best for you.

We talked about the different ways to build your professional network. The first option was being an open networker, where you connect with everyone who sends you a connection request. This enables you to create a very broad network so you have access to literally millions of connections in your first-, second-, and third-degree connections. Being an open networker lets you cast the widest net possible on LinkedIn with access to millions of LinkedIn members through your LinkedIn network. Open networking is a great option for recruiters, real estate salespeople, and some other sales professionals because you have indirect access to so many LinkedIn members. You are never more than two hops away from literally millions of LinkedIn members. The downside is that your network is unfocused, so you have to spend more time digging through your connections to find specific contacts or skill sets within your network. I'll discuss more of the pros and cons of open networking in a little bit.

Your other option is to cast a smaller net, which will bring you fewer opportunities but a more focused network. The audience will be highly targeted, so it's easier to connect with the right people. Building a small, focused network requires you to carefully review every connection request and vet every person who wants to join your exclusive professional network. This means you may opt to exclude some of your friends if they don't meet your stringent standards.

How big should your network be? As previously stated, studies conclude that it's impossible for a human to effectively manage a network of friends or colleagues if it gets too large. It's possible to effectively communicate with 100 to 150 people on a regular basis and maintain strong relationships. As your network increases in size, your ability to maintain strong relationships with your network members decreases significantly. If you build a network of 2,000 members on LinkedIn, you will not be able to maintain a strong relationship with everyone because you just don't have enough time.

Does this mean you should stop building your network at 150 members? Maybe. It depends what you are selling and how many people are in your target market. If you are selling a specialty product that is used only by senior bioinformatics scientists who reside in the United States, your target market is very small. It wouldn't make sense to connect with 1,500 other people just for the sake of connecting. Bigger is not always better.

The third option—and the most popular one—is to build a network somewhere in between the niche networker of 100 to 150 contacts and the Open Networker who may have more than 10,000 contacts. While most LinkedIn members have fewer than 500 connections, I see many LinkedIn members with somewhere between 500 and 1,000 connections. The longer you've been in the workforce, the more connections you have. I have more than 600 connections, most of which are current and former colleagues. I don't aggressively try to build my network right now because I'm employed at a company full time and I'm not trying to grow my personal business. If I were in sales, I would constantly be looking for quality connections to expand my LinkedIn network in order to generate more leads.

The Pros and Cons of Different-Sized LinkedIn Networks

Should you build a professional network that is small, large, or somewhere in between? It depends on what you are selling, whom you sell to, and how much time you want to spend on LinkedIn managing your network. Being an Open Networker gives you a lot of opportunities to connect with others, but you will have to dedicate at least an hour or two a day accepting connection requests and answering emails from your network. Open Networkers tend to be aggressive networkers, so they are constantly reaching out to their network, beating the bushes for new leads.

If you are a recruiter who fills jobs nationally or internationally, you need to build a huge network to keep your pipeline full. You have to be willing to dedicate up to half of your working hours working your LinkedIn network for leads to fill open positions and to find new jobs to post. There is nothing wrong with spending 20 hours a week networking on LinkedIn if it's your primary source to find job listings and quality candidates.

If you are selling niche products, it probably doesn't make sense for you to spend more than an hour or two a day on LinkedIn, if your target audience is small. You probably have a few key contacts on LinkedIn who can connect you with the right people, and you know which groups to participate in.

Most sales professionals choose the middle-of-the-road approach. They have their professional network of 500 to 1,000 members, which gives them tremendous access to millions of second- and third-degree connections. They also have their core members of their network, with whom they communicate on a regular basis. It's the old 80/20 rule: 20 percent of their network is most active, providing the majority of their leads and sales, while they occasionally benefit from some leads and sales from the other 80 percent.

Figure 20–1 on page 189 contains a table that describes some of the pros and cons of each style of LinkedIn networking. The optimal size of your LinkedIn network depends on a lot of factors that only you can determine. Every situation is different, so weigh the pros and cons of each networking style and determine which is best for the product or service you sell.

Of course, you can change your mind if you choose a style that's not working for you. If you start out as a niche networker, you can easily switch to be an Open Networker or a medium-sized network. The difficult transition is if you begin as an Open Networker and connections with 20,000 other professionals, it's hard to easily reduce the size of your network. It's a long, tedious process removing the connections that are not highly targeted. Some people even close their existing LinkedIn account and start over with a brand-new account and rebuild their network from scratch.

If you think building a smaller, more focused network is the way to go, you'll have to be more selective when connecting with others. There is a fine balance between keeping your network small and focused and also having access to those valuable second- and third-degree connections. Of course, you want to have as much access to second- and third-degree connections as possible, but you don't have time to maintain a huge network of first-degree connections.

Take a look at Figure 20–2 on page 190, which is from my profile. I have a network of 2,859 first-degree connections which is growing quickly. Next look at the size of my total LinkedIn network which include first-degree, second-degree, and third-degree connections. I have access to 22,902,063 professionals. The amount of potential connections I have access to grows exponentially. Imagine what these numbers would

	Pros	**Cons**
Small Niche Network	1. Targeted audience 2. Less noise/emails from connections 3. Fewer connection requests from people you don't know 4. New connection requests are usually more targeted because you are a niche networker	1. Limited ability to reach 2nd- and 3rd-degree connections 2. You may miss some sales opportunities because you don't have as many 1st-degree connections referring you to new connections
Medium-Sized Network	1. You benefit from having a targeted audience and an extended 2nd- and 3rd-degree audience 2. More opportunities to connect with prospects when you need introductions 3. More opportunities to receive referrals from your network	1. You may be limited when you try to reach out to 3rd-degree connections 2. You may receive a lot of connection requests from strangers or people who don't fit your professional network profile 3. You may receive a lot of unsolicited emails from connections
Open Networking	1. You have a very wide audience to sell to and to help refer you to prospects 2. You have access to millions of 2nd- and 3rd-degree connections 3. You are never more than two hops from millions of prospects	1. Your network is very unfocused so you have to work hard to find targeted prospects 2. You will receive a lot of unsolicited emails from your connections 3. You will have no personal relationship with over 90% of your network so you won't be able to refer them 4. You will receive a lot of requests to Recommend people in your network who you don't know very well

FIGURE 20–1. Pros and Cons of LinkedIn Networking Styles

Your LinkedIn Network

2,859 Connections

22,902,063 Professionals in your Network

FIGURE 20–2. My Network of Trusted Professionals

look like if I were an Open Networker. Looking at my numbers, it's easy to see why so many sales professionals are choosing this professional networking strategy.

As LinkedIn adds two new members every second, I don't have to add anyone to my first-degree connections to expand the potential reach of my second- and third-degree networks. As more of my second- and third-degree connections connect with others, my network is growing exponentially without my lifting a finger. When I started writing this book just two months ago, my total network had around 12 million members. It has almost doubled in size in two months, and I've added only a handful of first-degree connections.

The growth rate of LinkedIn shows no signs of slowing down, so by the time this book hits the bookstores, my total network could be well over 30 million people. Why would I want to take the time to grow my first-degree network when my second- and third-degree networks are growing like crazy automatically? If and when I need to reach out for new connections, I can easily tap into my second- and third-degree networks to connect with highly targeted connections.

SHOULD YOU GO ANONYMOUS?

I've seen blog posts and articles from LinkedIn experts recommending a technique where you go stealth by creating an anonymous profile and spy on your competitors. I leave it up to you to answer the ethical question. The technique will let you view others' profiles on a limited basis, monitor your competitor's company page and groups, and essentially be an anonymous LinkedIn member. You do this by creating a second LinkedIn account with a fictitious name and lock down your profile (see Chapter 5), so viewers will only see that Anonymous viewed their profiles. You probably won't be able to join your competitor's groups if they have to approve group memberships, but you can still learn a lot about them. LinkedIn changed their policy in 2013, which affects anonymous profiles. If you lock down your profile and do not share profile information with others, LinkedIn limits what you can see on other's profiles. Another technique is where people use fake names, company names, profile information, and even general stock photos as their profile pictures in their stealth accounts to make everything look real.

Again, I'll leave it up to you if you want to use this approach—but personally it's not for me. Oh, by the way, it's also against LinkedIn's terms of service so if you get caught, your will be removed from LinkedIn.

LEVERAGING YOUR COMPANY PAGE

Every B2B company should have a LinkedIn Company Page for many reasons. The obvious reason is that you are a member of the largest and most exclusive business networking site in the world. With more than 330 million members and growing by the second, you have a golden opportunity to get your brand in front of your target audience—for free! In Chapter 7, "LinkedIn for Companies," you learned how to set up and manage your LinkedIn Company Page. If you didn't set up your company page yet, go back and set one up right now.

Okay, let's assume you now have a LinkedIn Company Page or you have the right person working on it, so let's get back to the benefits of having a company page and how you can use it to increase your sales. As I mentioned in Chapter 7, your company is accessible to others on the internet even if they aren't a LinkedIn member. Take a look at www.linkedin.com/company/microsoft to see a sample company page. This page is accessible to both LinkedIn members when they are logged into LinkedIn and people who are not LinkedIn members. Your company page also shows up in Google search results, giving your company additional exposure on the internet.

LinkedIn Company Pages give you the ability to share new product announcements and company news in the Recent Updates section. You can post as many updates as you want. You can also recruit the best talent by posting your open positions in the Careers section. The best part of the company page for sales professionals is the Showcase pages section. You can create up to ten Showcase pages and feature your top products on their own Showcase page, which will also show up for both LinkedIn members and nonmembers. Your customers can write recommendations of your products, building social proof for your company that you can share with your LinkedIn network. If you were selling the Microsoft Dynamics CRM software, you could post links to the product and to the recommendations on your LinkedIn status in your LinkedIn profile and LinkedIn Groups. Here's the link to the Microsoft Dynamics CRM Showcase page so you can see what it looks like: https://www.linkedin.com/company/microsoft-dynamics?trk=biz-brand-tree-co-name.

LinkedIn Company Pages are like mini-websites for your company and your products that you can share with your LinkedIn network. When people see your products and recommendations, they can reach out to you on LinkedIn or visit your website to learn more about your products.

LEVERAGING YOUR COMPANY GROUP

LinkedIn Groups let you build an online community for your company within the larger LinkedIn community. Since most of your customers and prospects are already on LinkedIn, it makes perfect sense to give them access to your Company Group, where they can ask questions, find resources, and get to know your company better. The discussions on your Company Groups can give you insight into what your customers are struggling with and what they want more of. They'll also tell you what they like about your products, and they'll even help your other customers by answering their questions.

Sales professionals should always monitor their company's online communities to keep their finger on the pulse of their customers. If customers are complaining about the performance of your product on the discussion board, you can reach out and help them or get the right resources involved to help them out. Being proactive and helping unsatisfied customers is a great way to build strong customer relationships and show prospective customers that your company provides excellent customer service.

PROSPECTING ON LINKEDIN

Imagine having a Rolodex with more than 330 million names of the top business professionals in the world at your fingertips. In addition to the names of every business professional, you have a list of the employees of every major business in the world segmented by the company they work for. You have access to the top employees of companies such as Google, Facebook, IBM, Costco, Target, and every other Fortune 500 company. If you don't sell to large companies, you have access to thousands of small and medium-sized businesses instead. You even have access to consultants, coaches, and other solo-preneurs who are members of LinkedIn.

Never before has prospecting been so easy for a sales professional. In the past, you would have to purchase lists from list brokers and cold-call hundreds and thousands of people. Most of the time you reached the gatekeeper, who would play games with you and maneuver around until you finally got to the decision-maker. You spent countless hours on the phone trying to get five minutes of the decision-maker's time so you could convince him to meet with you for 15 minutes.

If you weren't purchasing lists, you were scouring the phone book or business directories looking for contact numbers of your target businesses. Prospecting was a lot of hard work and not for the faint of heart. You were essentially a telemarketer being rejected 99 percent of the time when you reached out to prospects.

Today, LinkedIn makes prospecting a lot easier. Using the Advanced Search features, you can find your target audience in seconds. Advanced Search is a fantastic LinkedIn tool, but there are even more ways to find new prospects on LinkedIn. By learning how to use other LinkedIn tools like Publishing and Groups, you'll know your prospects' frustrations and hot buttons so you'll know exactly how to approach them and get their attention immediately. People love to use the LinkedIn tools like Groups to get advice and guidance from their peers.

The key to successfully prospecting on LinkedIn is exactly the same way you network in person. Listen before you talk. You want to get to know a person who is struggling or frustrated and could benefit from your product or service. You'll know how to approach them with your solution when the time is right. The key to success is to hover in the background and observe before reaching out.

Prospecting in LinkedIn Groups

You can use LinkedIn Groups to find prospects because the groups have discussion boards where people reach out for support. The discussion boards in Groups are very similar to the now-defunct LinkedIn Answers, but the discussions are more focused. Since LinkedIn Groups are often focused on companies or specific products produced by a company, the questions and discussions go much deeper than they did on Answers.

For example, someone might ask a basic question about Photoshop on a LinkedIn marketing-related group. The questions tend to be more general in nature—like at the 10,000-foot level—and the answers and follow-up comments are very general. A typical question about Photoshop in a marketing-related group may be: "How do I crop a photo in Photoshop?" If you join the Photoshop group, the questions will be about the more advanced features of Photoshop, and the answers will be very detailed. You may get three or four great answers that show you how to accomplish the same task using different techniques. A typical question in the Photoshop group may be something like "JPG and RAW, of course, we all know the advantages of RAW. Is there anyone out there who will still use JPG format for professional work?" This question received 251 comments in one month from graphic artists, and the discussion shows no signs of slowing down. A very lively discussion results with many varying opinions and the debate continues. Obviously, this question struck a nerve with many graphic artists who seem to feel strongly one way or the other about which format to use for professional work. You see active questions like this frequently on the LinkedIn Groups focused on specialties and specific products. I highly recommend joining the groups related to your product and industry and the vertical markets that use your product or service.

You can also learn about industry trends and your competitors' new advancements in LinkedIn Groups. Companies often use LinkedIn Groups to announce new products and services. They also use the groups to gather feedback from customers about their products and services by conducting surveys. LinkedIn no longer uses their Polls feature, but you can post a question and lead people to an external survey tool like SurveyMonkey.

The same prospecting rules apply here as when networking in person. Be genuinely interested in helping others, and spend most of your time listening to their issues before you reach out. You can also monitor the groups to find top professionals in your industry. If you notice a certain person reaching out consistently and they're providing excellent advice, you can contact that person to see if he wants to connect on LinkedIn. If he is located in your area, you could invite him to meet for coffee or lunch to talk about industry trends or see if he wants to join a local networking group you belong to. Building relationships with other experts helps extend your professional network, which will help you gain more sales. Of course, you don't want to reach out to others if they are competitors or are connected to your competitors in any way—that could put you in an awkward position with your boss!

LinkedIn Company Groups

In addition to LinkedIn Groups related to specific topics and products, you can join LinkedIn Groups for specific companies. Most companies have LinkedIn Groups in addition to their Company page, so join both if you can. You can learn a lot about your competitors, your industry, and vertical markets where your product or service is used. People always ask me if it's appropriate to join your competitors' groups. Most of the time, the groups are moderated, so they will deny your membership request if they are carefully moderating the group. Occasionally, you can slip through the cracks, and they will grant you access. If that happens to you, I recommend being a silent participant in that group and just observe, so you can learn as much as possible about the issues your competitors are having with their products or services. You can use this information when selling against your competitors, which gives you a huge advantage. If you join the group and start participating in discussions, they will become aware that you are a competitor and will remove you from the group.

You should be able to join industry-related groups and vertical market groups without resistance. If you aren't monitoring the other groups in your industry or vertical market companies, you are missing out on a lot of relevant discussions that will help you discover potential sales opportunities. Remember, LinkedIn is one of the largest business intelligence databases available to you, so use it to your advantage to gather competitive information that will give you the upper hand in sales presentations against your competitors.

LinkedIn Company Pages

LinkedIn lets you "follow" companies similar to the way you can "like" a company page on Facebook. Once you follow a company on LinkedIn, anything it posts on its company page will be visible on your LinkedIn homepage. This is an easy way for you to monitor prospect companies (and even your competitors) to learn about new product announcements and company news. If you see one of your potential prospect companies just hired a new CIO, it may be a perfect opportunity to get your foot in the door at the company because often that means a clean slate, open to new vendors.

You can also monitor your prospect company pages to see what job openings they have. If you see a lot of new job openings or promotions in a certain department, it may be a great time to test the waters as the company and the new hires might be looking for new products or services.

You can infer a ton of great information from LinkedIn company pages, if you take the time to dig into the job postings, news items, and new product announcements.

LinkedIn Jobs

I touched on this in the previous section. You can learn a lot about a company's strategic direction by monitoring their job postings page. You know your target companies and perhaps even the key decision-makers. Spend a few hours a week (or have your assistant do this) and monitor your target companies' job postings. Use the Advanced Job Search features to hone in on the current job openings in the departments you sell to. When you see new job postings for key positions or a lot of listings for similar new positions, it's a sign that you may have an opportunity. If you see they are suddenly hiring 50 new C++ programmers, there must be a new product being developed that could mean a huge opportunity for you. With LinkedIn Premium accounts, you can save search criteria in Saved Searches so you can easily replicate your best searches on a regular basis.

LinkedIn Pulse

LinkedIn Pulse is a free newsfeed service where you can subscribe to popular news sources, such *The New York Times*, *The Wall Street Journal*, and industry-specific news. You can also follow LinkedIn Influencers who frequently post industry-related articles. I never used to log into LinkedIn on a daily basis until they added features like LinkedIn Pulse. Now I can log in to one website and learn the latest industry and financial news and keep up with my professional network from my LinkedIn homepage. Use LinkedIn Pulse to learn about the latest trends in your industry and world news in general. I always visit LinkedIn Today when I'm looking for ideas for my next blog post or article. I also use it to find great articles to tweet.

LinkedIn Mobile

The LinkedIn Mobile app has improved dramatically since it was initially released, as I mentioned in Chapter 17. The app lets you easily access your LinkedIn account from your mobile phone. Before you meet with a prospect in person, you can quickly review her LinkedIn profile, see the latest company news from her company page, and learn about the latest industry news by using LinkedIn Connected. You will be well prepared and make a good impression on your prospects.

Using LinkedIn Ads

You will learn everything you need to know about LinkedIn Advertising in Chapter 21, so I won't get into great detail here. I do want you to know that you can run precisely targeted ads to promote your business brand and advertise white papers, webinars, videos, and workshops for lead generation. The advanced targeting ability of LinkedIn advertising makes it one of the most efficient advertising platforms available online today. Your ads will be displayed only to the appropriate target company industry using, job title, specific keywords, and many other advanced targeting options available in LinkedIn Advertising.

Premium Sales Package

Of course, LinkedIn provides premium packages designed for sales representatives. These are designed to help sales professionals generate leads and manage their LinkedIn network. Figure 20–3 on page 197 shows you the features of the Sales Navigator and the Sales Navigator Plus packages.

InMail

I've talked about the pros and cons of InMail throughout this book, so I won't get into the details of how you can use InMail to your advantage. In Chapter 12, "Using LinkedIn InMail to Reach Out," you can learn how to use InMail to effectively reach out to second- and third-degree connections. With the Premium Business account or the Sales Plus account, you can receive up to 25 InMails every month, depending on which package you choose. There are many ways to connect with others without using InMail, but sometimes it's much easier and faster to just contact them directly via a personalized InMail message.

Compare Plans	Free	Business Your Current Plan	Sales Plus	Sales Executive
Pricing: Annual I Monthly ↖ Save up to 25%			US$47.99/MO[1] Billed annually [Start Now]	US$74.99/MO[1] Billed annually [Start Now]
Find Prospects				
Search Alerts Stay on top of new leads.	3 weekly	5 weekly	7 weekly	10 daily
Lead Builder Manage your pipeline to source and close deals.			✓	✓
Premium Search Pinpoint the right leads.[2]		4	4	8
Relate with Insight				
Full Profiles See full profiles of everyone in your network - 1st, 2nd and 3rd degree.	Limited Up to 2nd Degree	✓	✓	✓
Who's Viewed Your Profile Proactively manage inbound queries and interest in your profile.	Limited	✓	✓	✓
Full Name Visibility See full names of 3rd degree and group connections.				✓
Engage with Confidence				
Introductions Get warm introductions to inside sources at companies you're interested in.	5	15	25	35
InMail Messages Gain access to decision-makers. Response guaranteed.[3]		3 per month	10 per month	25 per month

FIGURE 20–3. Premium Packages for Sales Professionals

Lead Builder

Lead Builder allows you to create and save lists of prospects. As you search for prospects on LinkedIn using the Advanced Search features, you can save your searches in Saved Searches and also create lists of prospects in Lead Builder.

Premium Search Filters

A LinkedIn Premium account offers you significantly more search results than a free LinkedIn account when you perform Advanced Searches. This can be good news as well as bad news because you can be overwhelmed with search results that you have to manually sort through to find what you are looking for. The good news is that you also receive Premium Search Filters with your upgraded LinkedIn accounts. Figure 20–4 on page 198 shows you the Premium Search Filters you receive with the Sales Navigator and the Sales Navigator Plus accounts.

Access to Premium & Talent search filters help you quickly zero in on your ideal prospects.

Premium (4 filters)
- Seniority
- Company Size
- Interests
- Fortune 1000

Premium + Talent (8 filters)
- Seniority
- Company Size
- Function
- Interests
- Years of Experience
- Fortune 1000
- Your Groups
- New to LinkedIn

FIGURE 20–4. Premium Search Filters for Sales Navigator and Sales Navigator Plus

As you can see, it's worth upgrading to Sales Navigator Plus just for the additional search filters. Being able to filter your searches using the Premium + Talent search filters will save you time and provide more targeted searches.

Who's Viewed Your Profile

This is a vital feature of LinkedIn that lets you see who's been viewing your profile. As a sales professional, knowing who's viewed your profile can tip you off to customers who may be interested in your products or services. As you participate in LinkedIn Groups and establish yourself as a subject matter expert, people will click on your profile link to learn more about you. The simple act of a potential customer clicking on your profile link is better than if he opted in on your website to download a white paper. You'll find out a lot more about a client from his LinkedIn profile than you would just from the name and email address provided to you when he downloaded the white paper.

See More Profiles When You Search

I touched on this feature of LinkedIn Premium accounts a bit earlier. You can see up to 700 profiles when you perform an Advanced People Search, which helps you find more leads in less time. The combination of seeing up to 700 targeted profiles with the Premium Search Filters will help you find more prospects in a fraction of the time you spend today.

Saved Search Alerts

You already know about using the Saved Search feature in LinkedIn Premium accounts. As you identify the optimal search criteria to find your ideal prospects, you save them in the Saved Search section of the Advanced People Search page. The Saved Search Alerts takes the Saved Search feature to the next level by automating your searches. LinkedIn will automatically run up to ten of your saved searches every day and alert you when a prospect is found for you. This is another reason for you to upgrade to the Sales Navigator Plus account—you can receive all ten automated searches every day. With LinkedIn adding at least two new members every second, a new prospect could be signing up right now!

See Names of Your Third-Degree and Group Connections

Normally you will see only the first name and last initial of a contact when you perform a keyword search. If you are doing an Advanced Search for people with the keywords "content management system" in their profiles, by default you will see only their first names and last initials, so it's harder to learn more about them. If you upgrade to Sales Navigator Plus, you will see the full last name on all of your LinkedIn searches. This is yet another reason to upgrade to Sales Navigator Plus.

Get Introduced to the Companies You Are Targeting

Occasionally you try your hardest but, for one reason or another, you just can't make that connection with a key decision-maker in one of your target companies. LinkedIn Introductions will help you make that connection. As you know, you receive five LinkedIn Introductions with your free LinkedIn account. With the Sales Navigator Plus account, you receive up to 35 outstanding Introductions. You can learn more about Introductions in Chapter 11, "Connecting with Others."

Let Anyone Message You for Free with OpenLink

The reason you are on LinkedIn is to connect with as many prospects and customers as possible. Some people lock down their LinkedIn profiles so it's almost impossible to connect with them; this completely defeats the purpose of being on a business networking website. As you know, I'm all about opening up my LinkedIn profile so it's easy for people to get to know me, see that I'm an expert in my field, and connect with me. When you subscribe to any of the LinkedIn Premium accounts, you can enable OpenLink, which allows anyone on LinkedIn to send you a message without seeing your contact details. If you enable OpenLink and receive too many unsolicited messages from people you don't want to connect with, you can disable it at any time. I use OpenLink, and I receive only a few messages a month, and most are relevant opportunities. Remember, LinkedIn is a higher-quality network than most online networking websites, so you don't have to worry about being bombarded with spam.

CONCLUSION

As you see, LinkedIn provides many free and paid subscription levels. If you are in sales and serious about surpassing your number every month, you need to invest in Sales Navigator Plus to get the most out of LinkedIn. As LinkedIn continues to grow at staggering rates, you will need as many automated tools as possible to help you track down the right leads. The LinkedIn Premium subscriptions are worth the nominal fee you pay, and your return on investment will be exponential.

In the next chapter, we'll explore LinkedIn Advertising, one of the fastest-growing and most targeted ad networks today. You'll learn how to target your prospects with customized ads that will convert better than the industry average.

For additional updates and how-to videos, visit
www.tedprodromou.com/chapter20

Chapter 21

LinkedIn Advertising

I remember back in the late 1990s many internet experts were saying, "Banner ads are dead" and "Nobody clicks on internet ads." Based on Google's success—earning more than $50 billion in advertising revenue in 2013—I have to say things have changed. Internet advertising revenue is increasing about 16 percent every year and is showing no sign of slowing down as the internet continues to become an even bigger part of our lives.

LinkedIn is capitalizing on the popularity of internet advertising by offering a variety of alternatives. LinkedIn provides an affordable way to get your message out to a targeted audience using many easy-to-use options. Nowhere else on the internet can you create such laser-focused advertising at such an affordable price.

The beauty of LinkedIn advertising is the incredible targeting ability for your ads. You can display one set of ads on keyword-specific content, display another set of ads to specific LinkedIn Groups, and another a set of ads that are shown only to specific job titles, companies, and a host of other options covered in detail in this chapter. Since LinkedIn is already a targeted, business-oriented community, the ability to use targeted advertising makes your advertising dollar go a lot further and can provide extraordinary results.

LinkedIn members include highly educated, affluent, executive-level, and influential decision-makers in companies. According to The Nielsen Company, @Plan, almost 27 percent of LinkedIn members are business decision-makers, and more than 34 percent earn over $100,000/year. @Plan is the leading target-marketing platform for internet media planning, buying, and selling. @Plan uses more than 5,000 profile points and 19 profile categories to provide wide-ranging details about the U.S. adult online population.

@Plan also says three out of four LinkedIn members use LinkedIn to keep up with business news and industry trends because they trust the information they read. Over 64 percent of these executives believe LinkedIn helps develop business relationships and grow their businesses.

LinkedIn members are the perfect group to market to because they are receptive to relevant advertising and have the authority to take action when they see products and services that will solve their problems.

CONTENT MARKETING

With LinkedIn's commitment to becoming the largest content publishing website, now is the time to publish and promote your content on LinkedIn. With the recently launched Publisher option and new advertising options like Sponsored Updates, LinkedIn is making it easier than ever to get your content in front of your target audience. You can publish articles, blog posts, presentations, and even video on LinkedIn, then promote it so it appears in the newsfeeds of your ideal clients. Sponsored updates is one of the most affordable ways to get your brand in front of millions of potential customers.

ADVERTISING OPTIONS

Your LinkedIn advertising program options include:

- Self-service PPC advertising
- Premium Display Advertising
- Sponsored Updates
- Sponsored InMails
- Sponsored Groups
- Content Ads
- Social Display

Each of the above advertising options allows you the flexibility and affordability to reach your target audience, whether you are generating leads, growing your

LinkedIn network, recruiting new employees, or growing your LinkedIn Company Page membership.

Let's learn about the different advertising options available to you on LinkedIn, and then, in Chapter 22, I'll show you how to create powerful, laser-targeted ads that will convert like crazy.

LEAD COLLECTION IN LINKEDIN ADS

In the first edition of *Ultimate Guide to LinkedIn for Business*, I showed you how to use Lead Collection in your LinkedIn ads. This option automatically collected the LinkedIn profile details of everyone who clicked on your ad and wanted more information. Instead of having to fill out a form to receive a free report or more information about your product, the LinkedIn profile details were saved in your campaign. You could then reach out to the interested party through LinkedIn email. The downside of this option was you couldn't export the lead data and import it into your CRM. Because of this limitation, very few companies used this option in their ads. On July 15, 2014, LinkedIn discontinued the Lead Collection option.

SELF-SERVICE PPC ADVERTISING

LinkedIn Ads is a self-service advertising solution that allows you to create and place ads on prominent pages and page locations on the LinkedIn.com website.

You specify which LinkedIn members view your ads by selecting a target audience: by job title, job function, industry, geography, age, gender, company name, company size, or LinkedIn Group.

The Components of Your Self-Service Ads

- Headline (up to 25 characters of text)
- Description (up to 75 characters of text)
- From: (your name or any company)
- Image: (50 x 50 pixel image)
- URL (website people visit once they click on your ad)

Locations of Your Self-Service Ads

Your Self-Service ads, as seen in Figure 21–1 on page 204, will be displayed prominently at the top of the LinkedIn page as a text ad, and your full ad with an image will appear in the right sidebar.

FIGURE 21–1. Self-Service Ads

PREMIUM DISPLAY ADVERTISING

The rest of the LinkedIn advertising options are considered enhanced marketing solutions, and you need to contact the LinkedIn sales team for more information. The starting price for enhanced marketing solutions campaigns is $25,000, but it may be possible to negotiate and start campaigns at lower price points.

Below are the specifications for LinkedIn-approved formats when you run Enhanced Marketing Solutions campaigns:

- LinkedIn accepts iframe/Java script tags.
- LinkedIn accepts in-banner surveys—no floating layers or pop-ups.
- Third-party tags must be allowed so LinkedIn's ad server can track clicks via a click URL macro or redirect.
- All ad content must function uniformly on both Mac and PC formats as well as multiple browser versions of Firefox, Internet Explorer, Safari, and Chrome.
- LinkedIn does not allow the setting of "Flash cookies" (also known as Local Shared Objects, or LSO).

These are very standard ad specifications for those who are familiar with online banner advertising. LinkedIn also accepts the standard ad sizes of (in pixels) 160 x 600, 300 x 250, 728 x 90, and text links.

CONTENT ADS

Content ads are essentially mini-websites that let you display multiple advertising messages in one sidebar widget. You have the chance to display up to four advertising messages in different media formats, so you have more than one chance to catch the reader's eye. Content ads are similar to those rotating billboards you see on freeways where you see three different billboard advertisements as the panels turn.

Content ads come in just two sizes, 160 x 600 and 300 x 250, but you can add up to four tabs to your ad to create a multimedia experience. You can display your live Twitter feed in one tab, YouTube videos in another, and custom content in the last one. You can mix and match content to make highly interactive ads by offering white papers, podcasts, flash or image banners, or custom videos.

Content ads are a great way to reach many different audiences with just one ad. I like to use them to promote webinars or live events. On the first tab I promote the event with an image ad; on the second I show the live Twitter feed; on the third, I place YouTube videos of the event; and, on the last tab, I post PowerPoint slides from the event. I get to promote four elements of the event in just one ad, which is very effective.

Figure 21–2 shows a sample Content ads with three tabs. As you see, each tab provides the opportunity to display a separate offer or ad campaign.

FIGURE 21–2. Content Ads

SLIDESHARE CONTENT ADS

Presentations are an excellent way to engage LinkedIn members. In 2012, LinkedIn acquired SlideShare, a social media website where you can post PowerPoint presentations, infographics, documents, and articles. This lets you post content on the popular

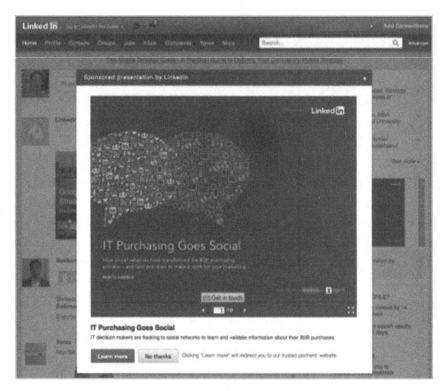

FIGURE 21–3. SlideShare Content Ads

SlideShare website and post the same content within your LinkedIn profile under your Summary or within each job posted in the Experience section.

With SlideShare Content Ads, you can now promote your content in sponsored updates. This lets you share your best content with your target audience who is looking for professional insights. In Figure 21–3 you see a sample SlideShare Content Ad being viewed.

Features of SlideShare Content Ads

- Delivers full SlideShare-based presentations within the 300 x 250 ad unit
- Enables direct interaction with your presentation content within the ad unit or in an expanded overlay player
- Supports the full suite of LinkedIn ad-targeting capabilities

Benefits of SlideShare Content Ads

- These ads provide a rich content experience using presentations and videos, which leads to longer viewer engagement.

- On SlideShare, the average viewer spends approximately five to six minutes viewing a presentation, according to SlideShare.
- This ad format lets you demonstrate your expertise and even generate leads through your presentations, which are tailored to your campaign goals.

SPONSORED INMAIL

Sponsored InMail lets you use InMail to deliver highly relevant messages to targeted audience segments. Sponsored InMail messages are different from the standard InMail message because they're designed to deliver a personalized marketing message to the recipient. When you send an InMail message to someone, you don't want to include a marketing message. The sole purpose of an InMail message is to establish contact with the person.

Sponsored InMail messages are personalized messages with space for extensive marketing copy on a co-branded landing page, one ad unit, and a call to action. Sponsored InMail messages are always delivered to the top of the member's LinkedIn inbox, increasing visibility and improving the open rate. LinkedIn members can receive only one partner message every 60 days, so they aren't overwhelmed with unsolicited emails.

When you send a Sponsored InMail Message, you have the ability to create messages personalized to very specific audiences because you can target any facet of the member profile. For this reason, Sponsored InMail Messages have an average open rate of 20 percent and a 20 percent clickthrough rate on the call to action. These are phenomenal open and clickthrough rates, well above the industry standard. Figure 21–4 on page 208 shows you a sample Sponsored InMail message.

SOCIAL ADS

The LinkedIn Social Ads are another new addition to the LinkedIn advertising family. Social Ads are a very effective way to encourage LinkedIn members to share messages and recommend your products. Social Ads use the same targeting other LinkedIn advertising options offers.

Social Ads let you leverage social proof throughout the LinkedIn community. The endorsements of trusted contacts are a highly effective way to add credibility and impact to your company messages. As we all know, it can be difficult to achieve social proof at scale.

LinkedIn's extensive range of social ads is designed to leverage the way members use the LinkedIn network to share ideas and information. Social Ads make it easy for

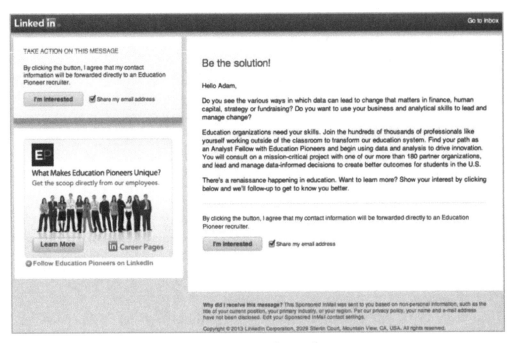

FIGURE 21–4. Sponsored InMail Message

members to endorse your company and share insights and updates. And they ensure that engagement with one member is quickly spread across his network.

LinkedIn Social Ads come in a variety of sizes, based on the type of social ad you're using.

Follow Company ads	300 x 250 or 160 x 600
Featured Company ads	300 x 250
Join Group ads	300 x 250 and 300 x 250 dynamic (ads with motion)

FOLLOW COMPANY ADS

LinkedIn Social Ads are a unique set of display ads that leverage a member's profile data to deliver a customized, personalized message to drive engagement with your Company Page. Follow Company ads gives companies the ability to target professionals, generate awareness for their Company Page, and convert them to engaged followers.

Figure 21-5 on page 209 shows you a sample 300 x 250 Follow Company ad.

FEATURED COMPANY ADS

In Figure 21-6 on page 209, you see a sample 300 x 250 Featured Company ad, which is very similar to the Follow Company ad. The difference is the Featured Company ad is

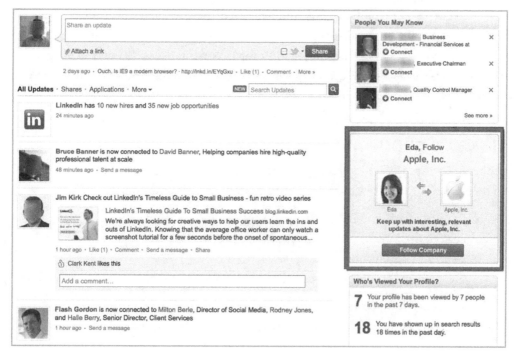

FIGURE 21–5. Follow Company Ad

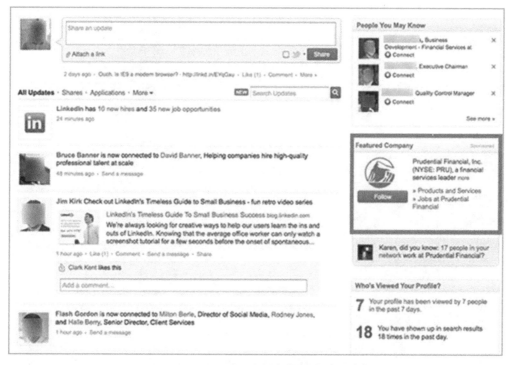

FIGURE 21–6. Featured Company Ad

associated with your Company page and lets you display links to the Product Showcase and Jobs pages on your Company page. The Featured Company ad is an organic-looking tool to generate awareness and interaction for Company Pages. It invites engagement directly from the ad unit and leverages member network connections to drive interest while the Follow Company ad only lets the viewer click on the Follow Company link.

LINKEDIN GROUP ADS

LinkedIn Group Ads are targeted, personalized, and relevant group-specific ads created to help promote and drive membership to custom group communities.

- Feature viewer-specific social graph information within the ad unit to build a personalized message
- Deliver Group recommendations
- Build trust through co-branded template and gain implied LinkedIn endorsement

Figure 21–7 shows you a Join Group ad, which helps you publicize and grow your LinkedIn Groups.

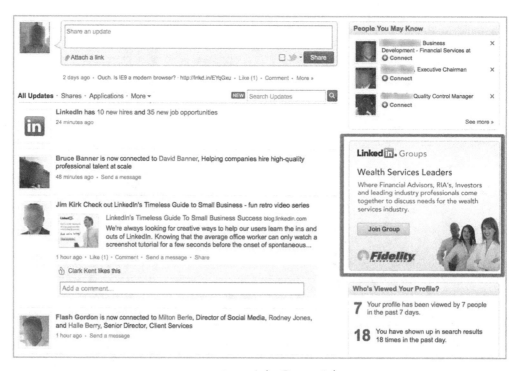

FIGURE 21–7. Join Group Ad

SPOTLIGHT ADS

A Spotlight Ad is a fully customizable Native Ad Unit that leverages the member profile image but can link to the advertiser's landing page. Native Ad Units are ads that look like content on the page and don't use the traditional ad formats. Since we are used to seeing ads in certain sections of web pages, "ad blindness" often occurs, and we gloss over the ads. Since Native Ad Units blend in with the content, we often click on them not realizing they are ads.

To submit a Spotlight Ad, you need to follow these specs:

- Logo image at 65 x 65 pixels
- Top text: 60 characters (including spaces)
- Bottom text: 70 characters (including spaces)
- Logo Title: max. 18 characters
- Call to action button: max. 18 characters
- Clickthrough URL (you can use a click tracker such as Google URL Builder)
- Optional: Secure Impression Pixel

Figure 21–8 shows a sample Spotlight Ad, which obviously targets job seekers. Spotlight Ads are designed to help someone find a job by associating their profile picture with a company logo.

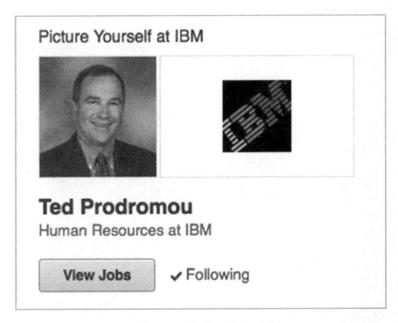

FIGURE 21–8. Spotlight Ad

These ads are very effective because they show your image in the ad under the headline, "Picture Yourself at Company" and your new job title under your name. This lets you visualize yourself in this position at a company you want to work for.

CONCLUSION

As you see, LinkedIn provides a variety of advertising solutions to help you generate leads, promote your company, and recruit new employees. LinkedIn ads are accurately targeted and effective since you have access to so much demographic data. This gives your advertising conversion rates that are often well above the industry average.

In the next chapter, I'll show you how to write LinkedIn ads that convert like crazy.

For additional updates and how-to videos, visit
www.tedprodromou.com/chapter21

Creating LinkedIn Ads That Convert Like Crazy

What makes one ad bring in sales better than another? We've all seen ads that grab our attention, and we can't wait to learn more. We've also seen ads that leave us speechless, wondering what the heck the advertiser was trying to accomplish.

Go back and read that last paragraph again. What is the difference between an ad that makes us want to learn more and an ad that leaves us confused? It's simple. Ads that grab our attention aren't visibly trying to sell us anything. Nothing turns us off more than someone giving us the hard sell like a used-car salesman. We like ads that grab our attention and teach us something or entertain us. Those ads turn off our noise filter so the advertiser can build a trusting relationship with us.

Apple is one of the very best at grabbing our attention. Watching an Apple commercial with the catchy background music is an experience that makes us feel cool and hip. Notice that Apple never tries to sell in their ads. Instead, they create an experience where average people just like you and I are enjoying a perfect life without a care in the world. They just happen to be using an iPad to surf the internet or talking to Siri on their iPhone while they're enjoying that carefree life. This makes us associate Apple products with enjoying a life without worry. As a result, we want to run out and buy an iPhone or iPad so we can be just like the people in the commercial. Who doesn't want to feel like that? Owning Apple products is a status symbol like driving a Mercedes or BMW.

On the other hand, have you ever watched a commercial or seen a banner ad that left you feeling angry or annoyed? Or maybe the ad was so offbeat that you had no idea what company produced it and what product they were promoting.

Ads with annoying jingles can turn us off. Annoying characters, such as Flo from Progressive Insurance—the woman with an irritating voice, wearing the white apron, selling insurance like it's a commodity product in a box—is always voted among the most annoying commercials.

Flashing banner ads with too much rapid movement are also ineffective. They may have a great message, but the fast, flashy movements turn us off.

Ads that confuse us often try to sell us something before we even know what the product is. Sometimes the ad does a horrible job explaining how the product can help us, so we get confused and tune out. It may be a product that we really need, but they lost us when they tried to close the sale before we were ready.

So how do we create text and banner ads on LinkedIn that seduce like the Apple TV ads do?

SELLING ON LINKEDIN

Did I say "Selling on LinkedIn"? Sorry about that!

When creating online ads for LinkedIn, you don't want to sell. You want to make a connection with the reader and build a long-term relationship. If you are selling business-to-consumer (B2C) products like you see on sites such as Amazon or Target, it's OK to sell in your advertising because you can entice people to make impulse purchases. The price point for B2C products is much lower, and the buying cycle can be seconds or minutes. LinkedIn isn't a great place to advertise B2C products, so you won't see ads for consumer products.

Business-to-Business (B2B) products and services have a much higher price point and a longer buying cycle—sometimes up to a year—so you have to build a long-term relationship with the buyer.

On LinkedIn, you may be running ads for many reasons including:

- Lead generation so your sales reps can follow up with the prospects
- Invitations to follow your company or join your group on LinkedIn
- Recruitment of new employees for your company
- B2B products or services promotions
- Client case studies or success stories promotions
- Brand promotions so people will become familiar with your company

LinkedIn advertising can be a very powerful tool if used correctly. As with any advertising campaign, whether it's on LinkedIn or not, you need to create a plan and an objective for your ad campaign. A well-executed advertising campaign will return huge dividends for your company.

CREATE LASER-FOCUSED CAMPAIGNS

If you are creating an ad campaign to generate leads, focus on generating leads. If you are running a branding campaign to publicize your company name, focus on the branding campaign. Do not try to kill two birds with one stone by combining a lead-gen campaign with a branding campaign. You will send a mixed message that will yield horrible results.

When you see an online ad, you should be able to tell if the campaign is designed to promote a brand, advertise a product, generate leads, gather information, recruit new employees, or build relationships. If the intent of the ad isn't obvious to you, the ad is probably a failure because it isn't conveying a crystal-clear message. Remember, people decide in a split second if an ad is relevant and move on if it's not.

Everyone sees thousands of advertisements every day, so it's hard to break through the clutter and grab someone's attention. You need to interrupt a viewer's thought pattern without being annoying. If you grab her attention and pique her interest, she'll click on your ad to learn more. If you don't grab her attention in a second or two, she moves on and can subconsciously block them in the future. This is why you need to carefully plan your advertising campaigns to get the most from your advertising dollar.

LinkedIn advertising has some of the most advanced targeting capabilities of any online advertising platform. You can display specific ads to specific job titles, companies, or LinkedIn Groups. A well-planned LinkedIn advertising campaign includes tracking your results so you know which ads and targeting demographics work best for your products and services.

If you are a web content management software company, you can create ad campaigns to target web developers, IT managers, marketing executives, project managers, and CEOs. You can display technical ads to the developers and IT managers; marketing-focused campaigns to the marketing executives; project-management-related ads to the project managers; and financial-related ads to the CFO and CEO.

Many advertisers don't take advantage of the targeting capabilities, and they display all ads to all job titles. The web developers will see ads designed for the CEO, and the CEO may see technical ads, which will result in a lower conversion rate. Creating relevant ads and displaying those ads to the appropriate target audience will improve your conversion rate significantly while reducing your advertising costs.

WRITING EFFECTIVE ADS

Remember when you were learning to ride a bike for the first time? You were probably nervous—maybe even scared—because you didn't know what to expect. You were afraid you would fall and get hurt. You thought people would laugh at you.

At first, you were unstable and fell a few times. Maybe you even fell a lot before you got the hang of it.

Eventually, you learned, and before you knew it, you were bombing down the street on your bike. The more you rode, the better you got, and your fear completely disappeared.

Copywriting, like bike riding, is a skill you need to practice on a regular basis to get better. We're not born expert copywriters. We get better at it by practicing and making mistakes. It doesn't hurt when you make a mistake when writing copy or ads. It just may cost you a few bucks because your ad didn't convert as well as you expected. Like learning to ride your bike, start slow and hone your skills. If you practice consistently and learn from your mistakes, you will get better.

There are many great books that will teach you the basics of copywriting and ad writing. Any book by Dan Kennedy will make you an expert in direct marketing and copywriting. I highly recommend his book *The Ultimate Sales Letter*, which teaches you how to write powerful, high-converting sales letters. You need to learn how to write these because a great ad does you no good if the landing page (the high-tech version of the traditional sales letter) doesn't convert.

Perry Marshall has co-authored two fantastic books, the *Ultimate Guide to Google AdWords* and *Ultimate Guide to Facebook Advertising*, that will teach you how to write great online ads. Perry, Mike Rhodes, and Bryan Todd study Google AdWords advertising religiously and know the ins and outs better than anyone I've ever met. Their greatest asset is they can take incredibly detailed, complex information and teach regular people like us in plain English. They are masters at simplifying the complex.

Perry, Keith Krance, and Thomas Meloche teamed up to write the *Ultimate Guide to Facebook Advertising*, which shows how to effectively reach your target audience on Facebook. Creating effective ads on Facebook requires a very different approach than reaching your audience on Google. Perry, Keith, and Thomas teach you how to write ads that connect with the Facebook community.

The most important thing you will learn from the above books is how to write sales letters and ads from the customers' perspective. The biggest mistake beginners make when writing copy and online ads is that they write from their own perspectives. They talk about the features and benefits of their products or services and tell you how wonderful your life will be when you purchase their products.

The key to writing successful online ads is to put yourself in the shoes of the person who is reading your ad. Imagine how they are feeling. Feel their pain points. Understand why they are frustrated. Once you get into their heads, you can write ads that will grab their attention instantly and make them feel comfortable with you and your products.

CREATING ATTENTION-GRABBING HEADLINES

Think back to one of your favorite commercials or advertisements. Great ads are more than just words. Great ads tell a story or create an unforgettable experience. The ad headline is the title of the story that makes you want to read more. In fact, great headlines make you have to read more, not just want to read more.

Well-converting headlines trigger emotions and pique your interest. How many times have you been standing in line at the grocery store and peeked at the cover of *Star* magazine or *Cosmopolitan*, hoping nobody you know would see you? These magazines are masters at creating attention-getting headlines that make you pick up the magazine to read the full story behind the headline.

Some sample ads from a recent issue of *Cosmopolitan* include:

- Would you date a dude who looked like this?
- How to turn an office crush into something more
- It drives him wild when I . . .
- Blow his mind every single time
- Five dates that will drive him wild
- The five new ways to lose weight

All these headlines trigger an emotion or grab your attention. Many single men and women have office crushes and don't know how to take the relationship to the next level, so they're going to read the article.

What guy isn't going to read the articles (in a secret location) about how a woman is going to blow his mind and the five dates that will drive him wild? He wants to know the tricks women are going to play on him!

If you are struggling with your weight and you've tried every diet imaginable, there is no way you are not going to read that article about weight loss.

Of course, it's unlikely your advertising on LinkedIn will trigger these same emotions, but you want to create the same effect when people see your ads. When they read your headline they'll have to read the rest of your ad and click to learn more.

FACTORS THAT GENERATE CLICKS

Here are five factors that can make your ads more clickable. Obviously there are other factors, but these work well in online advertising. Not all of these factors will result in clicks on ads for your product or service, so you have to test to see which ones convert best.

1. Curiosity
2. Benefit
3. Emotion
4. Credibility
5. Expectation

These factors seem pretty obvious, but let's explore them so you're clear on how you can use them in your headlines.

Curiosity

We are curious by nature and want to learn more about subjects that interest us. If you start your headline with phrases like "How I . . ." or "How do I . . ." the reader will be curious and want to read the entire headline. You can also use contradiction in your headline to confuse the reader so you'll grab her attention. Here are some sample headlines that use curiosity to grab attention:

- "How I turned my business around in the worst economy ever . . ."
- "How do I get top search rankings in Google for my business without spending a fortune?"
- "Social Media is NOT your only way to get web traffic"

Benefit

By providing a clear benefit in your headline, people will click on your ad to find out how they can benefit from what you are offering. You are implying that they will learn something new that may give them a competitive advantage. Some examples of benefit-driven headlines include:

- "Three Easy Ways to Increase Your Clickthrough Rate by at least 40 Percent"
- "How to Convert More Web Visitors into Raving Customers"
- "How to Work Less and Earn More"

Emotion

People respond to certain words, especially when they trigger an emotion. The right words will make people click on your ads and take actions. If you watch one of those Saturday morning infomercials, you will hear and see a steady stream of emotion-triggering words like *amazing, incredible, superb, excellent, free,* and on and on. You may hear them say something like "This amazing formula will help you feel superb, look incredible, and make you completely irresistible." Who wouldn't buy that product? Here are some examples of emotional headlines:

- "Eight Incredibly Simple Ways to Increase Sales by at Least 25 Percent"
- "Ten Free Social Media Tips That Will Generate More Incredible Comments on Your Blogs"
- "Easily Learn a New Language in Just 20 Minutes a Day!"

Credibility

Most people like concrete or tangible ideas because they are familiar and make sense to them. When you hear "1 + 1 = 2," that is tangible to you because you know it's true. When you hear "How large is space?" you don't feel comfortable because there is no definitive answer. Including familiar experts is an easy way to make your headline tangible and credible. Some examples of tangible headlines include:

- "Warren Buffett Shows You How to Invest Your Money Wisely"
- "Donald Trump Shares His Deepest Real Estate Investing Secrets"
- "How to Start a Social Network by Mark Zuckerberg"

Expectation

It's important to set reasonable expectations in your ad and not overpromise. You can't promise someone that you can get them top rankings in Google for all of their target keywords or guarantee they will lose at least 20 pounds with your home exercise program, unless you can really give them those results. It is just not realistic to promise results that you know everyone won't achieve, and it's illegal to make promises that you can't guarantee. You need to provide exactly what you are promising in the headline. If you promise a white paper showing seven steps, then you have to provide all seven steps in the white paper—not just one step and then coax the reader into purchasing the next six.

Here are some reasonable expectation-based ads:

- "Voted Best Restaurant in San Francisco Five Years in a Row by *Sunset* Magazine"
- "Seven Steps to Setting Up Your WordPress Blog"
- "Learn How to Recruit the Best Employees on LinkedIn"

You might like to create a spreadsheet to track which factors work best with each product. Figure 22–1 on page 220 demonstrates how you can track your ads. The best-converting ad is placed in the box that corresponds with the factor and appropriate product.

Factor	Product A	Product B	Product C	Product D
Curiosity				How I Turned My Business Around in the Worst Economy Ever . . .
Benefit		How to Convert More Web Visitors into Raving Customers		
Emotion	Easily Learn a New Language in Just 20 Minutes a Day!			
Credibility	Warren Buffett Shows You How to Invest Your Money Wisely			
Expectation			Learn How to Recruit the Best Employees on LinkedIn	

FIGURE 22–1. Tracking Factors of Successful Ad Conversion

So how do you create attention-grabbing headlines that convert like crazy? Here are a few techniques to help you get started.

BRAINSTORMING HEADLINES

Top copywriters like Dan Kennedy, Bill Glazer, and John Carlton teach you to sit down with a blank pad of paper and start writing headlines until you run out of ideas. Just put your pen on the paper and write every word that comes to mind. Don't stop until you've written at least 30 headlines. Most of them will be horrible, but by doing a complete brain dump, you will come up with a few good ones to test.

The Old Magazine Rack Trick

Another great way to get ideas for headlines is to go to your nearest bookstore or grocery store and check out the magazines like I did for the *Cosmopolitan* magazine headlines above. Your local bookstore will have huge magazine racks filled with hundreds of magazines in every niche—or you can search online.

Write down the headlines and article summaries that grab your attention, and use similar wording to create compelling headlines for your LinkedIn ads.

Let's say you sell computer security software and want to advertise on LinkedIn. You could create a targeted advertising campaign that is displayed only to IT professionals. You need some ideas for headlines and ad content, so you check out *PC* magazine for some ideas. In one issue of the magazine you see the articles shown in Figure 22–2 related to computer security. You hit the jackpot!

These are article titles and descriptions that could easily be modified to be powerful ads on LinkedIn to promote your products or white papers that describe your products.

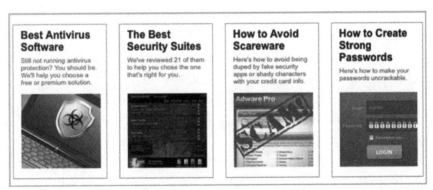

FIGURE 22–2. Article Titles

What if the first article was a LinkedIn ad? Would you click on this ad if you were in the market for a new antivirus program?

Best Antivirus Software
Still not running antivirus protection?
We'll help you choose the best solution

The headline "Best Antivirus Software" should catch their eye if they see this ad in the LinkedIn Groups section near a question about antivirus software. The simple question "Still not running antivirus protection?" will trigger an emotion if they aren't running an antivirus program or they're using an inadequate or free version that isn't protecting their computers. They're probably thinking, "I'm so stupid for not protecting my business data" or something to that effect. The last line of the ad, "We'll help you choose the best solution," triggers another emotion like "I'm not in this alone. This expert is going to save my business data."

Or, you could promote a white paper that you created to help people decide which solution is best.

Best Antivirus Software?
We reviewed the 21 best solutions
Free white paper helps you decide

This ad works the same as the first ad by grabbing attention and triggering emotions. The person who responds to this ad probably tried to figure out which antivirus program is best, but she was overwhelmed by too many choices or got lost in technical jargon. She feels great relief when she reads this ad and sees light at the end of the tunnel because this white paper will guide her to the best solution.

See how easy it is to create ads that resonate with people who are looking for what you are selling?

Create a Swipe File

All copywriters create what is known as a swipe file where they save articles, magazine headlines, newspaper headlines, and junk mail. Yes, I said junk mail. Those ads you receive in the mail every day are great sources for headlines and ad copy.

Create a file folder where you can save headlines and articles that caught your attention. If you run ads for many different niches or topics, create a separate swipe file for each topic. When you're ready to write new ads, pull out the swipe file for your niche and read through the clippings you've collected. After you read through all the clippings, do the brainstorming exercise I showed you earlier. Your brain is full of ideas from reviewing your clippings, so you should be able to crank out 30 to 50 headlines in a few minutes.

When I was a personal coach, I purchased a lot of personal development programs from Nightingale Conant at www.nightingale.com. It is the premier provider of personal development programs and masters of direct marketing. It sends daily motivational quotes via email that happen to have a promotion for a related personal development program. The emails have catchy subject lines, which act as the headline for the motivational tip and personal development program. I copy the emails and subject lines into a huge Word document as an online swipe file. They are also masters at direct mail promotion, so I receive at least two promotional postcards or sales letters in the mail every week. The envelope has a compelling headline that makes you rip it open to read the sales letter promoting the latest method for improving your life. I save every envelope and sales letter in my personal swipe file, so I have content to give me ideas when I'm ready to write ads or web copy.

WRITING YOUR AD COPY

Now that you have a headline, it's time to write your ad copy. Remember how I described the Apple ads that triggered the strong emotions? That catchy jingle, the cool tricks you can do with the iPhone, and the happy people in the ad make you feel happy and hip. When Apple shows you the cool iPhone tricks, it is visually describing the benefits of the product. Some Apple ads don't even show people. They just show an iPhone being held in one hand and a finger sliding across the screen, doing tricks like a magician. The simple, sleight-of-hand imagery is so powerful and makes the iPhone seem so easy to use, like all Apple products. What a huge benefit for a technology product when most people are overwhelmed by the complexity of technology!

Your ad copy should flow like a story that triggers an emotion in readers' minds so you catch their attention and they take your desired action. If your objective is to get them to download a white paper, they won't hesitate to fill out your web form because they know you are going to provide a solution to their problem.

The headline is the title of the story, the opening line of the ad should describe a benefit of your product or service, and the last line is your call to action or your offer.

Your ad should follow this template:

Headline

Describe a benefit of your product or service (paint a picture in the reader's mind).

Offer a solution to a problem in the call to action or offer.

THE POWER OF IMAGES

Images in advertising are almost as powerful as your headline and ad copy. Often, the image can be the most important aspect of your ad, depending on what you are promoting. The images you use in your ads are like a book cover. An attractive cover design for a book can increase sales exponentially, just like a compelling book title.

Advertisers have long realized the importance of images in advertising to create mental images in the buyer's mind. Claude Hopkins—one of the great innovators in advertising—was one of the first copywriters to discover that the combination of powerful benefit-driven copy and relevant images increased response rates significantly ("You'll wonder where the yellow went when you brush your teeth with Pepsodent"). This combination of copy and imagery also created a consistency in the response rates of advertising that never before existed. Creating advertising for products was always a hit-or-miss proposition until Hopkins revolutionized the advertising industry.

Selecting the right image for your ad can be up to 70 percent of the reason that someone clicks on it. Your image will make your ad stand out on the LinkedIn page and interrupt the viewer's attention. The image you choose must be relevant to your ad and to your offer. Deception may get viewers' attention and get them to click on your ad, but they will quickly become disappointed if your offer doesn't match the image.

Images of a real person—from the neck up—convert best on LinkedIn. The image size on the ad is only 50 by 50 pixels, so you don't have much real estate to work with. A simple headshot of a professional man or woman facing the camera works best. You don't want to use casual pictures of a guy in his baseball hat or a woman with a visor. You are targeting professional people on a business-oriented website, so you must choose appropriate photos.

I've done a lot of testing of images on ads in which I gave away white papers, and the results are not surprising. I've run the same ad headline and content and just changed the image in the ad. One ad had a picture of an average-looking professional woman. The second ad had an image of an average-looking professional man—the analyst who had written the white paper—and a third featured an image of the logo from the white paper. The ad with the woman received four times more clicks than those of the man or the logo. She had nothing to do with the ad or the white paper, but she had received more clicks.

The above result may sound sexist, but it's true that most of the time people will click on an ad with an image of a woman—even if she wasn't the author of the white paper. Recently, I ran the same three ads but changed the targeting from executives and managers to just a few LinkedIn Groups. The results changed dramatically. The ad with the picture of the analyst outperformed the other ads two to one. I'm assuming the people in the LinkedIn Groups were familiar with the analyst himself and for that reason clicked on his ad instead of the other ads.

FOLLOW EDITORIAL GUIDELINES

Be sure to adhere to LinkedIn's editorial guidelines because they approve every ad before it goes live. Here's a quick list of high-level guidelines for ads:

- Don't deceive or lie.
- Don't use nonstandard spelling, grammar, capitalization, punctuation, or repetition.
- Don't use inappropriate or unacceptable language.
- Don't deceive, confuse, or otherwise degrade the experience of members who click.
- Don't use trademarks that you aren't permitted to use.
- Don't use the LinkedIn name or logo.
- Don't use an ad to facilitate collection of members' data.

A/B SPLIT TESTING

I just showed you why it's important to always test your ads and measure the results according to the group you are targeting. You can never be 100 percent certain which headline, ad copy, or image will perform best. There are many factors that determine this, so you have to constantly test your ads and adjust accordingly.

Testing your ad combinations is commonly called A/B split testing. You are testing ad A against ad B to determine which one performs best. You always want to split-test different combinations of headlines, ad copy, and images until you find the highest converting combination. Once you know this result, use that ad as your control ad, and test new combinations of headlines, ad copy, and images until you beat your control ad (or not, as the case may be).

You never know what subtleties will make one ad perform better than another that is similar. Sometimes capitalizing every word works, and other times changing one word in the headline does the trick. Some things you can test in your ads are:

1. Create multiple ads for each campaign.
   - Use at least three variations of ads.
   - Try capitalizing every word in the headline and ad copy.
   - Try different calls to action.
2. You can create up to 15 ads per campaign and set different budgets and settings for each ad.
3. Ads that do best will start to be shown more often, or you can have all ads displayed equally.

Make sure you track your ads accurately so you know which ones are performing best. Your goal is to achieve the highest clickthrough rate (CTR) and conversion rate possible. The other important statistic to monitor is the number of impressions, which is the number of times your ads are displayed. You want your ads to be displayed as many times as possible, but they should be displayed to the appropriate audience so your CTR is highest, which reduces your cost per click (CPC).

TARGETING YOUR ADS

One of the most powerful features of LinkedIn advertising is your ability to target the audience where your ads will be displayed. You can create very specific ads for very specific demographics, so your response rate increases dramatically.

You can target your LinkedIn ads based on the following criteria:

- *Geography*. You can target specific regions, countries, states, and cities.
- *Companies*. You can target specific company names or categories of companies, including company size or by industry.
- *Job Title*. You can target specific job titles or categories of job titles, including job categories such as function or seniority.
- *Group*. You can display your ads only to specific LinkedIn Groups.
- *Gender*. You can display your ads to just men or women, as appropriate.
- *Age*. Display your ads to specific age groups.
- *LinkedIn Audience Network*. The LinkedIn Audience Network is a collection of partner websites that display LinkedIn Ads on their pages.

You are probably wondering how to determine where to find the demographic information about your target audience. LinkedIn provides that information for free in LinkedIn Groups. Join a group that is related to your industry or niche. In the right column of your group page you will see a widget, as shown in Figure 22–3.

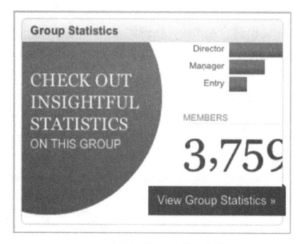

FIGURE 22–3. Group Statistics

Group Statistics is a gold mine of information if you want to run targeted ads. First of all, you can run one set of ads that targets your group, since they are all in your industry or niche. If you want to see the demographics of your group, View Group Statistics shows its seniority, function, location, and industry. This demographic information will let you create custom ad campaigns that should convert very well for you.

BIDDING

For each campaign, you set a payment method of cost per click (CPC) or cost per impression (CPM). You also set a bid for the maximum you're willing to pay for a click or for 1,000 impressions.

For CPC ads, you can enter a bid that's within the Suggested Bid Range. The Suggested Bid Range is an estimate of the current competing bids by other advertisers. The higher you bid within the range, the more likely it is for your ad to be shown and receive clicks. Once you become more familiar with how the bidding works, you can adjust your bids accordingly.

For CPM bidding, you enter the maximum you are willing to pay for 1,000 impressions of your ad. CPM bidding is different because you are paying for ad impressions, not clicks, while with CPC bidding you are paying for each click—not the number of impressions.

You should test CPC versus CPM bidding for your campaigns because sometimes you pay less for CPM bidding and get better results. This varies from campaign to campaign so you have to test it. If you are running a branding campaign to give your brand more exposure via maximum impressions and you don't care about the number of clicks, you should try CPM.

HOW TO MEASURE SUCCESS AND IMPROVE YOUR PERFORMANCE

It's important to define your advertising goals before creating your ad campaign. Clearly defined goals will help you create the right ads, target the right audience, and choose the best landing page.

- If your goal is to generate traffic to your website landing page at a certain cost per click (CPC), you can use the My Ad Campaigns section and Reporting section in LinkedIn Ads to track your performance. You can track the number of clicks you've received, which is the number of visitors to your website, and your total budget spent.
- If your goal is to generate leads, you need to track users' actions on your website using a web analytics tool like Google Analytics. Using web analytics, you can

Ad Name	Impressions	Clicks	CTR	Cost	Cost per Click (CPC)	Conversions	ROI
Ad 1							
Ad 2							
Ad 3							
Ad 4							

FIGURE 22–4. Ad Performance Tracking

track the number of web visits from LinkedIn, the number of conversions, and the conversion rate.

You can use a chart like the one in Figure 22-4 to manually track your ads and see which perform best. The chart shows you everything you need to know about your campaigns, including the number of conversions and your return on investment.

LINKEDIN SELF-SERVICE ADS

OK, now you know the basics of writing good ads, and you have some great resources that will make you an expert copywriter and ad writer. Let's explore LinkedIn Self-Service Ads and dig deeper into what it takes to write high-converting ads.

LinkedIn ads consist of the following components:

- Headline (up to 25 characters of text)
- Description (up to 75 characters of text)
- From: (your name or any company)
- Image: (50 x 50 pixel image)
- URL (website people visit once they click on your ad)

The headline and the image are the most important factors in your online ad. Most online advertising experts agree and say the headline can be 80 to 90 percent of your conversion rate. If you don't grab users' attention with a compelling headline or an eye-catching image, they'll never read the rest of your ad, let alone click on the link in your ad.

You could say the headline and image in your online ad is very similar to the title and cover of a book. Research has shown that the title of a book is one of the most important reasons people purchase a book. In 1924, F. Scott Fitzgerald wrote a book titled *Trimalchio in West Egg*, which was later retitled *The Great Gatsby*. Do you think the original title would have been dubbed a literary classic?

CONCLUSION

Online ads that convert best are relevant to the target audience and are written with clear, compelling words.

- Remember to use emotion-triggering words that grab the reader's attention in the headline.
- Make sure the description in your ad clearly describes the benefits of your offer.
- Use an image that readers will notice and is relevant to your offer.
- Always include a clear call to action like "download now" or "try it for 30 days" in your ad.
- Use special offers, trials, or free reports to entice them to click on your ad.

In the next chapter, we'll explore finding a job. You are likely a small-business owner and probably not looking for a job, but it's a good skill to know. If you understand the process of how others use LinkedIn to find a job, you'll be able to spot good talent more easily.

For additional updates and how-to videos, visit
www.tedprodromou.com/chapter22

Finding a Job on LinkedIn

Although this book is focused on LinkedIn for business owners and you probably aren't looking for a full-time job, you should always be prepared to do what you have to do to survive. The economy has been an absolute roller coaster over the past 15 years. We hit the highest of highs with the dotcom explosion, and we hit the lowest of lows with the economic collapse in 2008. Personally, my business collapsed twice in the past decade, and I had to give up my dream of owning my own business to return to the workforce full time to support my family. I had no choice because my business was focused on providing web marketing services to small businesses, and my clients either went out of business or stopped spending money completely when the economy tanked in 2008. I had to find a full-time job, or we would have faced foreclosure and bankruptcy. Luckily, I landed a great job, and while I miss the freedom and flexibility of owning my own business, the steady paycheck at this point in my life is just what the doctor ordered.

STARTING YOUR JOB SEARCH ON LINKEDIN

So, let's say you're looking for a job. I bet you joined LinkedIn because everyone says it's the best place to find a job. Almost every time I mention LinkedIn to someone, the person inevitably responds: "I signed up for

LinkedIn, but I never use it, because I'm not looking for a job" or "I signed up for LinkedIn a year ago to get a job, and I still don't have one." It seems like most people think LinkedIn is exclusively a job opportunity website like Monster.com. Of course I tell everyone that LinkedIn is a great job opportunity website—but it is so much more.

Yes, LinkedIn is a great place to find a job if you know what you are doing and you are willing to make the necessary effort. So many people think they just have to sign up for a LinkedIn account, and companies will magically find them and offer them a job. Well, I have some bad news for those folks: Just signing up for LinkedIn will not get them jobs. Like everything else in life, good things don't come to you unless you work for them. You need to put in the effort to find a job, whether it's on LinkedIn, another job website, or in person.

Finding a job is so much more than updating your resume, posting it on job websites, and responding to Craigslist ads. How many times have you applied for a job online that you knew you were perfect for, and yet you never heard back from the company? Most of the time, they don't even acknowledge they received your resume because it is so inundated with responses to their ads.

Standing Out Above the Crowd

To get a job in today's job market, you need to stand out above the crowd. You are competing against hundreds of applicants every time you apply for a job. You may be more qualified than most of the applicants, but somehow they get noticed by the employer and land the interview while your resume goes unnoticed. What are they doing that you aren't? Is their resume flashier than yours? Are they optimizing their resume, so it will get through the automated scanners that detect certain keywords? Do they know someone in the company who passed their resumes directly to the hiring managers?

The key to getting hired today is to catch the attention of the hiring manager. It's not about having more education or experience than other job applicants. Don't get me wrong. Education and experience are very important when you are looking for a new job. But there is so much more employers consider when they're looking to hire new employees. They are looking at the big picture, like your LinkedIn image where you demonstrate your skills and expertise in a variety of ways. You need to establish a presence on LinkedIn, as well as social media sites like Twitter, SlideShare, blogs, on article websites, and even YouTube.

Employers are looking for well-rounded, flexible people because jobs are so dynamic these days. Most jobs require a diverse skill set and adaptability because the business environment is changing so fast. The skills I use in my job as an online marketing and search engine optimization analyst didn't exist a few years ago. I had to learn these new skills to be qualified for my job, and these skills are changing constantly. In a few years, I will have to be an expert at an entirely different skill set because the tasks I do at work today will evolve into something completely different. I have no idea what skills I will be using in five years, but I know that the internet and online marketing will be very different. Google will probably be replaced by another company that doesn't even exist today. Employers are looking for employees who understand this and are willing to adapt quickly to the latest and greatest trends in their industry.

Who Are You Competing Against?

What can you do to rise above your competition for jobs? First of all, do you know who your competition is? What are their qualifications, experience, and skill sets that make them competitors when you're applying for a job? Why might they be more qualified than you for the position you are applying for? Let's go to LinkedIn and do a little research to find out who your competitors are and how you can rise above them.

Let's say you are looking for a position as a social media manager in a midsize business. This position is one of the hottest new jobs, and there are a lot of people competing for it. We should learn a lot from this example, since it's a job that didn't exist a few years ago, and it's an evolving career.

Let's start by searching for some job openings to see what qualifications these companies are looking for and comparing them with your skill set. This will tell you if you are qualified and what skills you need to learn to be a top candidate for an open position as a social media manager.

Go to the LinkedIn Search box, and in the dropdown menu, change People to Jobs. Let's start by searching just for "social media," so we don't limit our search results. You want to carefully review the qualifications and the responsibilities of the jobs you are interested in. Are you qualified? Can you quickly learn new skills you may be lacking? After reading the job responsibilities, is this a job you really want? Sometimes you have the skills for a position, but you don't like the responsibilities. Maybe the list of responsibilities is unfocused or includes tasks you don't want to perform. The good news is that there are plenty of jobs out there in high tech, so you can keep searching until you find the right job for you.

Below is a list of qualifications for a position as social media manager for a software company located in Silicon Valley. Competition for this job will be very stiff since Silicon Valley is full of social media experts, so you want to make sure you meet most, if not all, of the qualifications. Many times some of the qualifications are vague so you want to be sure to ask the hiring manager for clarification if you are lucky enough to get an interview. Let's go through these qualifications for the social media manager position and see if this is a job for you.

Job Qualifications

- Minimum of three to four years professional social media work experience, including demonstrated success using social media to grow a consumer or enterprise brand through creative, outside-of-the-box thinking that drives measurable results

- Strong project management or organizational skills

- In-depth knowledge and understanding of social media platforms and their respective participants (Facebook, LinkedIn, YouTube, Twitter, etc.) and how they can be integrated using tools and third-party applications

- Knowledge of blogging ecosystem relevant to Informatica's technology

- Experience using Radian6 preferred

- Team player, with the confidence to take the lead and guide other departments and team members when necessary

- Good technical understanding and can pick up new tools quickly

- Have a good knowledge of the principles of SEO

- Public relations, marketing, and community management experience a plus

- Candidates with past experience as a community manager are preferred; additionally, data integration and related industry experience are ideal

- A candidate's ability to forge strong connections cross-functionally and across business units will be key for success

- Advanced knowledge of how to leverage social networking sites, tools, plug-ins, video and photo-sharing sites, etc., is a plus

Most of these qualifications are very vague and full of jargon like "outside-of-the-box thinking," which you will see in many job descriptions. The good news is this is your first opportunity to rise above your competition! I'm sure you have some examples of times you "thought outside of the box" and created a unique and effective social media campaign. Of course you will add that successful "outside-of-the-box" campaign to your resume and to your LinkedIn profile, but to stand out, you need to show them the campaign in a creative way. You could create a YouTube video demonstrating how you executed the social media campaign. If the campaign is no longer active, you could create a narrated PowerPoint slideshow that explains the campaign in detail, including why you created the campaign, what you were promoting, and, of course, the fabulous results. Maybe your campaign resulted in 1,000 new Facebook likes, or 5,000 new Twitter followers. You can turn the narrated PowerPoint presentation into a YouTube video and promote the heck out of it on social media sites such as Twitter, Facebook,

LinkedIn, blogs, and other social media to help it go viral. You can measure the number of tweets, retweets, Facebook likes, and other social media measurements and share them in your PowerPoint and YouTube video. This demonstrates your ability to measure your social media activity, which is another requirement of the job. What would be more impressive than creating a successful social media campaign demonstrating your skills and creativity as part of your application process for the job?

Demonstrating your expertise in this manner gives you a huge advantage over your competitors. Submitting your resume with your education, qualifications, and experience has a fraction of the impact of creating your own multimedia social media campaign. Essentially, it becomes your video audition for the job, and it has the potential to grab the attention of the hiring manager if you do it correctly. If you can't catch the hiring manager's attention using social media, you need to rethink your desire to be a social media manager because that is the primary skill you need to succeed in the position.

Locking Down an Interview

OK, we know you are qualified for the position, and you've made a huge splash with your viral social media campaign—but that still may not be enough to get you an interview. As I mentioned before, competition is fierce for social media managers in Silicon Valley. Not only that, you may be competing against people from other areas, as companies are increasingly hiring remote employees. This means you are competing nationally—or even globally—for jobs, so you have to do everything you can to stand out.

Let's start by looking at the LinkedIn profiles of the top social media experts. They may not be in direct competition with you for this particular job, but if they are appearing at the top of a LinkedIn Search for "social media" you want to know how they got there.

Go back to the LinkedIn Search box, change the search type to People, and click on the Advanced link, so we can perform an Advanced People Search. Let's enter just "social media" in the job title and click Search to see who comes up. We'll leave the search filter on Relevance for now so we can see the most relevant search results. Figure 23–1 on page 236 shows our initial search results.

The first thing I notice about the top search results is that every social media expert is a Premium LinkedIn member and an OpenLink member. Remember, OpenLink members are open to receiving messages from any LinkedIn member, and they don't have to use InMail to reach out. Being a Premium LinkedIn member and using OpenLink should not affect your search rankings, but it does give people a great first impression of you. They see you are committed to LinkedIn and willing to pay for the enhanced features and

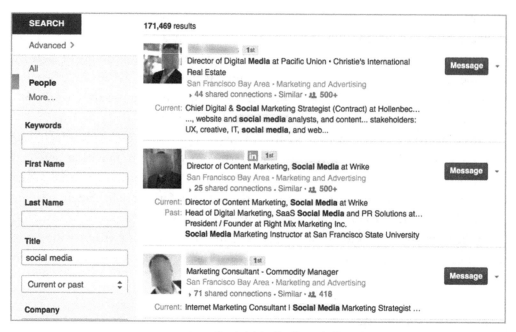

FIGURE 23-1. Social Media Search Results

networking capabilities. Being open to receiving messages from anyone tells everyone you are using LinkedIn to network with others to grow your professional network.

Notice the following common characteristics of the top search results:

- All the top search results use "social media" liberally in their Profile headline or in their current job title. If you view their full profile, you will see they use "social media" freely throughout their profile including their current and past position descriptions, their summary, and interests.

- All the top search results have at least 400 connections; this shouldn't affect their search ranking, but it shows viewers they are active LinkedIn members.

- Notice we have a lot of shared connections. This won't affect the search ranking, but it lets you know we have similar professional networks.

For this example, let's focus on the top search result, Tom Treanor, and dig into his profile to see if he is more qualified than you. Just because someone outranks you in a LinkedIn Search doesn't mean he is more qualified than you, but you can still learn a lot by reviewing his profile. You want to figure out what keywords, experience, or profile content made that person rise to the top of the search result, which is where you want to be. The best way to catch the attention of a hiring manager is to be one of the top search results for a job title.

My first impression of Tom's profile summary is very positive. The first thing I notice is his friendly profile picture. See his effective profile in Figure 23-2 on page 237.

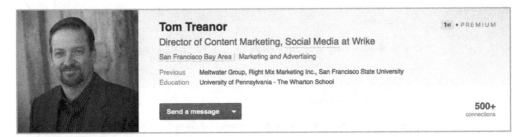

FIGURE 23–2. Tom Treanor Profile Snapshot

Tom makes it very clear that he does content marketing and social media by using his job title as his professional headline. I usually don't recommend using your job title as your professional headline, but in this case it works for me.

Let's dig deeper and see why Tom ranks so well for the search term "social media." Figure 23–3 shows Tom's summary with the term "social media."

FIGURE 23–3. Tom Treanor Profile Summary

Now I'm going to show you one of the secrets to ranking well in LinkedIn search results. As I mentioned in Chapter 8, "LinkedIn Search," the LinkedIn search algorithm isn't as sophisticated as the Google search algorithm, making it fairly easy to rank well.

The secret is to use your keywords in your job titles. The more job titles you have containing your keywords, the better your chance to rank well for those keywords. Take a look at Tom's experience in Figure 23–4 on page 238, and see how many times he has "social media" in his job titles and job descriptions.

Tom does a brilliant job establishing himself as an industry leader and expert in his field, telling you how he can help you, showing who he's helped in the past, and letting

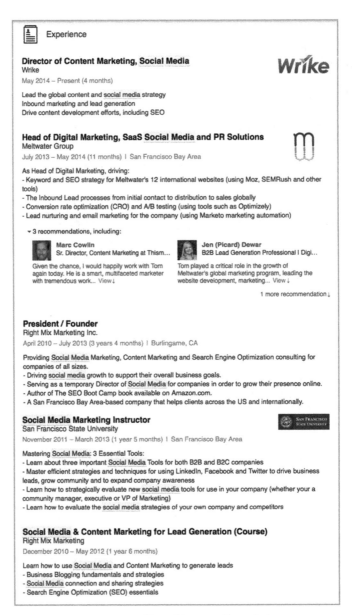

FIGURE 23–4. Tom Treanor Experience

you see his social media experience. This is the easiest way to rank well on LinkedIn. If you are a social media consultant, you need to create a profile as good or better than this in order stand out as an expert in your field.

If standing out as an expert is your goal, you need to demonstrate how you are a leader in your industry. Here are a few things that help: Join industry associations; become a board member in your associations; start a Meetup (www.meetup.com) group, if you want to attract small business owners; write a book; or become a public speaker to get your message out there.

Continue reviewing every section of your competitor's profile and see how you can improve yours and stand out. Don't make things up or exaggerate facts in your LinkedIn profile to look better than your competitors. Be honest and leverage your accomplishments. Set long-term goals and make a plan to increase your visibility in your industry so you will eventually be considered a leader in your field. Using the combination of LinkedIn and social media, you can quickly become known as a thought leader.

You get the idea. You know your top competitors, so do some surveillance work and check up on their online activity. Document what your competitors are doing well to promote their businesses online, and also note what they aren't doing so well. Take note of their weaknesses so you can stand out where they don't. With a clear plan of action and some hard work, you will eventually become a leader in your industry, and your business will never be the same. Employers or clients will be pursuing you instead of the other way around.

ACTION STEPS

We've covered a lot of material in this chapter, so in this section we will help you create your plan of action. The internet and social media make it relatively easy for anyone to get noticed and stand out above their competition. The key to success is to consistently post content online on LinkedIn, your blog, your website, Twitter, or Facebook. You can also be a guest blogger, write articles, and participate in LinkedIn Publishing and Groups. Sharing your expertise on a daily basis will help you rise in the LinkedIn and Google search results, which will make you appear as an expert in your field. Once you have reached that level, you will never have to look for a job again. Great opportunities will come your way on a regular basis, and you will have your choice of jobs.

Here is the process I use to identify my ideal job, the company I want to work for, and how I'm going to update my LinkedIn profile to attract attention from my target employers:

1. Identify your ideal job in great detail.
    a. What is your job title?
    b. What are your job responsibilities?
    c. Do you manage others?
    d. What is your boss like?
    e. What are your co-workers like?
    f. What is the company culture?

    g. Can you work from home or do you have to commute?

    h. Describe any other characteristics that make this your ideal job.

2. Identify the top five companies you want to work for.

3. Complete your LinkedIn profile! Fill out every detail of your profile, including the skills and accomplishments that are relevant to the jobs are you are pursuing. Go back and read Chapter 4, "Supercharging Your LinkedIn Profile," to make sure your profile is optimized so you will appear when people search for your expertise.

4. In your profile headline, add a statement that you are currently seeking a position in (fill in the job title you are looking for). Say something like, "Currently pursuing a senior management position in the biotech industry." The more detailed you can make it, the better.

5. Get at least three excellent references for each position you've held in the past ten years. The more excellent, relevant references you can get, the better. Coach the people you reach out to for the references, and let them know what skills and accomplishments you want them to highlight. We covered Recommendations in great detail in Chapter 10, "Giving and Receiving LinkedIn Recommendations," so feel free to go back and read Chapter 10 again to refresh your memory. Excellent references will open a lot of doors for you.

6. Add your LinkedIn badge on your website and blog to let people know you are an active LinkedIn member.

7. Add your Twitter account to your LinkedIn profile so your tweets will appear in your LinkedIn status.

8. Add your blog URL to your LinkedIn profile. Blog at least three times a week about current events in your industry to show hiring managers that you know what's happening. Don't just write a summary about current events. Give your opinion about the current events, and make predictions about industry trends so you establish yourself as a thought leader in your industry. Read the blogs of thought leaders such as Seth Godin or Chris Brogan to see how they convey their message. Create your unique style so you can differentiate yourself from other thought leaders in your field. Always tweet a link to your blog post to drive traffic to your blog.

9. Add the books you are reading to your LinkedIn profile, and share your thoughts about what you are reading with others. Read at least two books per month that are related to your industry or about business in general. Don't just post the books you are reading or want to read. Make comments on the books you list, and tell people why you are reading the books. Don't forget to let people know what you thought of the book after you finish it!

10. Add SlideShare content to your LinkedIn profile and share your best presentations. Create new presentations about relevant topics in your industry.

11. Upgrade your LinkedIn account to the Job Seeker Basic, Job Seeker, or Job Seeker Plus level. This lets people know you are looking for a job and gives you numerous tools to help you with your job search. I'll describe the various Job Seeker packages in detail at the end of this chapter.

Now that your profile is in order, it's time to start looking for your ideal job. I've covered LinkedIn Search and Advanced Search techniques numerous times in this book so you should be very familiar with them by now. If you are not familiar with them, what are you waiting for? Becoming an expert at LinkedIn Search is your key to leveraging LinkedIn to find a job, finding hot leads, reconnecting with colleagues, and building your professional network that will carry you to success. Start practicing your LinkedIn Searches now!

Create a detailed strategy for growing your professional network to help you achieve your career goals. Search for thought leaders and key decision-makers in your industry and connect with them. Don't be afraid to reach out to them or ask one of your connections for an introduction. You would be surprised how approachable many industry leaders are if you simply ask. Being associated with the leaders of your industry gives people a better impression of you. Remember, quality over quantity is best when you are growing your professional network. Don't connect with people unless you have a specific reason to add them to your network. LinkedIn is not a popularity contest where the person with the most connections wins. You want to connect with the right people, not with people who can't help you achieve your career goals.

Sometimes you aren't sure if you should connect with someone who is not in your industry or you may not see immediate value in connecting with them. See whom they are connected to and see if they are actively networking on LinkedIn. For example, it's OK to connect with someone who isn't in your industry or not a key executive, if they are connected with a key individual in your industry whom you want to meet through an introduction.

LET'S FIND A JOB!

I'm assuming your LinkedIn profile is at the All Star level, including your excellent recommendations that make you sound like the best thing since sliced bread. If your profile is not at the All Star level, stop reading right now and get to work on it, now! I know I keep harping on this fact, but it's so important to present a great first impression when a prospective hiring manager looks at your profile. If they see an incomplete or unprofessional profile, they're going to click right by you and move onto the next candidate.

In case you didn't know, many hiring managers search LinkedIn and monitor their industry-related groups and LinkedIn Pulse for exceptional people. It's not hard to spot the A-list players in your industry when they answer questions in LinkedIn Groups or write exceptional articles using LinkedIn Publisher. There are many wannabes that think answering hundreds of questions a week makes them more qualified for a job, but you will notice their answers are shallow and lack expertise. These people don't have time to answer in depth because they're answering a question every two minutes to meet their 150 questions per day quota.

When a hiring manager sees an exceptional person on LinkedIn, he will proactively reach out to this person and court her. Many times, a hiring manager will hire an exceptional person whether he has a job opening or not. Great companies proactively hire the best talent when they are available. If you haven't read the book *Good to Great* by Jim Collins, then make it your next read (after you finish this one, of course). In his benchmark book, Collins describes great companies as hiring the right people first, then putting them in their positions. He says, "Get the right people on the bus first, then decide where the bus is going." Most successful companies believe hiring the best people is the key to success. Microsoft overpaid for software engineers in the 1980s to get the very best. Today Google, Facebook, and other internet companies are paying premium wages and huge stock options to attract the very best talent.

Now do you understand why I keep harping on you to finish your LinkedIn profile? Hiring managers may be looking at your profile this very minute, so you want to impress the hell out of them on first glance; it may be your only one, so it had better be good.

Remember, you can see who has viewed your profile by looking at the Who's Viewed Your Profile widget in your sidebar. You see either limited information about who viewed your profile with your free LinkedIn account, or the full list of people if you are a LinkedIn Premium member. The full list is included with your paid Business account as well as the Job Seeker and Job Seeker Plus accounts. This is yet another reason for you to upgrade! If you are serious about wanting to get the most out of LinkedIn—whether you are looking for a job or building your professional network—you need to invest in a Premium account. It's a relatively small investment of a few hundred dollars a year, and it lets people know you are a serious networker.

When you are searching for a job and you find the perfect one, you will want to learn something about the hiring manager to determine if he or she is someone you want to work for. Once you click on the hiring manager's profile, it will register in their Who's Viewed Your Profile widget and she will most likely click on your profile link to check you out. Once she sees your outstanding LinkedIn profile that knocks her socks off, she's going to reach out to you. That's why it's important for you to let her see your full

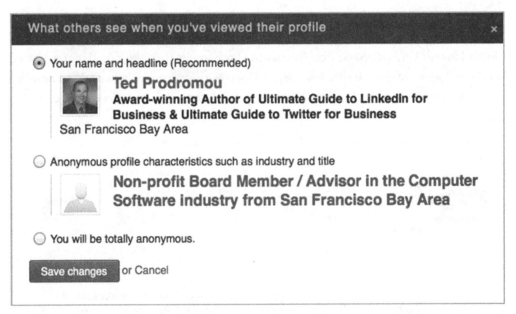

FIGURE 23–5. The Three Configuration Options for the What Others See When You've Viewed Their Profile

profile summary when she clicks on your link. Figure 23–5 shows you what she will see after clicking on your link.

It's hard to understand why anyone would want to remain completely anonymous or just show the company name in this situation. You are trying to find a job, so you want to be as accessible as possible so hiring managers can find you. If you remain anonymous, they'll never know you are a top performer in your industry and you are looking for a new opportunity.

You know what position you are looking for and the top five companies you want to work for, so let's start searching. First, let's see if any of those companies you want to work for have any job openings for you. Let's stay with the social media manager position we discussed earlier and assume the top five companies you want to work for are:

1. Google
2. Facebook
3. Salesforce
4. Cisco
5. Intuit

These are all great companies to work for, and you wouldn't mind being part of any of them. Your decision will mainly come down to your supervisor, the team you will be working with, the salary, the benefits, and perhaps other factors, such as the commute.

For now, let's assume the other factors won't be an issue—you can work virtually or relocate, if necessary—and you want to do some research on these five dream employers. Go to LinkedIn Advanced Search (you know how to get there by now!), enter "social media manager" in the job title field, select Cisco as the company, and click on Search.

As you see in Figure 23-6, there is one open job for a social media manager at this time.

FIGURE 23–6. Search Results for a Social Media Manager Job at Cisco

LinkedIn has partnered with Simply Hired, a job search network, to expand the LinkedIn Jobs Network. LinkedIn first searches the LinkedIn Jobs Network, and, if it doesn't find a match, it searches the Simply Hired partner job site. In this case, it looks like there's only one open social media manager position today at Cisco. Notice the job title is "Social Media Marketing Manager," not just "Social Media Manager." This is why you need to experiment with your search terms so you capture all open positions. You can also modify the job title to just "social media" to expand the search, since there may be a similar job title. You can also leave the title field blank and enter "social media" in the keywords. Try different combinations of searches because companies use different terminology in their job descriptions and titles. Sometimes you need to get creative, as job titles and job descriptions vary from company to company.

The job posting makes it easy to connect with the job poster who usually works in the HR department. That's great, but to cut through the clutter you need connect directly with the hiring manager because 145 other people already applied for this job. The cool thing about searching for jobs on LinkedIn is the way they help you connect with the hiring manager. In this case, four of my first-degree connections work at Cisco. I can reach out to my first-degree connections to see if they know the hiring manager. I can get feedback on the hiring manager and get my resume to the top of the pile if my connection knows him or her. If my first-degree connections don't know the hiring manager, they may know some of my second- and third-level connections who can connect me with the hiring manager. This is professional networking at its finest! This is so much easier than randomly submitting your resume to Craigslist ads and job sites and praying they'll see your resume. Figure 23–7 shows you the detailed job posting.

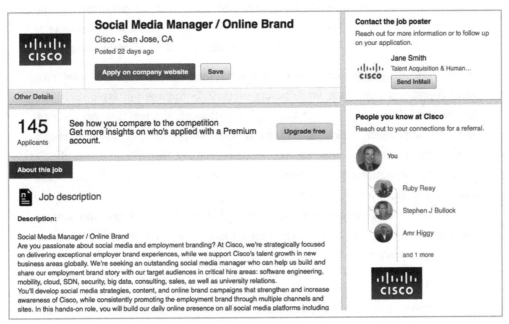

FIGURE 23–7. Details for the Social Media Manager Job at Cisco

Let's take a look at the job posting for Cisco's social media marketing manager position to see if it's a fit.

R915797 Social Media Manager/Online Brand

Cisco Systems—San Jose, CA

Job Description

Social Media Manager/Online Brand

Are you passionate about social media and employment branding? At Cisco, we're strategically focused on delivering exceptional employer brand experiences, while we support Cisco's talent growth in new business areas globally. We're seeking an outstanding social media manager who can help us build and share our employment brand story with our target audiences in critical hire areas: software engineering, mobility, cloud, SDN, security, big data, consulting, sales, as well as university relations.

You'll develop social media strategies, content, and online brand campaigns that strengthen and increase awareness of Cisco, while consistently promoting the employment brand through multiple channels and sites. In this hands-on role, you will build our daily online presence on all social media platforms including Facebook, Twitter, Pinterest, Google+, LinkedIn, SlideShare, Instagram, blogs, and others. You will create engaging content that's tailored to each social channel and work with Talent Acquisition, HR, Hiring Managers, and Marketing to develop and maintain a consistent employment brand voice. You'll track KPIs and report out on performance. Your in-depth understanding of social media best practices and the ability to implement new solutions will allow us to build meaningful relationships with new talent populations.

To be successful, you already need to be a social media maverick with a solid social network and social influence, while having successfully managed multiple social sites (at one time). You must have outstanding follow-through in a real-time environment, and have experience executing day-to-day site management, a social marketing background, as well as experience writing online content that will engage and build strong talent communities. Not only are you detailed-oriented, you're also action-minded, and you have a reputation for thinking outside the box when faced with complex global employment brand challenges that require a strategic and forward-thinking mindset. You also must also be a great manager of your time in an organization with a large remote workforce.

Job Requirements

- Seasoned experience implementing and maintaining complex social media strategies that increase brand awareness and user engagement

- Experience developing and facilitating online employer brand strategies, building talent networks, and driving engagement (producing results)

- Strong project management, follow-through, and decision-making skills

- Ability to multitask and complete projects accurately and on time

- Flex easily and effectively manage as well as lead change

- Deep understanding of social media best practices, online marketing, and recruitment/candidate attraction trends

- Four-plus years of in-depth, day-to-day management of all social media platforms (Twitter, Facebook, LinkedIn, Google, Instagram, Pinterest, YouTube, SlideShare), preferably in a high-tech business environment

- Background includes seven-plus years developing content strategies tailored to specific marketing channels; focused on building online communities

- Daily use of Hootsuite (or similar), editorial content calendaring, and blogging (e.g., WordPress)

- Competitive benchmarking, research, and analytics skills

- Actively use and understand the following in current role: Google AdWords, Google Analytics, SEO, SEM, A/B testing, PPC, and CTR

- Experience implementing emerging social media solutions

- Creative, innovative, and attentive to details

- Strong writing and social media content creation skills

- Exceptional communication and influence skills, as well as experience educating others on social media best practices

- BA/BS degree

#socialmedia

This looks like a pretty standard job description for a social media manager. You need to be well-versed in using social media platforms, such as Twitter, YouTube, Facebook, LinkedIn, and all the other popular social media channels. You need to use and understand Google AdWords, Google Analytics, SEO, SEM, and A/B split testing. They're looking for creativity, initiative, and the ability to manage the day-to-day activities of the social media team. I don't see any big red flags in this job description, so I think it's time to move to the next step, contacting the hiring manager.

Reaching Out to the Hiring Manager

It's not always easy to find out the name of the hiring manger, but I'll show you some tricks that may help. For this job posting on LinkedIn, you can see who posted the job in the right column of the page. See Figure 23–8 to see the Contact the Job Poster widget that shows who posted this job.

FIGURE 23–8. Contact the Job Poster Widget

In this case, Jane Smith is a third-degree connection to us. The most obvious option is to send Jane an InMail to learn more about the position, and maybe she will be willing to provide you with the name of the hiring manager. Some companies are very open and will tell you who right away, while other companies share that information only with people who make it past the initial screening process. Every company is different, and there is no rule of thumb how it will respond.

Before we send Jane an InMail, let's do some exploring to see if we can find this information on our own. By the way, if you don't care about the name of the hiring manager, you can go right to the Apply on Company Website button and apply right now. Most of the time you won't know the hiring manager in a huge company like Cisco, so it doesn't matter. If you have friends who work at Cisco, they may know the hiring manager and they'll warn you if it's a person you won't want to work for. If they do know the hiring manager and have positive things to say about him, they may be able to pass your resume on to him and put in a good word.

Let's take a look at Jane's profile to see if we're connected to anyone who can connect us with her in order to find out more about this job opening and the hiring manager. Figure 23–9 on page 249 shows us how we are connected to Jane or if any of our first- or second-degree connections are connected with her. It looks like we have no connections who can connect us directly to Jane.

At this point you have two options. You can send Jane an InMail to introduce yourself and learn more about the job, or you can click on the Apply on Company Website button and apply for it. I recommend the former for three reasons: First, when you send an InMail to someone, there is a very high chance you will receive a response from a recruiter, which increases your InMail rating and benefits you when you send future InMails; second, the recipient of the InMail knows it cost you money to send that InMail, so they know you are serious about the position; last, but not least, getting to know the recruiter before you apply for the position almost guarantees he or she will take a longer look at your application. Applying blindly, without reaching out to the recruiter or hiring manager first, is almost the same as blindly applying to jobs from Craigslist ads.

Before you send that InMail to Jane, let's check one more thing. I know you think I'm teasing you, but this is an important step. Let's click on the Apply on Company Website button and take a look at the job posting on the Cisco website to see if we can learn more about the position before reaching out to Jane.

The job posting on the Cisco website is exactly the same as the posting on LinkedIn, so we don't know which department this position resides in or the name of the hiring manager. These are good questions to ask Jane in the InMail because it shows her you've researched the job and have some very relevant questions. However, there is one fact on

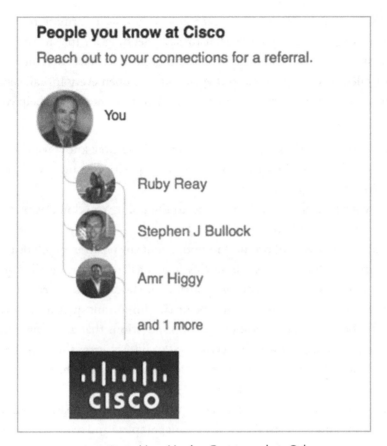

FIGURE 23–9. How You're Connected to Others

the Cisco website that we didn't see on the LinkedIn website. Figure 23–10 shows the job is located in San Jose, California, but there is an alternate work location in Richardson, Texas.

The fact there are two potential work locations suggests that this may be a job you can work from any town or city and telecommute. Many Cisco employees telecommute, which is a huge benefit. Not having to commute to and from work is priceless to someone with infants or school-age children at home. You can ask Jane about this when you reach out to her via InMail. The more relevant questions you can ask, the better. It shows you are doing your homework before you apply for the job. This gives you an advantage over the candidates who did not reach out in advance.

Job Title	Area of Interest	Primary Work Location	Alternate Work Locations ▲
Social Media Marketing Manager	Marketing	UNITED STATES.CALIFORNIA.SAN JOSE	"Richardson Texas"

FIGURE 23–10. The Primary and Alternate Work Locations

It looks like you aren't going to learn any additional information about the job online, so it's time to write your InMail to Jane. Sending an InMail to a recruiter is relatively easy because you should have a 100 percent open rate. Recruiters are always looking for talent to place in jobs so they're going to open every InMail sent to them, unless it has a horrible or offensive subject line. Here are some tips to help you write an InMail to a recruiter:

- Introduce yourself immediately, and let the recruiter know which job you are inquiring about. Include the job number or requisition number with the exact job title listed in the job posting.
- Keep your correspondence short and to the point. You don't want to waste the recruiter's time with idle chatter.
- Be curious and ask important questions about the position or job responsibilities that aren't included in the job posting. Don't ask too many detailed questions in the first correspondence because your intent should be to start a dialogue with the recruiter. Ask no more than one or two important questions in your initial InMail. Be careful not to ask very obvious questions that are answered in the job posting because it shows the recruiter you did not carefully read the entire job description. Remember, you want to start a dialogue with the recruiter so she can get to know you and remember you.
- Refer the recruiter to your LinkedIn profile so she can learn more about you. Since your LinkedIn profile is 100 percent complete and ready to knock her socks off, she should be sufficiently impressed.
- Follow up with the recruiter in a timely manner after she responds to you. Get back to her as soon as possible—definitely within 24 hours—to show her that you are a responsible person.
- If you are interested in the position, let the recruiter know you are interested and will be applying for the job online. Send her your resume and any other information she may request from you.
- Make sure you follow up with the recruiter a day or two after you apply for the position to let her know your application has been submitted. Also thank her for her time.

Reaching Out to Your Connections

I'm assuming you reached out to your first-degree connections at the company you're thinking of applying to see how they feel about the company and what they like about their job. It's always good to get feedback from the company's current employees to make sure the company culture is right for you. If you haven't reached out to your first-degree connections, this is a good time to contact them. Let them know you are thinking of applying for the position, and see if they know anyone in that department who can put in a good word for you. Since you've reached out to the recruiter and applied for the job, you know more about the position and which department the job reports to. Get as much information as you can about the department, other people who work on the social media team, and any other relevant information that may help you during the interview process. The more you know, the better prepared you will be for the interview process. Also, by learning about the department members and who's on the team, you can reach out to them in advance and familiarize them with your name and background, which will give you a leg up during the hiring process.

If your first-degree connections refer you to others in the company and help you get your foot in the door, don't forget to thank them for their effort. Even if you don't get the job, show your gratitude and offer to help them in the future.

Keep Going!

That seems like a lot of work to apply for one job, but that's how it works these days. You have to be proactive and aggressively go after the jobs you want. Being aggressive doesn't mean being annoying and bothering recruiters and hiring managers. Show them you are interested and keep in touch with them, but don't overdo it or you will ruin any relationship you have established.

Now that you applied for one job, go back to LinkedIn Job Search and keep looking. Try different keywords and job titles and follow the same process you just completed. Keep track of your activity in a spreadsheet so you know when you reached out to a recruiter, when you applied for the job, every time you followed up with her, and when you interviewed for the job. Also include any appropriate notes from your correspondence with the company, so you look and sound organized.

Keep following this process, and you will have the job of your dreams in no time. Don't get discouraged if you have to apply and interview over and over. Stay positive and keep networking. Persistence is the key to success.

JOB SEEKER PREMIUM

LinkedIn offers three premium packages called Job Seeker Basic, Job Seeker, and Job Seeker Plus. It can't be overstated: If you are serious about finding a job, you need to invest in yourself. The Job Seeker Basic, Job Seeker, and Job Seeker Plus give you additional tools that will accelerate your job search. I know most of you hesitate when it comes to paying extra when you get so many fantastic tools for free. The Job Seeker Plus subscription is $59.95 a month or $539.55 (25 percent off the monthly rate) for the entire year at once. If you are looking for a $100,000+ salaried job, don't you think it's worth investing $120 for a couple of months of the Job Seeker Plus subscription to get you a great job faster? That's an investment of one-tenth of 1 percent of your annual salary.

What You Get with Job Seeker and Job Seeker Plus

Here's what you get with your Premium Job Seeker packages so you can decide which package is best for you. Figure 23–11 shows the benefits of each package. Currently, I am a business member, and I receive some features that help with searching for jobs. Personally I'm not sure why you would invest in an Annual package because it shouldn't take you an entire year to find a job—even in today's economy—if you follow my approach.

There are many great features included in your free LinkedIn account when you are searching for a job. Each premium level gives you additional features, helping you find your dream job. Below is a list of the features included with the Premium Job Seeker accounts.

Compare Plans	Free Your Current Plan	Job Seeker Basic	Job Seeker	Job Seeker Plus
Pricing: Annual I Monthly		US$19.99/MO¹ Start Now	US$29.99/MO¹ Start Now	US$59.99/MO¹ Start Now
Get in touch				
InMail Messages Send direct messages to recruiters on LinkedIn. Response guaranteed.²			3 per month	10 per month
Who's Viewed Your Profile See the list of people interested in your profile.	Limited	✓	✓	✓
Get noticed				
Featured Applicant Move your job applications to the top of the recruiter's list.		✓	✓	✓
Premium Badge Stand out in search results with a premium icon on your profile.		✓	✓	✓
Get premium insights				
Applicant Insights See how you compare to other applicants for any job on LinkedIn.		✓	✓	✓
Salary Data See detailed salary info for each job.		✓	✓	✓
Job Seeker Group and Webinar Get support and advice on landing your dream job.		✓	✓	✓

FIGURE 23–11. Job Seeker Basics, Job Seeker, and Job Seeker Plus Comparison

■ *InMails.* This is a great tool for reaching out to others, but you can usually connect with someone you don't know through a first- or second-degree connection or by joining groups. I rarely have to use InMails to connect with others.

■ *Who's viewed your profile.* Viewing the full list is included in every package, including your business account.

■ *Featured applicant.* This option moves your job application ahead of nonpremium applicants. How valuable is that?

■ *Premium badge.* You can display a badge in your profile telling viewers you are looking for a job, and you'll stand out from other applicants.

■ *Applicant insights.* This feature lets you compare yourself to the other candidates to see where you stand in the application process.

■ *Salary data.* This is very useful information if you are looking for a job that pays more than $100,000 a year. Usually you can estimate what salaries will be based on the job title and responsibilities, though not always.

■ *Exclusive access to the job seeker community.* This is a nice benefit because the community can give you the additional support you may need to get a job. The community will help review your resume and your LinkedIn Profile; they will also give you interviewing tips and help cheer you up when you get discouraged.

■ *Job seeking on LinkedIn webinar.* You get great tips about using LinkedIn tools to find your perfect job.

CONCLUSION

As you see, there are some nice features and benefits in upgrading to the Job Seeker Premium packages. I'll let you decide which one is best for you. I may sound like I'm a salesman for LinkedIn, but I'm not. The Job Seeker Premium package is only $59.95 per month and one you should strongly consider, if your financial situation allows it. Most people are able to find a job in a couple of months, so the $120 investment is well worth it.

In the next chapter, we reach the end of this book but the beginning of a new phase of your career. If you implement just a portion of what you've learned in this book, your business will never be the same.

For additional updates and how-to videos, visit
www.tedprodromou.com/chapter23

LinkedIn Success Stories

While LinkedIn is growing by leaps and bounds, most members use the site very infrequently. I recently read a statistic on Social Media Examiner that the average LinkedIn member approximately spends only 17 minutes a month on LinkedIn.

Many of my clients and students tell me they don't know what to do on LinkedIn. Many still think LinkedIn is a site you use only when you're looking for a new job. LinkedIn has become THE place to find a new job or new employees if you're looking to hire, but there are so many other opportunities, as I've demonstrated throughout this book.

I decided to interview a few business owners who use LinkedIn daily and let them share their challenges, solutions, and results with you. Many of these business owners have had tremendous success while others are just seeing the benefits of LinkedIn (thanks to attending my training classes) and are seeing positive results quickly.

DAVE KERPEN, FOUNDER AND CEO OF LIKEABLE LOCAL

Dave Kerpen is the founder and CEO of Likeable Local, a social media software company serving small businesses, as well as the chairman and former CEO of Likeable Media, an award-winning social media and word-of-mouth marketing firm with triple-digit revenue growth for four consecutive years.

Following a sponsored wedding which raised over $100,000 including $20,000 for charity, Dave and his wife Carrie started and transformed theKbuzz (founded in 2007) into Likeable, one of Facebook's Top 65 Preferred Developer Consultants as well as the only three-time WOMMY Award winner for excellence from the Word of Mouth Marketing Association (WOMMA) and one of the 500 fastest-growing private companies in the U.S., according to *Inc.* magazine, for both 2011 and 2012.

The Challenge

Dave didn't have a specific challenge to solve when he joined LinkedIn in 2008. Since he owned a couple of social media companies and a social media agency, he thought he should join LinkedIn since it was an up-and-coming social media community.

The Result

Dave was invited to be a LinkedIn Influencer in 2013 and is one of the most popular Influencers. Dave has the second most popular article ever posted on LinkedIn with over 2.7 million views in a year and a half. Today almost 500,000 people follow Dave on LinkedIn, giving him tremendous visibility.

Dave's activity on LinkedIn has resulted in over a million dollars in revenue for the Likeable brands, and he has established himself as one of the most reputable social media experts.

Dave spends most of his time on LinkedIn through his mobile device and checks in periodically throughout the day. He checks comments on his articles and other articles that he has commented on. He typically shares one to two content items per day and checks the LinkedIn profiles of people he is meeting with during the day. He spends about one hour a week writing an article to post on the Publisher platform. Overall, Dave doesn't spend that much time on LinkedIn every day, but he maximizes the time he does spend.

KEVIN KNEBL, SOCIAL SELLING AND RELATIONSHIP MARKETING SPEAKER, AUTHOR, TRAINER, AND COACH

Kevin feels blessed to be The Most Recommended Business Speaker in the World among over 281,298 Business Speakers Worldwide (LinkedIn 2014). He speaks, trains, and coaches internationally on social selling, relationship marketing, networking, LinkedIn, and personal development from a relational perspective. His speaking and training style has been described as a blend of comedian, therapist, and stimulating teacher. Individuals and organizations significantly grow their networks, businesses, and revenues through his dynamic, inspirational, and humorous trainings, webinars, workshops, and individual and group coaching.

Kevin has over 1,600 client recommendations on LinkedIn, which is among the most, if not the most, out of the more than 330,000,000 LinkedIn users worldwide.

The Challenge

Kevin doesn't have a business challenge at this time because he was one of the original LinkedIn members and took full advantage of the opportunity. In fact, Kevin has too many opportunities at this time because he used LinkedIn to establish himself as one of the top authorities in his niche.

The Solution

Kevin works with companies like Transamerica, *The Wall Street Journal*, Standard and Poor's, State Farm, and other large companies in the financial services industry. He teaches them how to use social media, including LinkedIn, to engage prospects and increase their sales. He stresses that social media is not a sales tool. It is a tool to build relationships, which result in more sales.

Kevin's philosophy begins with being nice and helping people, which leads to stronger relationships and long-term clients. People live in either the world of competition or creation. You can look at other companies and view them as a competitor, where you are always fighting and struggling against each other. You could also choose to look from the perspective of creation, where you work together with your competition. Instead of fighting and backstabbing, you work together so both companies succeed.

Kevin starts every day by asking himself "Who can I add value to today?" He looks to help as many people as possible every day, with no expectation of anything in return. He truly lives the belief that the more you give the more you receive in life and business.

The Result

As I mentioned, Kevin has more business than he can handle at this time because he's such a generous person. By focusing on building relationships and adding value to others, you, too, can have more business than you can handle.

JONATHAN POWELL, SENIOR MANAGING PRINCIPAL OF CEG WORLDWIDE

CEG Worldwide takes a unique approach to delivering solutions to financial advisors and the institutions that serve those advisors. Its proprietary empirical research, combined with the experience of its highly successful principals, has shaped the company's thinking, practices, and programs in rich and meaningful ways. No other organization offers CEG Worldwide's combination of services.

Jonathan Powell's expertise in developing top-performing financial advisors is a great asset to the clients he serves through CEG Worldwide. Working with many of the nation's top financial firms, he enjoys helping financial advisors transform their professional and personal lives by implementing CEG Worldwide's research-backed principles.

Powell has hired and coached hundreds of the industry's top financial advisors—in multiple distribution channels—for more than 25 years. After starting his career as an independent financial planner in the San Francisco Bay area, he went on to spend more than two decades with Citigroup before deciding to pursue his passion for training and coaching.

The Challenge

Many financial advisors struggle to find new clients and grow their practice. They are experts at managing money, but they don't know how to market and sell their services.

The Solution

CEG Worldwide offers a full range of coaching solutions for financial advisors and their firms. They work with financial advisors who are already successful and want to become an elite financial advisor.

Jonathan uses LinkedIn to find prospects for his coaching programs, spending an average of 30 to 60 minutes every morning, which results in two to five constructive sales conversations each week with some of the top 5 percent of financial advisors throughout North America, Europe, Australia, and New Zealand. Each day, Jonathan receives five to seven connection requests, which he vets carefully. When he accepts a connection request, he takes a few minutes and sends them a personal message thanking them for connecting and invites them to have a short check-in call to get to know each other. As new leads come into the CEG Worldwide website, Jonathan reviews their LinkedIn profile to see if they're a fit and invites them to connect if he feels they are a potential client. These activities result in three to four sales conversations per day, all resulting from his 30- to 60-minute morning routine.

ANDY PETERSON, DIRECTOR OF BUSINESS DEVELOPMENT OF KAHUNA ACCOUNTING

Following a lifelong dream to be a pilot, Andy was able to pursue that with experience as a flight instructor, charter pilot, and corporate pilot. Shortly after Y2K, his position was eliminated, and an opportunity presented itself for him to manage an HVAC distribution warehouse and provide technical support to HVAC technicians out in the field. After a couple of years, another opportunity presented itself to manage a Dish Network installation team specializing in multifamily units. Shortly after joining, it was decided to dissolve this business, and Andy was absorbed into the parent company that built and managed website development and business applications on the web. He became the general operations manager, responsible for client acquisition and overseeing the translation of technical needs into more easily understood terms for clients to provide feedback in project development. Most recently, he was provided the opportunity to join a team focused on small business development acceleration. His focus now is on business development, identifying markets, clients, and collaborators to join in helping the small business community, with a current emphasis in outsourced bookkeeping services.

Kahuna Accounting provides outsourced bookkeeping for small businesses across the nation. For business owners who have too much on their plate, its professional staff of accountants provide bank reconciliations and key financial reports, so entrepreneurs can know what is happening with their business in real time.

The primary market Kahuna Accounting serves is solo and small-firm attorneys.

The Challenge

Being a new solution and a new name in the solo/small-firm market, Kahuna Accounting's biggest challenge was building its credibility. Attorneys have to know they can trust the company to consider it for their accounting needs. In addition, Kahuna Accounting has the challenge to educate its clients about what is possible, because many law firms are unfamiliar with the concept of outsourcing bookkeeping and cloud-computing accounting in general.

The Solution

Andy found that the solution to his company's challenges was to meet key influencers in the market and ask the right questions. LinkedIn provides an avenue for his company to learn from experienced experts in law practice management, and by understanding the needs of the market, it has been able to refine its communication and focus.

Kahuna Accounting wants to maximize its connections in the legal world so Kahuna becomes a recognized and trustworthy name. By following my suggestions, Kahuna learned to optimize its profiles to focus on the niche it was serving and thus gain a greater reach online.

Ultimately, LinkedIn is a tool where Kahuna can use thought leadership and connections to educate attorneys and entrepreneurs on the power of outsourced cloud accounting. By sharing blog posts, connecting with influencers, and meeting the exact profile of its target, Kahuna can gain the recognition and credibility to be the leader in this market.

JOEL HELFER, CEO OF QUOTEDAUTHORITY.COM

Joel Helfer has a lifetime of experience in the construction industry. For over 40 years, he was a partner in five commercial glass companies that each did well over a million in sales annually. He was an industry leader, and president of The Illinois Glass Association, and founder of the Glass Hall of Fame. He used modern-day marketing techniques to help build his businesses but didn't know it until he retired approximately five years ago and started studying marketing, specifically authority marketing. A serial entrepreneur, he started QuotedAuthority.com to help successful business owners and professionals move up to be recognized as the number-one authority in their marketplace.

QuotedAuthority.com provides systems and proven paths to help successful business owners, authors, speakers, coaches, doctors, dentists, lawyers, accountants, and other professionals gain and demonstrate authority in their marketplace. The company provides major media connections; opportunities for TV, radio, and podcast interviews; book creation and publishing services; targeted press releases; and a large array of other services.

QuotedAuthority.com's mission is to provide its clients with opportunities to both educate and become an advocate for their clients. This is done in a variety of ways to gain trust, likeability, and credibility and help develop their reputation as the go-to guy/gal in their field.

The Challenge

QuotedAuthority.com needed to engage new prospects and build relationships with and educate them. The company uses LinkedIn to engage people (in digital way) as if meeting them face to face for the first time, get them to respond, and then build a relationship that ultimately could lead to sales and profits for either them, QuotedAuthority.com, or both. The challenge was to find as many ways as possible to engage with new people, in a non-sales, nonthreatening, calm, and friendly manner.

The Solution

QuotedAuthority.com's initial strategy was to meet and engage as many people as possible with no immediate benefit other than the connection. The company used the following activities to engage people on LinkedIn:

- Make a positive comment on articles written by influencers.
- Share influencer articles among all QuotedAuthority.com's connections.
- Respond to each individual who viewed QuotedAuthority.com's profile and thank them.
- Offer contact information including phone number and an invitation to call QuotedAuthority.com.
- Offer a free, useful information report as a thank-you gift for connecting.
- Send a direct message to new connections asking about a career detail or specific accomplishment.
- Interact with people and offer practical solutions to their problems or situations.
- Endorse individuals and companies on Facebook and Twitter. This generated goodwill, thanks, replies, and phone calls.
- Publish blog posts.
- Publish individual chapters of a book.
- Provide informative, sometimes provocative, free information citing the benefits of what QuotedAuthority.com does to stimulate interest.
- Employees of QuotedAuthority.com engaged their colleagues, friends, and family in their LinkedIn activities and posts. The company found that third-party endorsements work like magic.
- Endorse people who view your profile if you feel they deserve to be endorsed for those particular skills.
- Provide recommendations to business associates of the company.
- Build out the company profile to an All Star rating. Add as many personal details as possible to make the company interesting and arouse the reader's curiosity.
- Use a question in the company profile headline that offers a benefit to the reader rather than just a boring "I'm the king of this and the god of that."
- Use advanced search to find targeted prospects the company wants to engage with.
- Send out InMail to engage prospects.
- Advertise on LinkedIn.
- Send out messages to the company's connections, which is like email, but much better, since these connections are targeted.
- Congratulate people on their birthdays, special occasions, job promotions, etc.
- Tweet special articles, successes, or newsworthy items about people the company wishes to engage with.
- Hashtag connections in the local area, create a special group, and offer an invitation for a Meetup group or even an individual "let's go for coffee" invitation.
- Persistence and a "rinse and repeat" attitude is the key to making these activities both beneficial and productive.

The Results

QuotedAuthority.com used all of its available solutions over a 60-day period, which proved very beneficial. The one activity that produced the most results was offering the contact information with the initial thank-you for connecting and an invitation to call if the new connection felt like it. This strategy produced 23 phone calls and 6 sales. The lifetime value of each sale is approximately $25,000. Furthermore:

- The company's connection base went from just over 3,000 to just over 5,000 connections.
- Joel's rank for the top 100 similar professionals went to number five.
- Joel's rank for all his connections was consistently in the top 25 percent. However, these rankings fluctuated on a daily basis, depending on the time he spent on LinkedIn and the interactions he had with others.
- Over 100 people viewed Joel's profile during each 30-day period.
- Joel found LinkedIn enabled him to produce personal relationships that would be more difficult to accomplish through Facebook, Twitter, and email.
- Joel discovered that people really enjoy a genuine "Hello, how are you?" or "Nice to meet you," without any pitch involved.
- When Joel sent out a friendly message, he found the response rate was over 90 percent.

MJ SCHWADER AND MICHELLE HUTCHINSON, CO-FOUNDERS OF INSPIRED APPS INC.

MJ Schwader and Michelle Hutchinson started working together when Michelle was exploring the idea of writing an ebook. Over the past 15 years, MJ had helped nearly 200 entrepreneurs become published authors through his writing coaching business and had suggested that Michelle put her books into an app to create another revenue stream.

Eventually they created Inspired Apps Inc., which is a mobile application development company, producing business and collaborative mobile apps for iTunes and Google Play stores. Founded in 2012, business partners MJ Schwader and Michelle Hutchinson pride themselves on personally working with each client to develop a creative and useful mobile app specific to each business.

The Challenge

MJ and Michelle's main challenge was reaching out to and educating people in their niche—coaches, speakers, and authors—and increasing the number of followers to their new company page.

The Solution

MJ and Michelle spent time each day on LinkedIn posting articles, writing articles, commenting on posts, and reaching out to people in their niche in several ways, including:

- Connecting with to people in groups where they shared a common interest
- Performing keyword searches in groups to find posts that had those words in their comments, and then following up with replies and informational comments
- Adding more activity to their company page by posting articles there and then sharing them with their personal networks
- Adding showcase pages
- Updating their company name to include their keywords
- Updating their description to include more of their keywords

The Results

By spending time making comments and getting involved in groups, MJ and Michelle were able to increase their reach by adding 54 new personal contacts within a matter of weeks. Many of these contacts came to them just from their increased participation through various posts and status updates. MJ, whose account had been silent for a while, noticed a huge increase in people reaching out from all the additional posts.

Writing articles and posting many comments on articles and group questions extended their reach and added a contact point. They estimate that every comment they made to a post resulted in a new contact reaching out to them.

Although the company page increased its followers by only four, the views and activity on the page did increase. MJ and Michelle are excited that new leads and connections are visiting and interacting with their information. They also noticed that the increase in the activity on the company page ranked them higher in the search results for their keywords.

Before engaging in all these activities they did not appear in the search results, but after just a week of constant activity on our company page they were listed on the first page as a mobile apps company in the LinkedIn search results.

DAVE BYRNES, FOUNDER OF EASIER NETWORKS

Dave Byrnes is the founder of Easier Networks, a startup providing LinkedIn strategies to help companies attract and engage audiences. Byrnes uses compelling stories coupled with LinkedIn's ability to reach audiences to attract customers and employees to his clients' businesses.

The Challenge

Dave's main goal was to understand the challenges faced by companies and recruiters for talent acquisition in Canada and position himself to provide strategies.

The Solution

Dave worked to gain authority and provide value to companies by producing an ebook of LinkedIn best practices for talent acquisition. He identified industry experts and contacted and solicited information from them through LinkedIn.

Dave used LinkedIn's Advanced Search features to identify representatives responsible for handling their company's LinkedIn strategy. He then contacted them through LinkedIn to request a short interview.

The next step was to use LinkedIn Groups to start discussions about best practices and challenges facing talent-acquisition professionals. He collected information through the discussions and established relationships with respondents to allow for more in-depth research into issues and best practices.

The final step was to become active in human resources, recruiting, and job-seeker groups by taking part in discussions, providing valuable feedback to people, and building deeper relationships with members of these groups.

The Results

Finding the representatives responsible for their company's LinkedIn strategy proved extremely difficult. There was no consistency from company to company for which department ran its LinkedIn strategy (human resources, marketing, communications, sales) nor was it mentioned on personal profiles.

Group owners of human resources and recruiting groups were also contacted at this point as they would have broad knowledge of trends from moderating the many discussions. This approach gained a reply from less than half the group owners contacted, and the responses were guarded about giving away "free" information.

Cold-contacting people produced a low response rate; the lesson learned was that asking for people's time and effort on the "first touch" was poorly received.

The next strategy of starting discussions in groups about issues regarding talent acquisition produced some feedback and conversation from industry members. Interestingly, about half the respondents were professionals having difficulty breaking back into the industry. The lesson learned was that connecting with people on the "second touch," after participating in a discussion with them, was far more effective.

At this point, Dave reached out to five existing connections who were in the industry and gained enthusiastic and in-depth feedback from each, including a face to face with one recruitment firm. The power of establishing relationships first and then looking to collaborate was a vital lesson.

Based on these learnings, his focus became heavy involvement in about 10 quality groups by commenting in discussions and adding value whenever possible. As he did this, he gained Top Contributor status in several groups, made numerous connections, and was directly contacted by people who either sought his advice or pointed him toward potential opportunities.

Several discussions he started provided useful background material for the planned ebook and sharpened the focus of the project. With a growing network of industry professionals the resources he could call on allowed the ebook to move forward and also provided the basis to publish posts on these subjects that will gain more attention, discussion, and connections.

Although Dave had often told clients and audiences about the need to build relationships first on LinkedIn, his time in the trenches with LinkedIn Groups showed how important this principle was and what happens when you stray from it.

DWAYNE JEFFRIES, CEO OF AUSTIN FOUND (AUSTINFOUNDIT.COM)

Dwayne Jeffries began his career in product development at age 13. His parents owned several gift and home décor shops. He was responsible for sanding and finishing the original products sold in the family store. After attending several trend shows in Atlanta in the early 1990s, a seed was planted. A passion for product took hold and propelled Dwayne into a career of selling and service. He was hired as a sales rep by OneCoast in 1999, and earned Rookie of the Year his first year, and several multimillion-dollar sales years coupled with continued upward growth put him in a key account position. He branched out into Asia, traveling with sourcing teams to support the strategic needs of major retailers like Cracker Barrel and Tractor Supply. Decades of immersive learning equipped Dwayne with the understanding of the product development and global sourcing complexities necessary to meet the challenges of servicing major retailers. In 2007, Austin Found was established.

Founded in 2007 by Dwayne Jeffries with the idea that "everyone is looking for *something*, and we can find it for you!," Austin Found is a company that specializes in designing, sourcing, and producing that "something." Dwayne's core business revolves around home décor, furniture, tabletop ceramics, kids' crafts, textiles, and general gift and tech products. It's challenging to know who to trust or even where to get started. Austin Found's network includes leading manufacturers throughout the United States, China, India, Southeast Asia, and Mexico. The company's well-established network of suppliers around the world offers its clients consistency, quality, and execution. Its aim is to make the product development process an exciting productive experience. Austin Found wants to climb outside of the box with its clients and explore options to meet current and future product development requests.

The Challenge

Global sourcing is difficult. It's often difficult to find and vet reputable manufactures to produce products that meet specifications. Achieving consistent quality that meets protocol testing and can be delivered on time is a hurdle for even the largest of retailers. In 2001 prior to establishing Austin Found, Dwayne worked with a customer to locate a supplier that could produce branded sling chairs. At the time, there weren't easy ways to review a supplier or vet them properly. Dwayne, young and adventurous, stepped out to try something he had never done before. He got the paperwork in order, sold the chairs, and waited for the product to deliver to the customer. Then 9/11 happened. Freight stopped. Everything stopped. The supplier called Dwayne and said that he had quoted him a delivered price, but that freight had went up and the customer owed an additional $4,000 to release the shipment. This was not what they had agreed to. Dwayne offered to forfeit his commission and asked the supplier to do the same to honor the price quoted to the customer. The supplier wouldn't help out. Dwayne ended up working personally to get the chairs to the customer. At the end of the day everything worked out, and the customer was thrilled with the product. The lesson learned was that the vetting process is key to protecting your investment in product production. Even in the digital age with verifications, reviews, and a flashy site, the real way to vet is in person, eye to eye.

The Solution

With well-funded sourcing companies offering global supplier verifications and aggressively pushing complicated sourcing models, Austin Found will create a business built on the development of great product, using reliable manufacturers that believe excellence can be achieved through consistency. Dwayne is using LinkedIn and other social media outlets to gain credibility with potential customers.

Each day Dwayne connects with new potential clients and business partners on LinkedIn. He finds them using LinkedIn Advanced Search and by searching LinkedIn Groups for specific keyword phrases. Dwayne is an active participant in LinkedIn Groups, helping others by answering questions and providing resources. The LinkedIn Groups give Dwayne valuable information about what problems businesses are having with their global suppliers or products they are manufacturing offshore.

Dwayne also uses LinkedIn Pulse to monitor breaking industry and company news. By following companies and subscribing to industry-related news sources, he knows exactly what's going on in the industry, giving him ideas for new content. Creating new content and sharing industry-related news in Status Updates helps Dwayne establish himself as an industry expert.

CONCLUSION

As you see, there are plenty of small- and large-business owners using LinkedIn effectively to grow their businesses. The key to LinkedIn success is to have a clear strategy and objective for using LinkedIn. Next, you need to execute your strategy every day on LinkedIn. Focus on helping others and sharing great content consistently, and in no time, you will see positive LinkedIn results.

For additional updates and how-to videos, visit
www.tedprodromou.com/chapter24

Commencement

M any authors call the last chapter of their books "Conclusion," "Wrapping It Up," or something to the effect that you've success- fully reached the end of the book. I prefer to call it "Commence- ment," because this is a new beginning for you—not the end. I want to be the first to congratulate you for reaching this chapter because you now know more about LinkedIn than 95 percent of all LinkedIn members.

As I mentioned many times throughout the book, most LinkedIn members never reach the milestone of seeing that magical message saying their profile is 100 percent complete. I hope your profile now says 100 percent complete, and if it doesn't, you need to commit to yourself that you will reach that milestone in the next day or so. You've seen the benefits of completing your profile completely, and it will make a world of difference to your business and career.

A lot of people still think LinkedIn is only a website for finding a job. After reading this book, you now know that LinkedIn is so much more than a job website. You learned how to use LinkedIn to give you a huge competitive advantage over your peers, co-workers, companies you are selling against, people you are competing against for jobs, or other consultants who are looking for new consulting engagements. It's time to put into practice what you just learned about LinkedIn and blow away your competition.

Throughout the book, I demonstrated the power of LinkedIn and how you can use it to rise above your competition. Here are a few of the highlights:

- Determine your reason for being on LinkedIn—whether it's to find a job, recruit new employees, prospect for new clients, connect with former colleagues, build your professional network, promote your company, or to become an industry thought leader.

- Use LinkedIn as a business intelligence search engine to find the best employees, find a new job, connect with key decision-makers, monitor trends in your industry, keep an eye on your competitors, or increase your sales.

- Optimize your LinkedIn profile so you and your company can easily be found on LinkedIn and Google.

- Build your professional network with the right people, whether you decide to become a LinkedIn LION with a massive network, build a small niche network, or somewhere in between.

- Use LinkedIn Tools so you can easily keep up with industry trends, connect with others, and automate many LinkedIn functions.

- Use LinkedIn Mobile Apps so you can easily access LinkedIn from your computer or mobile device to keep your LinkedIn profile up to date, read the latest industry news, connect with others, and find new prospects.

- Use LinkedIn Pulse to stay current by reading articles from other industry experts, then demonstrate your expertise by sharing and commenting on the content.

- Use LinkedIn Groups to build strong relationships with others, learn from other group members, and demonstrate your expertise.

- Establish a presence for your company on LinkedIn so others will learn about your products, your company employees, and culture; to recruit new employees; and to generate leads.

- Effectively use LinkedIn Advertising to promote your brand, generate leads, recruit new employees, and promote events.

- Use LinkedIn Premium services like Job Seeker, Business, Talent Finder, or Sales Navigator to help you get the most out of LinkedIn.

- And so much more! LinkedIn is constantly evolving, growing, and adding more great stuff, so stay tuned for developments as they occur.

Now that you qualify as an expert LinkedIn user, you have to use that knowledge on a regular basis to maintain the competitive advantage you just gained. I could create a generic 30-day LinkedIn plan for you, but since everyone uses LinkedIn for different reasons, I recommend you create your own that fits your needs. Keep your plan very simple and ease into LinkedIn gradually. In no time you'll be logging in to LinkedIn every day.

Some suggestions to get you started include:

1. Change the start page in your browser to LinkedIn.com so you automatically log in every time you open your browser.

2. Get in the habit of logging into LinkedIn every day, and check out LinkedIn Pulse to read your industry news.

3. Check out the People You May Know widget on your LinkedIn homepage, and connect with a few people every week.

4. Recommend one person every week.

5. Ask for recommendations from your current co-workers or past co-workers and bosses.

6. Read some of the new questions and content posted in your newsfeed.

7. Join a group and read some of the popular discussions.

8. Check out the profiles of people with the same job title as you, and update your profile so it's more focused than theirs.

9. Follow some companies that are leaders in your industry.

10. Check out the Jobs section and see what new opportunities are out there—even if you aren't looking for a job.

11. As you become more comfortable with the way group discussions work, try posting some provocative questions. When you're even more comfortable, start answering other people's questions. Remember, don't self-promote! Just answer the questions in an unbiased way.

12. Help at least one person every day on LinkedIn by answering questions or by giving recommendations.

13. Add new multimedia content to your profile every week so your profile becomes more robust.

14. Learn one LinkedIn tool every week so you can become more efficient with LinkedIn.

15. Install the LinkedIn mobile apps.

16. Set a goal of connecting with at least one key third-degree connection every week.

17. Practice using InMail by sending one to someone you know but aren't connected to. This will increase your chances of her opening it and replying, which helps your InMail score and lets you practice writing interesting InMails. Ask her for feedback, and see if she would have opened the InMail if you were a stranger. Practice with her and review her InMail messages in return for helping you.

18. Upgrade to at least the Business account after you become comfortable with the basic LinkedIn functions.

19. Do a Google search on your name and see if your LinkedIn profile comes up. If it does come up, does your profile headline let people know exactly what you do and how you can help them?

20. When you are comfortable with your LinkedIn profile, start promoting it by adding a link in your email signature, and add the LinkedIn badge to your blog and website.

Well, that was easy! There are 20 ideas to help you get started on LinkedIn. Do one item each day for the next 20 days, and you'll be hooked on LinkedIn.

The key to success in business is consistency. If you consistently use LinkedIn every day to grow your professional network, help others, and demonstrate your expertise by answering questions, participate in group discussions, and display your blog posts, articles, and SlideShare in your profile, there is a good chance you will be considered a thought-leader in your field. I've seen it time and time again on the internet—when someone consistently posts fresh, relevant content and helps others, they are soon considered a leading expert in their field. What's stopping you from becoming a leading expert in your field?

I really enjoyed sharing my LinkedIn experience with you, and I hope you use the information wisely. If you use just a fraction of the information I taught you, I guarantee your career will never be the same. Will you do me one more favor? When your career takes off because of what you learned in this book, please share your success story with me at ted@tedprodromou.com.

To your LinkedIn success!

For additional updates and how-to videos, visit
www.tedprodromou.com/chapter25

LinkedIn Glossary

Activity Broadcasts: Your status updates are sent to the Activity Feed and visible to others. You can edit your status updates.

Activity Feed: Displays your network activity such as joining/starting groups, comments, profile changes, and application downloads. You can control which activities appear in your activity feed in your LinkedIn settings.

Anonymous Viewers: You can choose to keep personal identification information private. Recruiters often choose to remain anonymous to remain discreet.

Applications: Applications can enhance your LinkedIn experience, by integrating other social media networks such as Twitter, Facebook, and WordPress, and by enhancing your professional profile with a reading list or portfolio app. Applications can be found under the More tab of your LinkedIn homepage.

Basic Account: A free LinkedIn account that most members use. The features of the Basic account are limited but meet the needs of most LinkedIn members.

Business Account: A Premium LinkedIn account which offers more features for business users. Business accounts include three InMails per month, enhanced profile search results, expanded profiles, and storage space.

Business Plus Account: A Premium LinkedIn account which offers more features for business users. Business Plus accounts include ten InMails per month, enhanced profile search results, expanded profiles, company introductions, and storage space.

Connection: LinkedIn members who have accepted an invitation to connect to become your First-Degree Connection.

Connections, First-Degree: LinkedIn members whom you've agreed to connect with. Your first-degree connections are usually friends, co-workers, or colleagues. If you are a LinkedIn LION, your first-degree connections are anyone who sent you a connection request since you want to connect with everyone. You can send messages to them directly without using InMail.

Connections, Second-Degree: A "friend of a friend," or the LinkedIn connections of your first-degree connections. You must request an introduction from a first connection if you want to connect with your second-degree connections. You can contact your second-degree connections only via an introduction or InMail unless you are members of the same LinkedIn Group.

Connections, Third-Degree: The connections of your second-degree connections. You must request an introduction or use InMail to contact your third-degree connections unless you are members of the same LinkedIn Group.

Events: LinkedIn Events is an application that allows you to see what events your LinkedIn network is attending and allows you to find events recommended to you based on your industry and job function. With LinkedIn Events, you can:

- Create an event
- Search for events
- Share an event
- See attendees and read comments about events

Executive Account: A LinkedIn Premium account that features 25 InMails per month, premium search results, maximum storage, third-degree connection info, and enhanced search filters.

Groups: LinkedIn Groups provide a place for professionals in the same industry or with similar interests to share content, find answers, post and view jobs, make business contacts, and establish themselves as industry experts. You can find groups to join in the LinkedIn Groups Directory or view suggestions of groups you may like. You can also create a new group focused on a particular topic or industry.

IDK response: When you receive a connection request, one of your options is to choose "I don't know this person" or IDK. If someone receives more than three IDK responses, his account may be suspended to prevent LinkedIn spamming. Always personalize your invitations with a greeting to let the person know why you want to connect with him and how you know him.

InMail: InMails are messages you can send directly to another LinkedIn member you're not connected to. Any member can purchase an InMail, or you can get them with a premium account.

Intermediary: The process whereby a first-degree connection must request an introduction from the secondary connection in order to connect to the third.

Invitations: Invitations are how you make connections on LinkedIn. When one LinkedIn user sends an invitation to another person who then accepts the invitation, they become first-degree connections. If the person receiving the invitation isn't a LinkedIn member, they'll be prompted to join LinkedIn in order to accept the invitation. Each new connection can increase your access to thousands of professionals in your network.

Job Seekers Account: A LinkedIn Premium account for people looking for a job. You can choose Job Seeker Basic, Standard, or Plus to enhance your job search. Job Seeker accounts let you get introduced to the companies you want to work for, you can be contacted by anyone using OpenLink, and you can post a Job Seeker's badge on your LinkedIn profile.

LinkedIn Influencer: LinkedIn Influencer is a designation given to approximately 500 professionals who've been invited to publish on LinkedIn. As leaders in their industries, geographies, and seniorities, they talk about broad topics of interest such as leadership, management, hiring and firing, disruption, how to succeed, and more. The list of Influencers includes Richard Branson, Bill Gates, Arianna Huffington, and Guy Kawasaki.

LION: An acronym of "LinkedIn Open Networker," which is usually posted on people's profile as an "open networker" or "LION." When you are a LION, you agree to connect with anyone, regardless of industry or connection, to increase your network size.

Local Connection: Connections that are in your local area listed on your account.

Network: Your LinkedIn professional network, which consists of a group of users that can contact you through connections up to three degrees away.

Network Statistics: The Network Statistics feature offers a variety of information about your network, including estimated size and regional and industry access. To learn more about the professionals in your network, move your cursor over Contacts at the top of your home page and click Network Statistics.

OpenLink Network: A network that Premium members can join, which allows any LinkedIn member to send them an InMail free of charge, regardless of relationship.

Profile: Creating a LinkedIn profile is an excellent way to establish and own your professional identity online. LinkedIn profiles typically appear among the top search results when people search by name.

Pulse: LinkedIn Pulse replaced LinkedIn Today. This is where you can customize news and content posted by LinkedIn Influencers. When you log into Pulse every morning, you see a snapshot of industry news created by influential LinkedIn members or from large media outlets.

Recommendations: A recommendation is a comment written by a LinkedIn member to endorse a colleague, business partner, student, or service provider. People interested in hiring or doing business with someone often consider recommendations in making their decisions.

Skills: The Skills page is found under the More menu at the top of your homepage. LinkedIn Skills helps you discover the expertise that other professionals have and see how the demand for these skills is changing over time. The skills information shown is based on data LinkedIn members enter on their profiles.

Index